Annals of Information Systems

Volume 12

Series Editors

Ramesh Sharda
Oklahoma State University
Stillwater, OK, USA

Stefan Voß
University of Hamburg
Hamburg, Germany

For further volumes:
http://www.springer.com/series/7573

Nasrullah Memon · Jennifer Jie Xu ·
David L. Hicks · Hsinchun Chen
Editors

Data Mining for Social Network Data

 Springer

Editors

Nasrullah Memon
University of Southern Denmark
Maersk Mc-Kinney Moller Institute
Campusvej 55
5230 Odense M
Denmark
memon@mmmi.sdu.dk

Jennifer Jie Xu
Department of Computer Information
  Systems
Bentley University
Forest St. 175
02452 Waltham Massachusetts
USA
jxu@bentley.edu

David L. Hicks
Department of Computer Science
  and Engineering
Aalborg University Esbjerg
Niels Bohrs Vej 8
6700 Esbjerg
Denmark
hicks@cs.aaue.dk

Hsinchun Chen
University of Arizona
Eller College of Management
E. Helen St. 1130
85721 Tucson Arizona
430Z McClelland Hall
USA
hchen@eller.arizona.edu

ISSN 1934-3221   e-ISSN 1934-3213
ISBN 978-1-4419-6286-7   e-ISBN 978-1-4419-6287-4
DOI 10.1007/978-1-4419-6287-4
Springer New York Dordrecht Heidelberg London

Library of Congress Control Number: 2010928244

Printed on acid-free paper

Springer is part of Springer Science+Business Media (www.springer.com)

Contents

Contributors

Reda Alhajj Department of Computer Science, University of Calgary, Calgary, AB, Canada; Department of Computer Science, Global University, Beirut, Lebanon, alhajj@ucalgary.ca

András A. Benczúr Data Mining and Web search Research Group, Informatics Laboratory, Computer and Automation Research Institute, Hungarian Academy of Sciences, Budapest, Hungary, benczur@ilab.sztaki.hu

Noah Cepela Department of Communication, University of Illinois, MC 132, 1007 W. Harrison St., Chicago, IL 60607, USA, ncepela72@gmail.com

Hsinchun Chen Eller College of Management, University of Arizona, 430Z McClelland Hall, E. Helen St. 1130, Tucson, AZ 85721, USA, hchen@eller.arizona.edu

Jiyang Chen Department of Computing Science, University of Alberta, Edmonton, AB, Canada T6G 2E8, jiyang@cs.ualberta.ca

Wesley W. Chu Computer Science Department, University of California, Los Angeles, CA 90095, USA, wwc@cs.ucla.edu

James A. Danowski Department of Communication, University of Illinois, MC 132, 1007 W. Harrison St., Chicago, IL 60607, USA, jimd@uic.edu

Randy Goebel Department of Computing Science, University of Alberta, Edmonton, AB, Canada T6G 2E8, goebel@cs.ualberta.ca

Dominique Haughton Department of Mathematical Sciences, Bentley University, 175 Forest Street, Waltham, MA 02452, USA, dhaughton@bentley.edu

Jianming He Computer Science Department, University of California, Los Angeles, CA 90095, USA, jmhek@cs.ucla.edu

David L. Hicks Department of Computer Science & Engineering, Aalborg University Esbjerg, Niels Bohrs Vej 8, 6700 Esbjerg, Denmark, hicks@cs.aaue.dk

Guangying Hua Department of Mathematical Sciences, Bentley University, 175 Forest Street, Waltham, MA 02452, USA, ghua@bentley.edu

Siddharth Kaza Department of Computer and Information Sciences, Towson University, Towson, MD, USA, skaza@towson.edu

Keivan Kianmehr Department of Computer Science, University of Calgary, Calgary, AB, Canada, mkkian@ucalgary.ca

Negar Koochakzadeh Department of Computer Science, University of Calgary, Calgary, AB, Canada, nkoochak@ucalgary.ca

Miklós Kurucz Data Mining and Web search Research Group, Informatics Laboratory, Computer and Automation Research Institute, Hungarian Academy of Sciences, Budapset, Hungary, mkurucz@ilab.sztaki.hu

Iltae Lee Department of Computer Science, University of Calgary, Calgary, AB, Canada, itlee@ucalgary.ca

Yutaka I. Leon-Suematsu National Institute of Information and Communications Technology (NiCT), 3-5 Hikaridai, Seika-cho, Soraku-gun, Kyoto 619-0289, Japan, yutaka.leon@acm.org

Nasrullah Memon Maersk Mc-Kinney Moller Institute, University of Southern Denmark, Campusvej 55, 5230 Odense M, Denmark, memon@mmmi.sdu.dk

Tsuyoshi Murata Department of Computer Science, Graduate School of Information Science and Engineering, Tokyo Institute of Technology, W8-59 2-12-1 Ookayama, Meguro, Tokyo 152-8552, Japan, murata@cs.titech.ac.jp

Bruno Pouliquen World Intellectual Property Organization, 34, chemin des Colombettes, CH-1211, Geneva 20, Switzerland, poulique@gmail.com

Jon Rokne Department of Computer Science, University of Calgary, Calgary, AB, Canada, rokne@ucalgary.ca

Jörg Sander Department of Computing Science, University of Alberta, Edmonton, AB, Canada T6G 2E8, joerg@cs.ualberta.ca

Ralf Steinberger IPSC, T.P. 267, Joint Research Centre – European Commission, Via E. Fermi 2749, 21027 Ispra, Italy, ralf.steinberger@jrc.ec.europa.eu

Yingjie Sun Department of Biomedical engineering, Boston University, 44 Cummington Street, Boston, MA 02215, USA, yjsun@bu.edu

Hristo Tanev IPSC, T.P. 267, Joint Research Centre – European Commission, Via E. Fermi 2749, 21027 Ispra, Italy, htanev@gmail.com

Jennifer Jie Xu Department of Computer Information Systems, Bentley University, Forest St. 175, 02452 Waltham, MA, USA, jxu@bentley.edu

Kikuo Yuta Crev Inc., Keihanna-Plaza Laboratories, 1-7 Hikaridai, Seika-cho, Kyoto 619-0237, Japan, y@crev.jp

Osmar R. Zaïane Department of Computing Science, University of Alberta, Edmonton, AB, Canada T6G 2E8, zaiane@cs.ualberta.ca

Vanni Zavarella IPSC, T.P. 267, Joint Research Centre – European Commission, Via E. Fermi 2749, 21027 Ispra, Italy, zavavan@yahoo.it

Chapter 1
Social Network Data Mining: Research Questions, Techniques, and Applications

Nasrullah Memon, Jennifer Jie Xu, David L. Hicks, and Hsinchun Chen

1.1 Introduction

Decision-making in many application domains needs to take into consideration of some sorts of networks. Examples include e-commerce and marketing [6, 10], strategic planning [21], knowledge management [12], and Web mining [5, 13]. Since the late 1990s a large number of articles have been published in *Nature*, *Science*, and other leading journals in many disciplines, proposing new network models, techniques, and applications (e.g., [3, 22, 25]). This trend has been accompanied by the increasing popularity of social networking sites such as FaceBook and MySpace. As a result, research on *social network data mining*, or simply *network mining*, has attracted much attention from both academics and practitioners.

Unlike conventional data mining topics, such as association rule mining and classification, which are aimed at extracting patterns based on individual data objects, network mining is intended to examine relationships between objects, thereby extracting valid, novel, and useful structural patterns in networks ranging from the Internet [7], the World Wide Web [2], metabolic pathways [11], to social networks [25].

However, because this area is still young and evolving, there has not yet emerged a widely accepted research framework that offers a holistic view about the major research questions, methodologies, techniques, and applications of network mining research. The goal of this special issue is to move one step forward in the area of network mining by reviewing and summarizing research questions from existing research, providing examples of new techniques and applications, and illuminating future research directions.

N. Memon (✉)
University of Southern Denmark, Maersk Mc-Kinney Moller Institute, Campusvej 55,
5230 Odense M, Denmark
e-mail: memon@mmmi.sdu.dk

N. Memon et al. (eds.), *Data Mining for Social Network Data*,
Annals of Information Systems 12, DOI 10.1007/978-1-4419-6287-4_1,
© Springer Science+Business Media, LLC 2010

1.2 Network Mining: Research Questions

There are two major streams in network mining research: static structure mining and dynamic structure mining. Static structure mining focuses on the "snapshot" of a network, that is, nodes and links observed at a single point in time. Dynamic structure mining, in contrast, analyzes a network based on data observed at multiple points in time. Static analysis is aimed at discovering the structural regularities in the specific configuration of the nodes and links of a network at the time of observation. Dynamic analysis is aimed at finding the patterns of changes in the network over time. The focus of static analysis is on structure, while the focus of dynamic analysis is on the processes and the evolutionary mechanisms that lead to the structure [3].

1.2.1 Static Structure Mining

There are three major research questions in the area of static network structure mining: (a) How to locate critical recourses in networks? (b) How to reduce the network complexity and generate the "big picture" of a network? and (c) How to extract topological properties from networks?

Locating critical resources. A network can be viewed as a collection of recourses [17]. The critical recourses in a network are those important nodes, links, or paths it contains. On the World Wide Web, for example, the contents of Web documents can be viewed as information resources. Users search for quality Web pages whose contents match their information needs. The key people, documents, relations, and communication channels in a network often are critical to the function of the network. Existing techniques for locating critical resources have been used in a number of applications, such as finding high-quality pages on the Web [13], locating cables and wires whose failure reduces the robustness of the Internet [14, 24], and searching for experts for a specific problem in collaboration networks [12, 18].

Reducing network complexity. A network can be very complex due to the large number of nodes and links it contains. Understanding the structure of a network becomes increasingly difficult when its size becomes large. For example, a marketing manager may get lost when he/she faces a network consisting of thousands of existing and potential customers. A researcher may find it difficult to understand the intellectual structure of an unfamiliar discipline when studying its citation networks containing hundreds of papers or authors. Therefore, it is desirable to extract the "big picture" from a complex network by reducing it into a simpler image while preserving the intrinsic structure. To achieve this goal, a network can be first partitioned into subgroups, each of which contains a set of nodes. The between-group relationships can then be extracted. A number of applications can benefit from this technology. In particular, network partition methods have been employed to find communities on the Web [8, 9], major research topics and paradigms in a discipline in citation networks [23], and criminal groups in criminal networks [26].

Extracting topological properties. Recent years have witnessed an increasing interest in the topological properties of large-scale networks. A few factors have contributed to this trend. First, data collection and analysis of extremely large networks have become possible due to greatly improved computing power. The size of the Web studied, for example, has been up to several million nodes [15]. Second, the recently proposed small-world and scale-free network models [3, 25] have motivated scientists to search for the universal organizing principles that may be responsible for the commonality observed in a range of networks. Third, social networking sites such as FaceBook and MySpace have become more popular motivating academics and practitioners to study the network phenomenon.

Static structure mining provides a means of discovering structural patterns in networks. However, networks are not static but constantly change. How to reveal the dynamics of networks and the evolutionary mechanisms leading to a certain topology is the focus of the dynamic structure mining area.

1.2.2 Dynamic Structure Mining

Networks are subject to all kinds of changes and dynamics. New nodes may be added to the system and old nodes may be removed. New links may emerge between originally disconnected nodes and old links may rewire or break. Understanding the dynamics and the process of evolution in networks is of vital practical importance. The evolutionary mechanisms that lead to a specific type of network topology have direct impact on the function of a system. There are two general research questions in this area: (a) How to describe the dynamics? and (b) How to model and predict the dynamics? Descriptive approaches are relatively simple and are based on capturing and observing the changes in a network over time using a set of topological statistics such as changes in average degree and clustering coefficient.

The modeling and prediction of structural dynamics is much more challenging. Presently, the research focus is primarily on the evolution process of scale-free topology because the structures of many empirical networks are scale free [7, 11, 19]. The core research question is, What are the mechanisms responsible for the power-law distribution in degree [1]? Several mechanisms, such as growth and preferential attachment [3], competition [4], and individual preference [16, 20], have been proposed to explain the emergence of scale-free topology in real networks.

The research on network dynamics is a recent development and fairly new compared with static structure mining research. More innovative approaches and models are expected to be added to this line of research in the near future.

1.3 Network Mining: Techniques and Applications

The ten chapters published in this special issue collectively represent and demonstrate the latest development in network mining techniques and applications in a wide range of domains.

The chapter "Automatic expansion of a social network using sentiment analysis" by Tanev et al. presents an approach to learning a signed social network automatically from online news articles. The proposed approach is to first combine a signed social network with a second, unsigned network of quotations (person A makes reference to person B in direct reported speech), to train a classifier that distinguishes positive and negative quotations. The authors then apply this classifier to the Quotation network. The authors identify the polarity of sentiments between two people and automatically label quotations which are likely to express the same sentiment between these two properties. In the chapter, "Automatic mapping of social networks of actors from text corpora: Time series analysis", Danowski and Cepela present a time series analysis of social networks obtained from data mining, and use political communication theory to generate some hypotheses to add further meaningfulness to the analysis.

In the next chapter, "A social network-based recommender system (SNRS)" Chu and He present a system which makes recommendations about an item's general acceptance by considering a user's own preference and its influence on the user's friends. The authors propose to model the correlations between immediate friends with the histogram of friend's rating differences. The influences from distant friends are considered with an iterative classification strategy. Hua et al. next present a study of the United States air transportation network, which is one of the most diverse and dynamic transportation networks in the world. The study reveals that the network has the features of a scale-free small-world network with the degree distribution following the power law.

Chen and Kaza next describe how they have modeled knowledge flow within an organization and identified high-status nodes in the network with the help of unique characteristics which are not commonly used in determining node status. The authors propose a new measure based on team identification and random walks to determine status in knowledge networks. In the next chapter Murata proposes a new measurement for community extraction from bipartite networks. Experimental results show that bipartite modularity is appropriate for discovering communities that correspond to the community of other vertex types and the degree of correspondence can also be used for characterizing the communities.

Chen et al. propose a general definition of communities in social networks and a list of requirements for a good similarity metric that can be used to detect those communities. The authors provide an analysis of existing metrics based on those criteria and then propose a new similarity metric R which satisfies all of those requirements. A visual data mining approach for overlapping community detection in networks is then proposed based on the metric R. The authors show by experiments that the approach can be used effectively in real large networks to identify the overlap among the communities. In the next chapter, Leon-Suematsu and Yuta describe new improvements to Clauset, Newman, and Moore (CNM) algorithms which yielded positive results in terms of modularity and speed. The authors describe the inefficiencies in CNM along with its mostly used modifications and prove their verdicts on practical large-scale networks available like Facebook, Orkut.

Kurucz and Benczúr in their chapter entitled "Geographically organized small communities and the hardness of clustering social networks" identify the abundance of small-size communities connected by long tentacles as the major obstacle for spectral clustering. These sub-graphs hide the higher level structure and result in a highly degenerate adjacency matrix with several hundreds of eigen values very close to 1. The results on clustering social networks, telephone call graphs, and Web graphs are twofold. The authors show that graphs generated by existing social network models are not as difficult to cluster as they are in the real world. In the next chapter, Lee et al. demonstrate that fuzzy logic can be applied to deviation value using genetic algorithms. The authors describe converting deviation value to the restructuring factor value and define the initial random fuzzy memberships using the WPR index, the log rank index, and the restructuring factor value. The membership functions are also optimized using genetic algorithm techniques. The authors derive fuzzy rules for each page using the best chromosome (optimal fuzzy membership functions) and select general fuzzy rules from them.

1.4 Conclusions and Future Directions

Future research in network structure mining will include at least three major areas: theoretical, technical, and empirical. In the theoretical realm, a more comprehensive research framework is needed as research on network structure mining matures. New research questions, techniques, and findings should be incorporated into the framework. For example, research on the diffusion of information, innovation, or disease in networks is a very interesting and promising area. Research on network evolution is also highly desirable in order to develop new models and reveal new mechanisms that are responsible for network evolution. Such research will contribute to theory building regarding networks.

In the technical area, future research may aim at the development of additional techniques and methods for mining structural patterns in networks. Existing techniques such as the network partition methods still lack efficiency, limiting their capabilities of extracting group structures in very large-scale networks such as the Web.

In the empirical category, the significance and impact of this new field of network structure mining in terms of its roles for supporting knowledge management and decision making in real-world applications, together with the impacts of network mining technology on users, organizations, and society, still remain to find. A large number of empirical studies are needed in order to evaluate the significance and impact and also demonstrate the value of this new field.

Acknowledgements The editors would like to gratefully acknowledge the efforts of all those who have helped create this special edition. First, it would never be possible for an edition such as this one to provide such a broad and extensive look at the latest research in the field of social network mining without the efforts of all those expert researchers and practitioners who have authored and contributed papers. Their contributions made this special issue possible. In addition, we would like to thank the reviewers for their time and effort in the preparation of their thoughtful reviews. Their support was crucial for ensuring the quality of this special issue and for attracting wide readership. oreover, we would like to thank the series editors, Ramesh Sharda and Stefan Voß, for their valuable advice, support, and encouragement. We are also grateful for the pleasant cooperation with Neil Levine and Matthew Amboy from Springer and their professional support in publishing this volume.

References

1. Albert, R. and Barabási, A.-L. Statistical mechanics of complex networks. *Reviews of Modern Physics*, 74(1):47–97, 2002.
2. Albert, R., Jeong, H. et al. Diameter of the World-Wide Web. *Nature*, 401:130–131, 1999.
3. Barabási, A.-L. and Albert, R. Emergence of scaling in random networks. *Science*, 286(5439):509–512, 1999.
4. Bianconi, G. and Barabási, A.-L. Competition and multiscaling in evolving networks. *Europhysics Letters*, 54:436–442, 2001.
5. Chau, M. and Xu, J. Mining communities and their relationships in blogs: A study of hate groups *International Journal of Human-Computer Studies*, 65:57–70, 2007.
6. Domingos, P. and Richardson, M. Mining the network value of customers. In *The 7th ACM SIGKDD International Conference on Knowledge Discovery and Data Mining*, San Francisco, CA: ACM Press, 2001.
7. Faloutsos, M., Faloutsos, P. et al. On power-law relationships of the internet topology. In *Annual Conference of the Special Interest Group on Data Communication (SIGCOMM '99)*, Cambridge, MA, 1999.
8. Flake, G.W., Lawrence, S. et al. Efficient identification of web communities. In *The 6th International Conference on Knowledge Discovery and Data Mining (ACM SIGKDD 2000)*, Boston, MA: ACM Press, 2000.
9. Gibson, D., Kleinberg, J. et al. Inferring web communities from link topology. In *The 9th ACM Conference on Hypertext and Hypermedia*, Pittsburgh, PA, 1998.
10. Janssen, M.A. and Jager, W. Simulating market dynamics: Interactions between consumer psychology and social networks. *Artificial Life*, 9:343–356, 2003.
11. Jeong, H., Tombor, B. et al. The large-scale organization of metabolic networks. *Nature*, 407(6804):651–654, 2000.
12. Kautz, H., Selman, B. et al. Referralweb: Combining social networks and collaborative filtering. *Communications of the ACM*, 40(3):27–36, 1997.
13. Kleinberg, J. Authoritative sources in a hyperlinked environment. In *The 9th ACM-SIAM Symposium on Discrete Algorithms*, San Francisco, CA, 1998.
14. Kleinberg, J., Sandler, M. et al. Network failure detection and graph connectivity. *The 15th Annual ACM-SIAM Symposium on Discrete Algorithms*, New Orleans, LA, Society for Industrial and Applied Mathematics, Philadelphia, PA, 2004.
15. Lawrence, S. and Giles, C.L. Accessibility of information on the web. *Nature*, 400: 107–109, 1999.
16. Menczer, F. Evolution of document networks. *Proceedings of the National Academy of Science of the United States of America*, 101:5261–5265, 2004.
17. Nahapiet, J. and Ghoshal, S. Social capital, intellectual capital, and the organizational advantage. *Academy of Management Review*, 23(2):242–266, 1998.
18. Newman, M.E.J. The structure of scientific collaboration networks. *Proceedings of the National Academy of Science of the United States of America*, 98:404–409, 2001.
19. Newman, M.E.J. Coauthorship networks and patterns of scientific collaboration. *Proceedings of the National Academy of Science of the United States of America*, 101:5200–5205, 2004.

20. Pennock, D.M., Flake, G.W. et al. Winners don't take all: Characterizing the competition for links on the web. *Proceedings of the National Academy of Science of the United States of America,* 99(8):5207–5211, 2002.
21. Powell, W.W., White, D.R. et al. Network dynamics and field evolution: The growth of interorganizational collaboration in the life sciences. *American Journal of Sociology,* 110(4):1132–1205, 2005.
22. Singh, J. Collaborative networks as determinants of knowledge diffusion patterns. *Management Science,* 51(5):756–770, 2005.
23. Small, H. Visualizing science by citation mapping. *Journal of American Society of Information Science,* 50(9):799–813, 1999.
24. Tu, Y. How robust is the Internet? *Nature,* 406:353–354, 2000.
25. Watts, D.J. and Strogatz, S.H. Collective dynamics of "small-world" networks. *Nature,* 393(6684):440–442, 1998.
26. Xu, J.J. and Chen, H. CrimeNet Explorer: A framework for criminal network knowledge discovery. *ACM Transactions on Information Systems,* 23(2):201–226, 2005.

Chapter 2
Automatic Expansion of a Social Network Using Sentiment Analysis

Hristo Tanev, Bruno Pouliquen, Vanni Zavarella, and Ralf Steinberger

Abstract In this chapter, we present an approach to learn *a signed social network* automatically from online news articles. The vertices in this network represent people and the edges are labeled with the polarity of the attitudes among them (positive, negative, and neutral). Our algorithm accepts as its input two social networks extracted via unsupervised algorithms: (1) a small signed network labeled with attitude polarities (see Tanev, *Proceedings of the MMIES'2007 Workshop Held at RANLP'2007*, Borovets, Bulgaria. pp. 33–40, 2007) and (2) a quotation network, without attitude polarities, consisting of pairs of people where one person makes a direct speech statement about another person (see Pouliquen et al., *Proceedings of the RANLP Conference,* Borovets, Bulgaria, pp. 487–492, 2007). The algorithm which we present here finds pairs of people who are connected in both networks. For each such pair (P_1, P_2) it takes the corresponding attitude polarity from the signed network and uses its polarity to label the quotations of P_1 about P_2. The obtained set of labeled quotations is used to train a Naïve Bayes classifier which then labels part of the remaining quotation network and adds it to the initial signed network. Since the social networks taken as the input are extracted in an unsupervised way, the whole approach including the acquisition of input networks is unsupervised.

2.1 Introduction

Social networks provide an intuitive model of the relations between individuals in a social group. Social networks may reflect different kinds of relations among people: friendship, co-operation, contact, conflict, etc. We are interested in social networks in which edges reflect expressions of positive or negative attitudes between people, such as support or criticism. Such networks are called *signed social*

H. Tanev (✉)
IPSC, T.P. 267, Joint Research Centre – European Commission, Via E. Fermi 2749, 21027, Ispra, Italy
e-mail: htanev@gmail.com

N. Memon et al. (eds.), *Data Mining for Social Network Data,*
Annals of Information Systems 12, DOI 10.1007/978-1-4419-6287-4_2,
© Springer Science+Business Media, LLC 2010

networks [25]. Signed social networks may be used to find groups of people [27]. Groups can be identified in the signed networks as connected sub-graphs in which positive attitude edges are predominant. Then, conflicts and co-operation between the groups can be detected by the edges which span between the individuals from different sub-graphs. In the context of political analysis, sub-graphs with predominant positive attitudes will be formed by political parties, governments of states, countries participating in treaties, etc. Analysts can use signed social networks to understand better the relations between and inside such political formations.

Automatic extraction of a signed social network of sentiment-based relations from text is related to the field of *sentiment analysis* (also referred to as *opinion mining*). The automatic detection of subjectivity vs. objectivity in text and – within the subjective statements – for polarity detection (positive vs. negative sentiment) is an active research area. For a recent survey of the field, see Pang and Lee [17]. Within the fields of information retrieval and computational linguistics, sentiment analysis refers to the automatic detection of sentiment or opinion using software tools. These are frequently applied to opinion-rich sources such as product reviews and blogs. Opinion mining on generic news is uncommon, although the results of such work would be of great interest. Large organizations and political parties often keep a very close eye on how the public and the media perceive and represent them.

News articles are an important source for deriving relations between politicians, businessmen, sportsmen, and other people who are in the focus of the media [25]. State-of-the art information extraction techniques can detect explicit expressions of attitudes (like "P_1 supports P_2," see [23]). However, in some cases, detection of attitude descriptions may require deep analysis and reasoning about human relations, which is mostly beyond the reach of state-of-the-art natural language processing technology. In this chapter, we concentrate on the more feasible task of automatically extracting and classifying explicit attitude expressions and of automatically constructing signed networks from such expressions.

There are two main ways in which the attitude of one person toward another is reported in the news:

1. The news article may contain an explicit expression about the relation between the two people, such as *"Berlusconi criticized the efforts of Prodi."*
2. The article may contain direct reported speech of one person about another, such as *"Berlusconi said: 'The efforts of Prodi are useless'."*

The first way of reporting attitudes is more explicit about their polarity: usually straightforward words and expressions like "criticize," "accuse," "disagree with," "expressed support for," "praised," are used in the news articles to report negative or positive attitudes. However, it is nevertheless difficult to automatically detect such phrases due to the many ways in which an attitude can be expressed and due to the usage of anaphora (e.g. "he" in *"He criticized Prodi"*) and other linguistic phenomena. As a consequence the coverage of approaches which rely on attitude statements of this kind is rather low. For example, Tanev [23] shows that automatically learned patterns to detect a support relationship (expressing a positive attitude) in the news recognize only 10% of the cases in which human readers sense such a relationship when reading the same article.

On the other hand, quotes are easier to find even using superficial patterns like "PERSON said '....'". Pouliquen et al. [19] describe a multilingual quotation detection approach from news articles based on such superficial patterns. This method finds statements of one person about another person. These quotations are then used as edges of a directed graph where vertices are the persons.

The problem with attitudes expressed through direct reported speech is that the polarity of such attitudes is more difficult to be derived, since it contains comments about the qualities of a person, about his/her actions, etc.

Based on the two aforementioned approaches, we have built automatically two social networks out of the data extracted by the Europe Media Monitor (EMM) news gathering and analysis system (see section "EMM news data") [22]:

The first one, so-called *signed network of attitudes (signed network* for short*)*, was described by Tanev [23] and Pouliquen et al. [20]. It detects in news articles interpersonal relations of support (positive attitude) and criticism (negative attitude). The edges in the signed network are obtained by applying syntactic patterns like "P_1 supports P_2," "P_1 accuses P_2," etc. The edges are directed and labeled with the corresponding attitude polarities. Due to the problems of this approach already mentioned, this network has relatively low coverage (595 edges and 548 vertices). See also Tanev [23] for implementation and evaluation details.

The second network is the so-called *quotation network* in which a pair of people P_1 and P_2 is connected with a directed edge (P_1, P_2), if in the news it is reported that P_1 makes a direct speech statement about P_2. The edges are labeled with a reference to the set of quotations of P_1 about P_2. This directed graph is much bigger than the first one (17,400 edges); however, the attitudes of the quotations are not specified.

The signed social network and the quotation network express attitudes in a mutually complementary way: the signed social network specifies the attitude polarity, but captures a relatively small number of person pairs, while the quotation network captures many expressions of attitude, but does not specify the polarity. It was quite natural to combine the information from the two networks in order to derive more relations of specified attitudes between people.

The effort described in this chapter targets information-seeking users who are looking for sentiment expressed toward persons and organizations in the written media.

This chapter is organized as follows: the next section describes characteristics of both input sources, i.e., of the signed social network and the quotation network, and it summarizes the algorithm used to expand the existing signed social network with new edges. This is followed by a third section focusing on the experiments carried out and their evaluation. The fourth section summarizes related work and motivates some of the decisions taken in our approach. The last section concludes the chapter and points to possible future work.

2.2 An Algorithm for Expanding a Signed Social Network of Attitudes

The whole learning process is outlined in Fig. 2.1. Before we run the expansion algorithm which we present in this chapter, we run two unsupervised algorithms – for relation and quotation extraction. These algorithms produce the two social networks, which our algorithm takes as its input: (i) the signed social network of expressed positive and negative attitudes between people and (ii) the quotation network. Our expansion algorithm trains a Naïve Bayes classifier, which classifies the quotations and labels automatically some of the edges in the quotation network with attitude polarity.

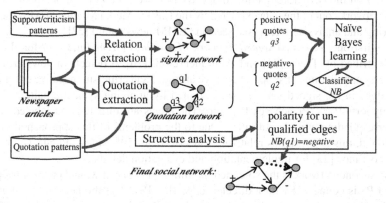

Fig. 2.1 Process overview: from news we extract the two networks. A classifier is learned out of quotations between signed edges (here q2 and q3). The remaining quotations are automatically classified (here q1). If necessary, we take advantage of the structure of the network. Finally the tool generates a signed social network taking advantage of the two techniques

The newly labeled edges can be added to the signed social network and increase its size. Structure analysis can be used to achieve higher confidence for some of the learned new edges. In the example in Fig 2.1, one new edge is added to the signed network after classifying the corresponding set of quotations q1. Since the two networks are completely automatically learned, and the classifier learns from these (which may have a certain number of incorrect edges), the learning settings are completely unsupervised. In the rest of this section we will explain the structure of the two networks and the expansion algorithm in more detail.

2.2.1 Signed Social Network

The signed social network used in our algorithm is a directed graph of attitudes between people. The network is represented by a directed graph where vertices represent people whose names are detected in the news, and the directed edges between two people represent expressions of positive or negative attitude of the first person toward the other one (polarity). We consider the cases when there is one predominant attitude during a certain period of time. In case the attitude is controversial or significantly changes during that period, there should not be an edge between the two people. Since the relations among people may change over time, it makes sense to build a network of predominant attitudes for not very long periods. In our experiments, we used a period of 3 years and it turned out that in this period there were not many cases, when both positive and negative attitudes are expressed between the same people.

More formally, our signed social network of attitudes is a signed directed graph $A_{\pm}(V, E, F)$ with a set of vertices V, a set of directed edges E, and a labeling function $F: E \rightarrow \{+,-\}$ attaching a positive or negative valence or polarity to each edge in E. Each vertex is labeled with the name of the corresponding person. Each directed edge e between two vertices v_1 and v_2 shows that there were one or several expressions of attitude of the person represented by v_1 toward the person represented by v_2 and this is reported in the news articles, published in a certain time period T. The edge e is labeled with the predominant polarity of the attitude of v_1 toward v_2.

We will illustrate this with an example. Let us consider the following set of news fragments:

1. *Hassan Nasrallah* said: "The one who must be punished is the one who ordered the war on Lebanon. *Bush* wants to punish you because you resisted."
2. *Silvio Berlusconi* wrapped up a 2-day meeting yesterday with *George Bush* at the President's ranch near Crawford, Texas, a reward for Italy's strong support.
3. *Berlusconi* criticized *Prodi*.

Ideally, we would like to have in the signed social network all the relations of attitude between people, reported in these three fragments. So a complete signed network $A_{\pm}(V, E, F)$ about these texts will have the following nodes (represented here by the names of the corresponding people):

$$V = \{Hassan\ Nasrallah,\ George\ Bush,\ Silvio\ Berlusconi,\ Romano\ Prodi\}$$

Here we suppose that the creator of the network (analyst or a computer program) may successfully resolve the full names of the people. The directed edges labeled with attitude polarities will be the following:

$$E = \{(Hassan\ Nasrallah,\ George\ Bush,\ negative),$$
$$(Silvio\ Berlusconi,\ George\ Bush,\ positive),$$
$$(George\ Bush,\ Silvio\ Berlusconi,\ positive),$$
$$(Silvio\ Berlusconi,\ Romano\ Prodi,\ negative)\}$$

The symmetry of the attitude between Nasrallah and Bush cannot be derived directly from the text of the chapter. The second sentence implies a mutually positive attitude of Berlusconi toward Bush and vice versa. The third sentence reports an expression of negative attitude by Berlusconi with respect to Prodi.

Automatic extraction of signed social network of attitudes is not an easy task. It requires co-reference resolution, e.g., *Bush = George Bush*, and a sentiment detection algorithm to derive the polarity and the direction of the attitudes. Additionally, world knowledge and deeper syntactic processing are necessary to infer, in the second sentence, that the relation between Berlusconi and Bush is positive on the basis of the fact that the visit of Berlusconi is a reward for Italy's strong support. Some of the necessary tools, like co-reference resolution and sentiment detection algorithms, already exist. However, automatic reasoning systems as the one required to resolve the attitude in the second sentence go beyond the capabilities of state-of-the art natural language processing systems. Therefore, we feel that such indirect expressions of sentiment and attitude go beyond the scope of our current work.

In Tanev [23], we showed how to acquire automatically, in an unsupervised way, a signed network of positive and negative attitudes. This approach was based on syntactic patterns: For example, *X criticized Y* implies that *X* has a negative attitude toward *Y*, where *X* and *Y* are person names. From the third sentence in the example above, this approach may infer that Silvio Berlusconi has a negative attitude toward Romano Prodi. The resolution of the full names of the two leaders is done with a co-reference resolution tool (see [22]). Building on this method, a working system for the automatic acquisition of social networks was implemented and a signed social network of positive and negative attitudes was automatically acquired from news corpora. The problem with the detection of these syntactic patterns is that – due to the many ways in which support or criticism can be expressed – a relatively low part of the expressed attitudes are captured in this way (low Recall). This approach cannot capture important sources of attitude expression like direct reported speech.

2.2.2 Quotation Network

We use a tool for the automatic acquisition of a quotation network, described in Pouliquen et al. [19]. This approach uses surface linguistic patterns like *PERSON said "QUOTATION"* to extract direct speech in newspaper articles in many languages. Other methods, like Krestel et al. [13] or Alrahabi and Descles [3], use more sophisticated patterns, but these are harder to extend to further languages. In addition, the chosen system also recognizes if a person name is mentioned inside the quotation. The system has the advantage that it extracts the opinion holder (the speaker) and the opinion target (the person mentioned inside the quotation) unambiguously when the holder and the target are named persons. Our experiments with online news articles extracted by the EMM system show that the precision of recognition is high enough (99.2% on random selection of multilingual quotes from EMM data) to build a social network based on persons making comments on each other using direct speech. Out of 1,500,000 extracted English quotations, 157,964 contain a reference to another person.[1]

We produce a directed graph $Q(V,E)$ in which vertices V represent people, mentioned in the news in the same way as it is with the signed network of attitudes. Each directed edge $e = (v_1, v_2)$ from E represents the fact that at least one news article contains a quotation of the person v_1 in which this person makes reference to v_2. If we consider again the fragments from news articles shown in the previous section, then the following edge can be derived from the first sentence: {(*Hassan Nasrallah, George Bush*)}. This edge will be labeled with a reference to the quotation of Nasrallah. In general, the edge between two people will be labeled with a reference to a list of all the quotations of the former about the latter, e.g., all the statements of Nasrallah about Bush reported in the news.

A daily updated version of the quotation network is published on http://langtech. jrc.it/entities/socNet/quotes_en.html

We found that quotations about other persons often express an opinion. As stated in Kim and Hovy [11], a judgment opinion consists of a valence, a holder, and a topic. In our case, the holder is the author of the quotation, whereas the topic is the target person of the quote. We apply natural language techniques to try to extract automatically the valence of the quotation.

2.2.3 Automatic Expansion of the Signed Social Network

We present here the algorithm, which automatically expands the signed social network of attitudes. It automatically labels some of the edges from the quotation network with attitude polarity and adds them to the signed social network. For illustration purposes, we will use two small networks presented in Fig. 2.2 and Table 2.1: the signed social network of attitudes $A_\pm(Va, Ea, F)$ and the quotation network $Q(Vq, Eq)$. The symbols "+" and "–" on the edges of A show the polarity of the attitude represented by the corresponding edge. The numbers on the edges of Q are references to the rows in Table 2.1, each of which contains a set of quotations, related to the corresponding edge.

The algorithm performs the following basic steps:

1. It takes as its input the two automatically extracted social network graphs: $A_\pm(Va, Ea, F)$ and $Q(Vq, Eq)$ (see Fig. 2.2).
2. It finds all the pairs of people, who appear in both social networks A and Q and are connected in the same direction. In such a way, we find pairs of people for which the polarity of the attitude is defined in A and at the same time the quotations of the first person about the second can be taken from Q.

---

[1]The system is restricted to only one person per quotation. It is assumed that the first person mentioned in the quotation is the main person to whom the quotation refers.

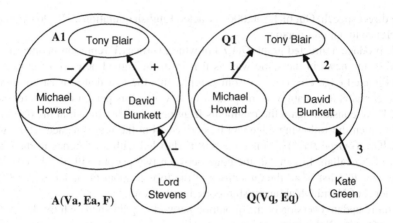

Fig. 2.2 Signed network of attitudes $A_\pm$ (*Va, Ea, F*) (*left*) and a quotation network $Q(Vq, Eq)$ (*right*)

Table 2.1 Quotation sets for the quotation network Q in Fig. 2.2

Reference label, author	Quotation set
1, Michael Howard	Mr. Blair's authority has been diminished almost to vanishing point
2, David Blunkett	2.1 And it is good, because anybody with any ounce of understanding about politics knows that when Tony Blair and Gordon Brown work together we are a winner
	2.2 Tony Blair and Gordon Brown can accept that there will be a transition, that there is a process and whatever the timetable, they can work together
3, Kate Green	David Blunkett was committed to the aim of ending child poverty

3. More formally, we find A_1– a subgraph of A and Q_1– its isomorphic subgraph in Q, whose corresponding vertices are labeled with the same person names. Each directed edge $e_1 = (va_1, va_2)$ from A_1 has a corresponding edge $e_2 = (vq_1, vq_2)$ from Q_1, such that the labels va_1 and vq_1 represent the same person P_1, and the same holds for va_2 and vq_2, which represent person P_2.

   The label on e_1 shows the polarity of the attitude of P_1 toward P_2 and the label on e_2 is a reference to a list of statements of P_1 about P_2. For example, in Fig. 2.2 A_1 and Q_1 represent the same triple of British politicians. These people are connected in the same way in both subgraphs. The only difference between A_1 and Q_1 is the labeling of the edges. For example, in A_1 the edge corresponding to the pair (*Blunkett, Blair*) is labeled with the sign "+," which stands for positive attitude, while the edge in Q_1 for the same pair is labeled with "2," which is a reference to row number 2 in Table 2.1, which contains all the quotations of *David Blunkett* about *Tony Blair*.

4. For each pair of people (P_1, P_2), represented in Q_1 (e.g., *Blunkett, Blair*), we find the set of quotations of P_1 about P_2 from Q_1. In this example there are two

quotations of *Blunkett* about *Blair*, which are in row number 2 of Table 2.1. At the same time (P_1, P_2) will be represented also in the signed network A_1 and, from it, the algorithm takes the polarity of the attitude of P_1 (e.g., *Blunkett*) toward P_2 (e.g., *Blair*). The polarity may be positive or negative. The outcome of this step is a set of pairs (q, a), where q is a set of quotations of one person about another person (e.g., the two quotations of *Blunkett* about *Blair*) and a is the attitude polarity between these two people (positive in this example). We can assume that the predominant attitude polarity of the quotations in q is equal to a.

5. The algorithm uses the quotation–polarity pairs obtained from the previous step as a training set and trains a Naïve Bayes classifier, which finds the predominant polarity of a quotation set. As features, we use words and word bigrams from the quotation set. The categories are two: positive and negative attitudes. For example, one training instance from the example in Fig. 2.2 and Table 2.1 will be a vector of words and bigrams extracted from the comments of *Blunkett* about *Blair*. This training instance will be labeled with the category "positive attitude." From the example in Fig. 2.2 and Table 2.1, we can extract two training instances: one of them we already mentioned and the other one is obtained from the quotation of *Howard* about *Blair* (row 1 in Table 2.1), labeled with negative polarity, defined from network A.

6. The Naïve Bayes classifier is then applied to the set of quotations of each directed edge from Q between two people P_1 and P_2 that was not used during the training stage. In our example these will be the pair (*Green, Blunkett*). The classifier returns two probabilities $pp(P_1, P_2)$ – the probability that the person P_1 has a positive attitude toward P_2 – and $pn(P_1, P_2)$ – the probability that the attitude is negative.

7. If $pp(P_1, P_2) > pn(P_1, P_2)$ and $pp(P_1,P_2) > minpp$," then the pair is added to the signed network A and a positive attitude edge is put between the vertices representing P_1 and P_2 in A. If $pn(P_1, P_2) > pp(P_1, P_2)$ and $pn(P_1,P_2) > minpn$, the new edge between P_1 and P_2 is labeled with negative attitude. If pp and pn are not beyond the necessary thresholds (*minpp* and *minpn*, set empirically on the training set), then the pair (P_1, P_2) is not added to A. In our example, if the pair (*Green, Blunkett*) is correctly classified as belonging to the category "positive attitude," a new vertex will be added to A which represents *Kate Green*, and an edge labeled with "+" will be added between *Kate Green* and *David Blunkett*.

2.3 Filtering the Results Using Output Network Structural Properties

We also wanted to test whether the performance of the Naïve Bayes classifier could be significantly improved by adding constraints on structural properties of the output signed network. As an example, if a person A likes person B which in turn likes person C, but person A dislikes person C, then we will discard the triple ABC as inconsistent.

There is rich research literature showing how certain kinds of social networks can be globally characterized by a number of structural properties and how these properties can in turn be derived from local constraints like the aforementioned. Consider a signed graph $A_\pm(V, E, F)$: this represents a simplified model of our signed social network, where the assumption is made that attitude polarities between two persons are always reciprocated: that means it cannot be that person A likes person B while B dislikes A, therefore we can ignore the directions of the edges.

Each of the sub-graphs of $A_\pm(V, E, F)$ consisting of 3 nodes and 3 edges, or complete *triads*, can be in one of the 8 states drawn in Fig. 2.3, A.-H.

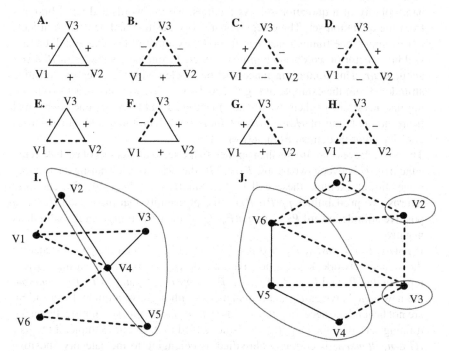

Fig. 2.3 Triad configurations and graph clustering. A.-H.: possible configuration of triads in a signed graph. I.: bipartition of a balanced signed graph into two clusters; edges stand for positive attitudes, dashed edges for negative attitudes. J.: a partition of a clusterable signed graph into multiple clusters of nodes

The polarity configurations of the triads in the top row are commonly taken as "minimizing the tension" between the participant nodes or, in other words, as *balanced*. As an example, when interpreting graph signs as affective attitudes such as liking/disliking, network actors v_1 and v_2, who like each other, would expect to agree on attitudes toward a third actor v_3 and would take as highly inconsistent to have conflicting attitudes on it. Viewed from the other side: for actor v_3 it would look like inconsistent to find a positive attitude between two persons on which he has inconsistent attitudes.

More formally speaking, the triads on the top row can be viewed as positive sign cycles, where the sign of a cycle in a graph can be calculated as the product of signs on the single edges. If we generalize this to cycles of length larger than 3 we can derive a definition of balance for signed graphs [25][2]:

D1: A signed graph is balanced iff all its cycles have positive signs.

An intuitive consequence of this property is that vertices of the graph can be partitioned into two clusters, that is two subsets V_1 and V_2 of V such that any edge between V_1 and V_2 is negative and any edge within V_1 or V_2 is positive, as in graph I in Fig. 2.3.

As we found this hypothesis too strong for our application domain, we relaxed some of the constraints of balance and evaluated a more general property of clusterability, as defined in Davis [6]:

D2: A signed graph has a clustering iff the graph contains no cycle with exactly one negative edge.

Referring again to triad types, the only unbalanced configuration to be additionally allowed now is the one with three negative signs (Fig. 2.3.H).

Clearly, the signed graph on quotation pairs output by the Naïve Bayes classifier does not fully satisfy the clusterability principle as such; rather, we tried to enforce statistical tendency toward it and evaluate the precision gain with respect to pure Naïve Bayes. Namely, for each edge $e = (v_i, v_j)$, we consider all triads in the graph including e: for each such triad (v_i, v_j, v_k), we check polarities on edges (v_i, v_k) and (v_j, v_k) and apply clusterability conditions[3] to derive an expected polarity p for (v_i, v_j). For each edge we denote with $C(+)$ the number of triads which imply positive expected attitude for this edge and with $C(-)$ the number of triads which imply negative expected attitude.

We then compute a ratio $R = C(+)/C(-)$ of the expected "+" counts over the "−" counts. Next we take into consideration only the edges for which $C(+)$ and $C(-)$ are significantly different and $R > \alpha$ or $R \leq \beta$, where $\alpha \geq 1$ and $\beta \leq 1$. In this way we predict $p = +$ if $R > \alpha$, $p = -$ if $R \leq \beta$, and do not consider the edges for which $\alpha \geq R > \beta$, since the ratio does not allow for clear prediction.

Finally, we discarded actual values on edge (v_i, v_j) which were different from p. Our hypothesis is that, if clusterability is in place in networks of positive or negative attitudes between people, aligning output to it should result in increased accuracy.

---

[2]The original definition was actually formulated for directed graphs and made use of the notion of "semi-cycle", that is a closed directed walk of at least three nodes on the graph which is traversed ignoring the direction of the edges.

[3]Namely, if (v_i, v_k) and (v_j, v_k) are both positive, we enforce "+" on (v_i, v_j), while if (v_i, v_k) and (v_j, v_k) have conflicting signs, then we enforce "−" on (v_i, v_j).

2.4 Data, Experiments, and Evaluation

We carried out several experiments and evaluations in order to prove that our approach to automatically expand signed social networks is feasible.

2.4.1 The News Data

The source of the data on which relation extraction, quotation recognition, and sentiment analysis is carried out are the English language news articles gathered by the *Europe Media Monitor* (EMM) news gathering and analysis system. EMM currently monitors an average of 90,000 news articles per day from about 2,200 news portals around the world in 43 languages, as well as from commercial news providers including 20 news agencies. About 15,000 of these articles are written in the English language. To access the various EMM-based online applications, see http://press.jrc.it/overview.html. These public web sites are accessed by an average of 40,000 distinct users per day, with approximately 1.4 million hits per day.

News-based social network data is mostly being produced to serve the information needs of political analysts and journalists. Social networks are one of many ways to look at media information.

2.4.2 The Social Networks Used as Input

We used a signed social network and a quotation network, built automatically from English language news articles, published in the 2.5-year period January 2005–July 2007. The signed social network contains 548 vertices and 595 edges. In order to ensure higher reliability for the training of the Naïve Bayes classifier, we considered only those edges that are supported by at least three articles (see the algorithm description in the section *Signed Network*). We also excluded the edges which are marked both positive and negative, which can be caused by expression of both positive and negative attitude between the same people. In the period January 2005–July 2007, a daily average of 4.36 pairs involving criticism and 3.52 pairs involving support was found as part of the daily news analysis.

The quotation network was extracted from the same period. It has 11,353 vertices and 17,423 edges. During the reporting period, a daily average of 1159 English quotes was found, of which 51 made reference to other named persons. Due to an increase in the number of articles processed, the number of relations and quotations detected every day is approximately double at the time of writing this chapter (early 2009).

Two hundred seventy-five edges were common between the signed network and the quotation network.

2.4.3 Evaluation Criteria

The task on which we want to evaluate the system is the automatic expansion of the signed social network by deriving attitude polarities from a quotation network. We thus trained the classifier, applied it to new quotes, and then evaluated whether the automatically assigned sentiment polarity is correct. There are two issues to be considered:

First, our main task was the expansion of the signed network; the quotation network was used only as an auxiliary resource. For this reason, we did not aim at high recall in the classification of the edges of the quotation network; we rather wanted to get better precision. Second, for our purpose, we are only interested in subjective quotations, i.e., those in which sentiment polarity is expressed, while we do not consider quotations with neutral sentiment. Subjectivity detection is thus the first step, which will eliminate those quotations that are neutral. Polarity detection is then the second step, i.e., the detection of quotations that express either a positive or a negative attitude.

The neutral quotes can be of three different types: (i) neutral or factual quotations that clearly do not express attitude toward the other person, e.g., *Bonaiuti said "Today Mr. Berlusconi visited Washington"*; (ii) quotations which may express an attitude, but out of the context, it is – even for human judges – not possible to recognize the attitude, and therefore the quotation itself can be regarded as neutral; (iii) sets of quotations in which sentiment is being expressed, but either the sentiment is neither positive nor negative (e.g., expression of a strong sentiment that things are *normal*, or *average*) or expressions of positive and negative attitudes are balanced.

The predominant attitude of a person P_1 toward P_2 can be derived from all the quotations of P_1 about P_2. This is not trivial, since sometimes we have changing attitudes between people (*balanced sentiment*), so we may have quotations of P_1 about P_2, which are positive, negative, and neutral. We adopted the following evaluation approach: we ignore the neutral quotations of P_1 about P_2. If no subjective quotations remain, then we consider that the attitude of P_1 toward P_2 is not defined. For the subjective quotations, we first ignore duplicates or near-duplicates and then count the number of positive and negative quotations. If there are more positive than negative quotations, then the predominant attitude is considered positive; if negative quotations prevail, then we consider the predominant attitude to be negative. In the rare case when the number of positive and negative quotations is the same, we consider the attitude of P_1 toward P_2 not defined.

Precision was defined as the number of assigned labels for which the human judgment coincides with the decision of the system divided by the number of edges for which the system makes a decision.

2.4.4 Experiments and Evaluation

There were about 17,400 ordered pairs of people in the automatically extracted quotation network. We took a random sample of 176 pairs and evaluated manually their distribution into the three classes: positive attitude, negative attitude, and neutral attitude. We found the following distribution: 32.3% positive, 28.4% negative, and 39.2% neutral. A baseline system which labels all the pairs as positives will thus have around 32.3% precision.

As we pointed out earlier, 275 of the ordered pairs of people from the quotation network were common with the signed network. In the signed network, 111 of these pairs were labeled with positive attitude and 164 with negative attitude. However, we think that there is no reason for the negative quotations to be considered more probable in the quotation network. The manual calculation of the distribution mentioned in the previous paragraph confirmed our hypothesis. Presumably the tool simply identified more negative relations because the patterns for this relation are more comprehensive. Considering this, out of the 275 common pairs we produced a balanced training set of 111 positive and 111 negative ordered pairs, by randomly selecting 111 of the negative pairs. Using this set, we trained a Naïve Bayes classifier (see step 5 of the algorithm).

To find the best values for *minpp* and *minpn* we used a development set of about 100 pairs of people from the quotation network. We empirically found two settings for *minpp* and *minpn* which were likely to give reasonable precision combined with a reasonable number of classified pairs. One of the reasons to test the approach with two settings was the fact that we used a relatively small development set to define the parameters, so we were not sure to what extent the optimality of the found parameters will be generalized across the whole collection.

In parameter settings A, *minpp* = 0.9199 and *minpn* = 0.969 In parameter settings B, *minpp* = 0.9599 and *minpn* = 0.9899.

We ran the algorithm with both parameter settings on 10,000 randomly chosen pairs of people who do not appear in the signed social network and who were not included in the development set. The system output only those pairs which it succeeded to label as positive or negative. Next, two judges evaluated the output of the system in terms of precision, the percentage of correctly labeled pairs. The coverage was calculated as a percentage of those pairs out of these 10,000 which were given a (correct or incorrect) label by the system. A pair was considered correct only if both the system and the evaluator both labeled it with the same positive or negative label. If a pair was present in the output of the system, but the evaluator considered it neutral, then it was counted as an error, independently of the system-generated label. The evaluation of the algorithm with settings *A* was carried out on 96 randomly selected pairs. When choosing settings *B*, 57 out of these 96 pairs remained, the rest were filtered out by the algorithm as being neutral. The results are reported in Table 2.2. All the reported precision figures are significantly over the baseline precision of 32.3%, with the exception of the evaluation of judge B of the performance of settings *A*. With settings *B*, the precision goes 15–17% beyond the baseline, which shows the feasibility of our unsupervised approach. The kappa agreement between judge A and judge B on the run with settings *A* is 0.67 and with settings *B* the kappa is 0.70 – both values correspond to significant agreement.

If we exclude the 39.2% neutral cases from the quotation network, then we can evaluate our algorithm on the more classic task of polarity detection (is the statement positive or negative?). For this task, a baseline approach which classifies

Table 2.2 Precision and coverage of the algorithm. The baseline is 32.3%

	Precision judge A (%)	Precision judge B (%)	Coverage (%)
Settings *A*	44.8	37.5	24.8
Settings *B*	49.1	47.3	15.9

every pair as positive will have a precision of 53.2%, considering the distribution of positive and negative quotations. We used the evaluated data and took out the pairs which the judges labeled as neutral, then we recalculated the precision on the remaining pairs. The results are shown in Table 2.3.

Table 2.3 Precision of the algorithm for the task of polarity detection. The baseline is 53.2%

	Precision judge A (%)	Precision judge B (%)
Settings *A*	55.8	52.17
Settings *B*	62.2	61.4

It can be seen that, with settings *A*, the algorithm produces results close to the baseline, which means that it does not work in practice when selecting between positive and negative pairs. However, with settings *B*, the precision is 9–10% above the baseline.

We evaluated also the recall of both settings on the task of identifying positive and negative edges from the quotation network. From 100 randomly taken edges, we found 54 which express positive or negative attitude. Taking into consideration these 54 edges, the following figures were found for the two parameter settings:

Settings *A*: 20.4% recall

Settings *B*: 18.5%. recall

Even if the recall seems to be a bit low, it should be taken into account that, from a quotation network with more than 17,400 edges, this still means extraction of over 3,200 additional edges which can be added to the signed network together with the people, represented by their adjacent vertices. Considering the initial size of the signed network, the level of recall which our method achieves allows for six times increasing the size of the initial signed network.

Finally we evaluated the precision of the algorithm when boosted by the network structural constraints introduced above. We first run the Bayes classifier with settings *A* on about 17,000 edges from the quotation network, assigning positive or negative labels to around 4,000 edges. Then we applied the filtering procedure based on the clusterability hypothesis, eventually extracting 199 labels. Precision rate counted on a random sample of 100 labels was 59%.

Among the labels filtered out, there were some which were participating in at least one triple in the network: we tried to include them all in another output evaluation: interestingly, while slightly outperforming the pure Bayes classifier, the precision rate in this case was significantly reduced with respect to the structural filtering (45.7%), suggesting that participation in some specific types of triads, rather than generic degree of connectedness of the pair nodes, has a crucial role in improving the performance.

2.5 Related Work

Our work touches on various disciplines and areas: sentiment analysis, relation extraction, text classification, quotation extraction, and social networks. We will thus discuss related work for each of these one by one.

Apart from the immediate usefulness of this work for the main target user group, sentiment analysis on reported speech (quotations) is also needed for generic sentiment detection in documents. First, for an overall document sentiment assessment, it is important to identify passages (such as quotations) with different sentiment [17, p. 6]. Second, news articles are relatively likely to contain descriptions of opinions that do not belong to the article's author, e.g., in the case of quotations from a political figure [17, p. 55f], making opinion holder or opinion source detection in the document an important task. According to Mullen and Malouf [16] and Agrawal et al. [1], it is common to quote politicians at the other end of the political spectrum. Authors can thus be clustered so that those who tend to quote the same entities are placed in the same cluster [17, p. 49], similarly to using co-citation analysis to group publications (e.g., [8, 15]). The work in this chapter contributes to opinion holder identification.

The algorithm described in the previous section detects subjectivity and polarity in a one-step process: only those cases classified with a Naïve Bayes output above certain thresholds are considered as expressing positive or negative opinion, while cases below that threshold are considered neutral. Among the neutral cases, we do not distinguish between objective statements, i.e., those that are more factual and do not express any sentiment and those that are subjective, but where the polarity is balanced (a balanced mix of positive and negative statements). These choices are motivated by our objective, which is the detection of social networks with support and criticism relations. However, it is not uncommon to split subjectivity and polarity detection explicitly and to separate sentiment from polarity, as someone may for instance express a strong feeling that something or someone is mediocre. Mihalcea et al. [14] found that subjectivity recognition is more difficult than the subsequent step of polarity detection, while Yu and Hatzivassiloglou [28] report achieving 97% accuracy with a Naïve Bayes classifier to distinguish more neutral Wall Street Journal reports from the more opinionated editorials. To distinguish neutral from emotionally balanced reports, Wilson et al. [26] worked on intensity classification.

In our algorithm, we use automatically extracted information on support and criticism relations to perform lexicon induction, i.e., to identify positive and negative lexicon entries. Alternatives would be the manual compilation of positive and negative lexicon entries, or lexicon induction by using positive and negative seed words such as "good" and "bad," for which the polarity is known (e.g., [9, 24]). According to Allison [2], using only positive and negative words does not consistently improve the classification results, compared to using all words.

Another choice of ours is to use a Naïve Bayes classifier. We did not invest in comparing different classifiers, as Allison [2] has compared Naïve Bayes with SVM and other classifiers and concluded that differences in performance depended on the amount of training data and on the document representation more than on the choice of classifier. On the other hand, the advantage of the Bayes classifier is that it returns the probability distribution of every instance between the two attitude polarity classes – positive and negative. This distribution can be considered to be a measure for the reliability of the classifier decision, i.e., the bigger the difference in the two probabilities is, the more reliable is the decision of the classifier. We used this fact, in order to leave some unreliably classified instances as unclassified and increased the precision in such a way.

Regarding the representation of the quotations, we opted for a bag of unigrams or bigrams, where we used term presence rather than term frequency or term weight. We base this choice on the insights of Pang et al. [18] and Allison [2], who both achieved better sentiment analysis results using term presence. Pang and Lee [17, p. 33] reckon that term presence may work better for sentiment analysis, while term frequency may work better for topic classification.

We achieved better results using a combination of word unigrams and bigrams rather than using only unigrams. This is in line with the results by Dave et al. [5], who came to the conclusion that, in some settings, word bigrams and trigrams perform better for product review polarity classification.

We did not investigate the usage of more linguistic information or patterns that would detect phrases, negations, syntactic structures, parts-of-speech, and the like. The reason for this is that EMM applications always aim at being highly multilingual. Achieving high multilinguality, while working in a small team, is only possible by keeping language-specific information to a minimum and by trying to use language-independent methods and resources to the largest extent possible [22]. At least regarding the non-usage of part-of-speech information and syntax, we have reasons to believe that this choice does not have a negative impact on the results achieved: While Hatzivassiloglou and Wiebe [10] found that adjectives are good indicators to determine sentence subjectivity, Pang et al. [18] found that adjectives alone perform less well than the most frequent word unigrams, and their usage of part-of-speech information did not improve results compared to simply using word forms. Regarding the usage of syntax, Pang and Lee [17, p. 35] found that – for sentence level sentiment classification tasks – using dependency trees did work better than approaches using bags of unigrams, but the results were comparable to experiments using word n-grams with $n > 1$. Generally speaking, the advantage of using bag of n-gram representations is that the methods are likely to be easily adaptable to further languages, although it is intuitively plausible that at least negation should be considered in sentiment analysis applications. For approaches to considering negation, see Pang and Lee [17, p. 35ff].

Studies on balance and its effects on global structure of networks of person mutual attitudes can be traced back to the origins of social network analysis [25].

In social cognition research, evidence was found that human representation of social links is *biased* by the balance hypothesis, resulting in lower error rates in recalling and learning tasks on actually balanced structures with respect to unbalanced ones [4]. On the other hand, while balance theory proved successful in modeling collaborative relations in political communities and international relations [12], sociometrical data collected from a range of social networks was not always found fitting the balance structure, leading researchers to look for weaker hypotheses, like clusterability, ranked clusterability and transitivity [7].

Given the unsupervised nature of our approach and resulting noise in the output data, extracting structural properties from a statistical analysis of the returned networks was not an option for us. On the contrary, we exploratively assumed a minimal constraint on the global structure of the attitude networks (clusterability) and evaluated how much this helped the classifier to better fit data from human annotation.

A relative novelty of our approach is the usage and combination of information from two different networks produced with different means, and the fact that the directed graphs of the social networks (produced in unsupervised fashion) are used for unsupervised training of the classifier. However, Riloff & Wiebe [21] also used some type of bootstrapping: They used the output of two available initial classifiers (one to identify subjective sentences, the other to identify objective sentences) to create labeled data, which was then used to learn more syntactic patterns to recognize sentence subjectivity.

2.6 Conclusions and Future Work

We have presented work on automatically expanding existing signed social network graphs. The proposed method is to first combine the signed social network with a second, unsigned network of quotations (person A makes reference to person B in direct reported speech), to train a classifier that distinguishes positive and negative quotations, and to then apply this classifier to the quotation network. By doing this, we managed to add over 3,200 additional edges to the initial smaller network consisting of 548 vertices and 595 edges. Experiments showed that, with the best parameter settings, the classification precision of the added edges in this unsupervised approach is about 62%, when ignoring the neutral quotations. This result is very encouraging as it was produced in an unsupervised setting with input data taken from automated processes for social network generation, but it goes without saying that it could be improved.

Although other methods use bootstrapping for sentiment detection, we did it in a way, which to the best of our knowledge was not previously used: We identified the polarity of the sentiment between two people and then automatically labeled quotations which are likely to express the same sentiment between these two people. We were able to use our approach to identify attitudes between people, organizations, and topics, in this way significantly augmenting the size of the signed social network.

A major advantage of the proposed method is its independence of language-specific procedures, as no linguistic information was used. It is thus, in principle, possible to combine the monolingual signed social network of support and criticism relations with the highly multilingual data of the quotation network in EMM: Quotations are currently being identified in 13 languages, and an average 3326 new multilingual quotations are found every day, of which 176 make reference to other persons. As positive and negative attitudes between persons should not differ according to the reporting language, it is reasonable to assume that the monolingual English support and criticism relationships can be combined with multilingual quotation relationships. The advantage would be a generous expansion of the existing social networks. Assuming that the two social networks overlap enough to have enough training data, exploring this multilingual extension is on our agenda for future work.

Next steps will thus be to test a range of further methods to reduce the error rates for subjectivity recognition and polarity identification.

One issue to tackle is the fact that changes in attitude of persons over time (like *Hillary Clinton* and *Barack Obama* during the electoral campaign) are currently not considered because all quotations for a pair of persons are put into one bag, thus mixing positive, negative, and neutral statements. We thus plan to evaluate whether increasingly reducing the time span of input source news for both signed social network and quotation network could result in a significantly improved accuracy of the trained classifier.

One of the open avenues would also be to evaluate how differently the alternative structural constraints on the output network can contribute in refining the results. We also have the intention to make the postulation of structural properties more grounded on a statistical analysis of the extracted attitude networks.

Users are very interested in a news bias analysis. We would therefore like to investigate whether the subjectivity of quotations differs from one news source to another, and also from one news source country to another. The question is thus, Do the media of one country show more positive or negative quotations for given pairs of persons.

Finally, feeding social networks from live media is an excellent way of feeling the pulse of daily politics. It would thus be particularly attractive to engage in group mining and group dynamics detection focusing on changes that occur over time.

Acknowledgments We would like to thank the whole team working on the Europe Media Monitor for providing the valuable news data. Their research and programming effort laid the foundation which made this experimental work possible.

References

1. Agrawal, R., Rajagopalan, S., Srikant, R., and Xu, Y. Mining newsgroups using networks arising from social behavior. In *Proceedings of World-Wide Web Conference*, Budapest, Hungary, pp. 529–535, 2003.
2. Allison, B. Sentiment detection using lexically-based classifiers. In *To Appear in Proceedings of TSD'2008 Brno*, Czech Republic, 2008.

3. Alrahabi, M. and Desclés, J.P. Automatic annotation of direct reported speech in Arabic and French, according to semantic map of enunciative modalities. In *Proceedings of GoTAL conference*, Gothenburg, Sweden, pp. 40–51, 2008.
4. Crockett, W.H. Inferential rules in the learning and recall of patterns of sentiments. *Journal of Personality*, 47(4):658–676, 1979.
5. Dave, K., Lawrence, S., and Pennock, D.M. Mining the peanut gallery: Opinion extraction and semantic classification of product reviews. In *Proceedings of World-Wide Web Conference*, Budapest, Hungary, pp. 519–528, 2003.
6. Davis, J.A. Clustering and structural balance in graphs. *Human Relations* 30:181–187, 1967.
7. Davis, J.A. The Davis/Holland/Leinhardt studies: An overview. In P.W. Holland and S. Leinhardt (eds), *Perspectives on Social Network Research*, New York, NY: Academic, pp. 51–62, 1979.
8. Efron, M. Cultural orientation: Classifying subjective documents by cociation [sic] analysis. In *Proceedings of the AAAI Fall Symposium on Style and Meaning in Language, Art, Music, and Design*, Washington, DC, pp. 41–48, 2004.
9. Hatzivassiloglou, V. and McKeown, K. Predicting the semantic orientation of adjectives. In *Proceedings of the Joint ACL/EACL Conference*, Madrid, Spain, pp. 174–181, 1997.
10. Hatzivassiloglou, V. and Wiebe, J. Effects of adjective orientation and gradability on sentence subjectivity. In *Proceedings of the International Conference on Computational Linguistics*, Saarbrücken, Germany, pp. 299–305, 2000.
11. Kim, S.M. and Hovy, E.H. Identifying and analyzing judgment opinions. In *Proceedings of the HLT-NAACL conference*, New York, NY, pp. 200–207,2006.
12. Knoke, D. *Political Networks: The Structural Perspective*. New York, NY: Cambridge University Press, 2003.
13. Krestel, R., Witte, R., and Bergler, S. Minding the source: Automatic tagging of reported speech in newspaper articles. In *Proceedings of LREC conference*, Marrakech, Morocco, 2008.
14. Mihalcea, R., Banea, C., and Wiebe, J. Learning multilingual subjective language via cross-lingual projections. In *Proceedings of the ACL Conference*, Prague, Czech Republic, pp. 976–983, 2007.
15. Montejo-Ráez, A., Ureña-López, L.A., and Steinberger, R. Text categorization using bibliographic records: Beyond document content. *Procesamiento del Lenguaje Natural*, 35: 119–126, 2005.
16. Mullen, T. and Malouf, R. Taking sides: User classification for informal online political discourse. *Internet Research*, 18:177–190, 2008.
17. Pang, B. and Lee, L. Opinion mining and sentiment analysis. *Foundations and Trends in Information Retrieval*, 2(1–2):1–135, 2008.
18. Pang, B., Lee, L., and Vaithyanathan, V. Thumbs up? Sentiment classification using machine learning techniques. In *Proceedings of the Conference on Empirical Methods in Natural Language Processing*, Morristown, NJ, pp. 79–86, 2002.
19. Pouliquen, B., Steinberger, R., and Best, C. Automatic detection of quotations in multilingual news. In *Proceedings of the RANLP Conference*, Borovets, Bulgaria, pp. 487–492, 2007.
20. Pouliquen, B., Tanev, H., and Atkinson, M. Extracting and learning social networks out of multilingual news. In *Proceedings of the SocNet workshop*, Skalica, Slovakia, pp. 13–16, 2008.
21. Riloff, E. and Wiebe, J. Learning extraction patterns for subjective expressions. In *Proceedings of the Conference on Empirical Methods in Natural Language Processing*, Morristown, NJ, pp. 105–112, 2003.
22. Steinberger, R., Pouliquen, B., and Ignat, C. Using language-independent rules to achieve high multilinguality in Text Mining. In F. Fogelman-Soulié, D. Perrotta, J. Piskorski and R. Steinberger (eds). *Mining Massive Data Sets for Security*, pp. 217–240. Amsterdam: IOS Press, 2008.

23. Tanev, H. Unsupervised learning of social networks from a multiple-source news corpus. In *Proceedings of the MMIES'2007 Workshop Held at RANLP'2007*, Borovets, Bulgaria. pp. 33–40, 2007.
24. Turney, P. Thumbs up or thumbs down? Semantic orientation applied to unsupervised classification of reviews. In *Proceedings of the Association for Computational Linguistics*, Philadelphia, PA, pp. 417–424, 2002.
25. Wasserman, S. and Faust, K. Social network analysis: Methods and applications. Cambridge: Cambridge University Press, 2008.
26. Wilson, T., Wiebe, J., and Hwa, R. Just how mad are you? Finding strong and weak opinion clauses. *Computational Intelligence*, 22(2):73–99, 2006.
27. Yang, B., Cheung, W., and Liu, J. Community mining from signed social networks. *Transactions on Knowledge and Data Engineering* 10:1333–1348, 2007.
28. Yu, H. and Hatzivassiloglou, V. Towards answering opinion questions: Separating facts from opinions and identifying the polarity of opinion sentences. In *Proceedings of the Conference on Empirical Methods in Natural Language Processing*, Morristown, NJ, 129–136, 2003.

25. Tanev, H.: Unsupervised learning of social networks from a multiple-source news corpus. In: Proc. Workshop on Multi-source Multilingual Information Extraction and Summarization, pp. 33–40, 2007.

26. Turney, P.: Thumbs up or thumbs down? Semantic orientation applied to unsupervised classification of reviews. In: The Meeting of the Association for Computational Linguistics Foundations, Inc., pp. 417–424, 2002.

27. Wasserman, S., and Faust, K.: Social network analysis: Methods and applications. Cambridge University Press, 2004.

28. Wilson, T., Wiebe, J., and Hwa, R.: Just how mad are you? Finding strong and weak opinion clauses. Computational Intelligence 22(2):73–99, 2006.

29. Yang, H.: Cheung, W., and Liao, L.: Community mining from signed social networks. IEEE Transactions on Knowledge and Data Engineering 19:1333–1348, 2007.

30. Yu, H., and Hatzivassiloglou, V.: Towards answering opinion questions: Separating facts from opinions and identifying the polarity of opinion sentences. In: Proceedings of the Conference on Empirical Methods in Natural Language Processing, Vol. 10, pp. 129–136, 2003.

Chapter 3
Automatic Mapping of Social Networks of Actors from Text Corpora: Time Series Analysis

James A. Danowski and Noah Cepela

Abstract To test hypotheses about presidential cabinet network centrality and presidential job approval over time and to illustrate automatic social network identification from large volumes of text, this research mined the social networks among the cabinets of Presidents Reagan, G.H.W. Bush, Clinton, and G.W. Bush based on the members' co-occurrence in news stories. Each administration's data was sliced into time intervals corresponding to the Gallup presidential approval polls to synchronize the social networks with presidential job approval ratings. It was hypothesized that when the centrality of the president is lower than that of other cabinet members, job approval ratings are higher. This is based on the assumption that news is generally negative and when the president stands above the other cabinet members in network centrality, he or she is more likely to be associated with the negative press coverage in the minds of members of the public. The hypothesis was supported for each of the administrations with the Reagan and G.H.W. Bush having a lag of 1, Clinton a lag of 4, and G.W. Bush a lag of 2. Automatic network analysis of social actors from textual corpora is feasible and enables testing hypotheses over time.

3.1 Introduction

Political and communication science has long valued a network analysis approach to conceptualizing and measuring phenomena. Among the earliest to map the networks of political actors were the studies of political communication among voters [29]. At the level of community, others have investigated networks of political power [10, 27, 34]. Organizations have been conceptualized in political economy terms using social network analysis frameworks [24, 37]. A sweeping explication of political networks ranging from individual through international levels has placed

J.A. Danowski (✉)
Department of Communication, University of Illinois, MC 132, 1007 W. Harrison St., Chicago, IL 60607, USA
e-mail: jimd@uic.edu

N. Memon et al. (eds.), *Data Mining for Social Network Data*,
Annals of Information Systems 12, DOI 10.1007/978-1-4419-6287-4_3,
© Springer Science+Business Media, LLC 2010

network concepts at the center of political processes [30]. Of particular relevance to the current study, presidential cabinets have been seen in network terms [22], although have yet to be measured from this perspective.

Here we introduce a method of automatic identification of the networks among presidential cabinet actors. Mining large volumes of news and web documents for evidence of the identities of social actors and their relationships is increasingly feasible. Moreover, because most online information has time stamps, it is possible to construct time series analyses of how social networks change over time, and how the network variables are associated with other kinds of variables over time. This can give two of the three necessary conditions for causality: (1) association and (2) time order, leaving for the analyst's further examination: (3) ruling out rival explanations as potential causes of the response variables of interest.

To illustrate the measurement of association and time order from social network mining, we use as an example the relationships among members of the US presidential administration cabinets for Presidents Reagan, G.H.W Bush, Clinton, and G.W. Bush. We identify the networks among the cabinet members based on their co-occurrence in news stories. The network centrality of each actor and of the entire network is indexed and examined in association with the job approval ratings of the president over the course of the administrations.

One of the features of data mining for such networks is that the time slices can be readily set according to the situational conditions of the processes being studied. For example, for Clinton, the Gallup job approval ratings were measured on average 30 days apart, while for the G.W. Bush administration they were 22 days apart. Network time slices can be set according to the time intervals of the response variable, as is done in this study, increasing the interval validity of the research design.

Political scientists and communication scholars have studied predictors of presidential job approval and favorability for several decades. In the most recent wave of research, media variables are increasingly examined as predictors of presidential job approval and favorability [25]. The current research is an example of this. Rather than looking only at the amount of coverage within nominal categories of content, we take a more refined approach of automatic content analysis of the networks among cabinet members portrayed in the press within time slices.

Regarding our response variable, presidential job approval, prior research has found that job approval and favorability, measured separately in the Gallup polls, is very highly correlated. Few respondents hold inconsistent attitudes, such as reporting that a president is doing a bad job yet that they strongly like him [9]. In the current research, therefore, we use only the job approval variable.

In theorizing and measuring the effects of news coverage on public opinion, researchers have taken a variety of approaches. A network approach was central to the two-step flow model 66 years ago when researchers proposed that opinion leaders in social networks mediated news coverage effects on public opinion of the electorate [31]. Since that time, research on news coverage and political attitudes has mainly set aside concern with social networks and conceptualized the agenda-setting process of news coverage, investigating the extent to which the amount of news coverage of an issue is associated with how important the public perceives the issue to be [32]. Recently, still in an individualistic framework, news has been studied in terms of narrative framing and its effects [19], although investigators have returned to conceptualizing network variables in modeling news coverage effects on sentiment [20]. Nevertheless, the focus of attention is on communication networks of elites in influencing media framing, rather than on networks contained within the content itself. We propose that networks among presidential cabinet members represented in the news mediate framing's influence on public attitudes toward the presidency.

The negative information orientation of the press is well documented [20]. Positive events are not nearly as likely to be considered "news" as are negative events or negative characterizations of processes or personalities. Given a generally negative valence to news, our theoretical argument derives from the research on "divided presidencies" [33], where one party holds the White House and another holds the Congress. Studies have found that this results in higher job approval ratings for the president. Investigators have reasoned that this is because of added uncertainty resulting from less ability to assign blame to the president for lack of political progress or failed initiatives. This uncertainty weakens the normal situation in which there is a negative bias in the media toward political actors and therefore increases the chances that the population perceives the president more positively, absent the normal flow of negative information being specifically tied to the chief executive.

We further reason that when the president is portrayed as a more central figure in the administration, he is more clearly the "lightning rod" for the generally negative information orientation of the press. Absent countervailing information, this negative coverage of the president results in audience members perceiving the president to have lower job performance, and thus they give him lower job approval ratings. On the other hand, when the president is less central in the administration network, as other cabinet members are more central, this structural dispersion makes it more difficult for the media to successfully tag the president in a negative manner. The negative "lightning" of media messages is more diffuse with multiple smaller bolt strikes. As a result, when the average centrality of cabinet members is higher, which lowers the centrality of the president, the job approval of the president is higher. The president is more likely to "fly beneath the radar" from the perspective of media audiences and with less connection of negative news with the identity of the president himself, job approval will increase. So, in addition to expecting that when average network centrality of cabinet members is higher presidential approval is higher, we also expect to find that when the president has higher network centrality, job approval is lower. Stating this more succinctly, the following hypothesis is offered:

H1: *The greater the similarity of the centrality of the president and his cabinet members, the higher the job approval ratings for the president.*

The contemporary speed with which these effects can be expected to occur is related to the substantial shortening of the news cycle since the growth of online news sources. These have affected all media such that the media cycle is no longer weekly or daily, it is hourly and even minutes/seconds in periodicity. The cycle was longer during the Reagan, G.H.W. Bush, and Clinton administrations. The "web" was launched in the middle of Clinton's two terms and was still in early stages of development through the late 1990s. For the G.W. Bush presidency, on the other hand, the online news cycle had shortened [17], political blogs grew rapidly in his first term [1] and exerted increasing power on media framing through his second term [21]. We therefore expect that the relationship between administration network centrality and presidential job approval is longer for the Reagan through Clinton administrations than it is for the G.W. Bush administration.

H2: *The lag between centrality similarity of president and cabinet members and an increase in job approval ratings for the president is shorter for the G.W. Bush administration than for the Reagan, G.H.W. Bush, and Clinton administrations.*

3.2 Methods

We have network analyzed the cabinets of each of the presidencies since Nixon aggregated across their respective terms [8]. All Lexis-Nexis news stories in the *New York Times* and the *Washington Post* during the administrations that mention at least one of the cabinet members were captured in full text form. A separate search was done for each cabinet member during the time of the presidency. We then aggregated all of these files into one text file for each administration. There were 26 Mb of text and 30,194 stories for Nixon and his cabinet, 16.7 Mb and 18,432 stories for the short Ford term, 163 Mb and 46,586 stories for Carter, 653 Mb of text and 135,996 stories for Reagan's two terms, 93 Mb of text and 17,265 stories for G.H.W Bush, 674 Mb of text and 114,511 stories for the two Clinton administrations, and 504 Mb and 89,810 stories for the two G.W. Bush administrations. Although G.H.W Bush's administration generated relatively little press coverage, considering that the president is the single most covered news source [20] this would appear to be the result of a press strategy or of some other systematic variation.

For the current analysis four separate text files were created in UTF-8 format. Each file was then analyzed using WORDij 3.0 [15, 16] to measure the co-occurrence of actors mentioned within 400 words of each other. Each output file was then put into UCINET [7] to measure average network centralization, individual centrality scores for each member, and NetDraw [5] to create the static network visualizations. WORDij 3.0 produces time series movies of networks, but these cannot be shown in such a paper.

WORDij was originally designed to analyze large numbers of co-occurring words to create semantic networks. Nevertheless, social actors' names are indeed words and mining for their co-occurrence is no different. WORDij 3.0 not only has a stop word list or drop list but also has its opposite, an *include* list that will map the network only among words on it. Additionally, some features to aid in multi-node type analysis including people, organizations, places, and formal concepts and objects are enumeration of proper nouns and automatic creation of include lists from them. For this chapter, using WORDij 3.0's string replacement and include list functions, all aliases we created for each cabinet member's name were converted to a single string and then proximity-based co-occurrences were computed.

3.2.1 Link Coding with Proximities not "Bag of Words"

The extent to which cabinet members co-occur within large numbers of documents is the basis for defining the link in the social network with more co-occurrences indicating higher link strength. This co-occurrence indexing is proximity based so it avoids the problems of the simplistic "bag of words" approaches common from Information Science and Information Retrieval. Those treat all words in an entire document as having a link with one another, regardless of how far apart these terms might be in the document. While such word bags are useful for document retrieval they blur social meaning by ignoring or masking the more precise relationships of social units within the texts, whether these units are words, people, or other entities. More reflective of social structure are methods using a proximity criterion to define co-occurrence of links within a relatively short distance as introduced by Danowski [11, 13, 14].

3.2.2 Optimal Window Size for Actor Social Networks

We performed tests with different window sizes, using as a criterion the overall network structure. Windows of 3, 10, 25, 50, 100, and 200 were used. The window size of 3 produces the same network results as the other windows sizes, for example, having a QAP correlation coefficient of .997 with the network resulting from a window size of 200. The reason for this is because with the include file approach (opposite of a stop list or drop file) the WordLink subroutine of WORDij drops all words from the initial text except for the strings on the include list. So, the window of 3 when using an include list has face and predictive validity.

3.2.3 Actor Co-occurrence Segmentation Software

We use the software package WORDij 3.0 that has a graphical user interface in java but runs fast on Windows, Mac, and Linux/Unix operating systems because all of the network analysis computations are done in C++ not java, unlike some other similar software such as AutoMap [18]. Among the many options for analysis in WORDij 3.0, relevant here is the option to produce Pajek [2] formatted output files because we wished to import these to UCINET for centrality computations.

3.2.4 Network Centrality Measures

The most often used centrality measure in social network analysis is "betweenness centrality" [26]. Nevertheless, use of this measure developed by Freeman [23] has been shown to be very often inappropriate in terms of its operational assumptions in relation to conceptual definitions [6, 35]. The betweenness measure assumes that messages flow through a network along a single shortest path, moving sequentially from one node on this path to the next. No weighting is assumed for the strength of each link in terms of its overall frequency of activation, bandwidth, or channel capacity. Accordingly it treats only dichotomous links, so even if strength or vertex valued data is available, the measure removes such information and codes each link as either present or absent. Sometimes analysts do this dichotomization by binarizing the data with a split at the median into 0 and 1 codes for each link. In the betweenness centrality model, it is not possible for a node to receive messages from more than one other node nor can a node send out the same message to multiple nodes. These assumptions do not fit well with our conception of presidential cabinet networks. We assume that our representations of networks have an association with the actual communication among the actors.

Organizational communication is such that some relationships are stronger than others, with these stronger links more frequently activated. In addition, it is common for individuals to communicate the same basic message to more than one node, sometimes simultaneously as would occur in situations such as group meetings, or email copied to multiple recipients. In such a model, individuals may receive the same basic content from more than one source. The centrality most appropriate for these assumptions is "flow betweenness" [6]. It indexes the degree to which each node is present on all possible paths among the nodes in the network, weighted for link strength values. Thus flow betweenness centrality was used in the current study.

Alternatively, eigenvector centrality [4] is consistent with a social influence model similar to that described as guiding this investigation. Nevertheless, with the relatively small numbers of nodes that are in a cabinet network the eigenvector solutions can produce anomalous results as indicated by features including negative eigenvectors, which occur when the triangular inequality principle of node relations in Euclidean spaces is violated. In such distance models if A is linked with B at a particular distance based on vertex strength, and A is linked with C at a particular distance, then the B and C link is determined, yet does not empirically correspond to the formulation. Flow betweenness is the best measure of centrality for the current research.

3.2.5 Time Segmentation

TimeSlice is a utility in the WORDij 3.0 software package that allows one to segment the larger corpus into sections of any width, such as by number of days, weeks, quarters, or years. The time sliced files are in turn input into the WordLink program in WORDij that generates basic information for each time slice in eight output files for words, for word pairs, and for statistics such as entropy and mutual information, and in various formats, such as the .net Pajek format.

3.2.6 Creating the String Replacement and Include Lists

The first step in preparing the list of names for the network analysis in WORDij 3.0 is to create a string replacement list, an advanced option. This converts aliases for each name into a unigram. Table 3.1 shows an example.

Table 3.1 Examples of string replacement (partial file for Nixon cabinet)

Richard Nixon->richard_nixon
richard nixon->richard_nixon
nixon-richard_nixon
President->richard_nixon
president->richard_nixon
Vice President->spiro_agnew
vice president->spiro_agnew
Spiro Agnew->spiro_agnew
spiro agnew->spiro_agnew
agnew->spiro_agnew
Gerald Ford->gerald_ford
gerald ford->gerald_ford
ford->gerald_ford
William Rogers->william_rogers
william rogers->william_rogers
rogers->william_rogers
Henry Kissinger->henry_kissinger
henry kissinger->henry_kissinger
kissenger->kissinger
David Kennedy->david_kennedy
david kennedy->david_kennedy
kennedy->david_kennedy
John Connally->john_connally
john connally->john_connally
connallh->john_connally
George Shultz->george_shultz
george shultz->george_shultz
shultz->george_shultz

The new strings created from the string replacement file are input as an include file in the WordLink identification of co-occurring words, in this case name unigrams. The include list is the opposite of a stop or drop list. Rather than removing certain words from the network analysis, the include list contains all of the words to be network analyzed and co-occurrences are indexed only for these terms, in this case name unigrams (Table 3.2).

Table 3.2 Example include
list for Nixon cabinet

caspar_weinberger
claude_brinegar
clifford_hardin
clifford_hardin
david_kennedy
earl_butz
elliot_richardson
frederick_dent
george_romney
george_shultz
gerald_ford
henry_kissinger
james_hodgson
james_schlesinger
john_connally
john_mitchell
maurice_stans
melvin_laird
peter_brennan
peter_peterson
rich._kleindienst
richard_nixon
robert_finch
rogers_morton
spiro_agnew
walter_hickel
william_rogers
william_saxbe
william_simon
winton_blount

3.2.7 Post-Processing of Link Data for Centrality Measures

The WORDij 3.0 program has the option of producing a network file in the .net Pajek format. This is one of the import file types that UCINET accepts and converts to its system files. We chose UCINET because it is widely accepted in the social network analysis community and we wished to use common, validated centrality indices to profile the structures of the cabinets. Given the status of UCINET and the ease of output importing we felt no need to incorporate centrality measures into WORDij. This Pajek format is one of the import file types in UCINET, which is where we compute the centrality statistics for each time slice.

In the current study, within each time slice we compute the flow betweenness centrality statistics for each of the cabinet members appearing in the social network in the time period and also compute the average of such centralities across all admin-istration members. To index the extent to which the president stood apart from the cabinet in centrality we divided the president's centrality by the average centrality of cabinet members so that higher values indicate the president more likely stands above the other cabinet members and serves as a media "lightning rod" to which negative stories connect to the identity of the president. Lower values indicate it is more likely that the president is "below the radar" of negative public opinion formation as there is less likelihood of audiences linking the negative stories to the president per se.

Presidential job approval ratings were obtained from the Roper Public Opinion Center Archives (http://www.ropercenter.uconn.edu/). For each presidency we computed the average time interval between such measurements and used this as the time slice criterion to produce time series data.

3.2.8 Time Series Statistical Analysis

For Reagan the interval of job approval rating was 22 days, resulting in 132 time intervals; for G.H.W. Bush it was 13 days and 121 intervals; for Clinton it was 30 days and 98 time intervals; and for G.W. Bush it was 22 days and 133 time intervals. To test the hypotheses we created for each administration a data file in SPSS where we entered columns of data for president centrality, average administration (cabinet) centrality, and job approval from the polls. We used the statistical function of differencing adjacent time series to remove serial autocorrelation ($d = 1$) and computed cross-correlations to examine seven lags before and after each centrality variable period to see what the relationship between centrality and job approval might be.

3.2.9 Combining Visualization with Statistical Centrality of Actors

A fundamental tenet of data analysis is to first visualize it. WORDij 3.0 has VISij for creating static or time series movies of changes in network composition and structure, although NetDraw has more options for rendering static networks such as having larger circles for more central nodes. We used node centrality to visually render the nodes' network size. For link strength we used the maximum available range of thickness of links, from 0 to 12. Our larger array of strengths was converted to this scale.

3.3 Results

To give the reader a sense of the differences between the four cabinets in overall network structure, Figs. 3.1, 3.2, 3.3, and 3.4 show the aggregate cabinet social networks for the cabinets of Reagan, G.H.W Bush, Clinton, and G.W. Bush administrations.

The centrality of the president in the cabinet network was divided by the average centrality. This ratio represents the extent to which the president stands out in centrality compared to the others. Figure 3.5 shows this ratio for each president. It was noteworthy that the G.H.W. Bush administration was unique in having a high

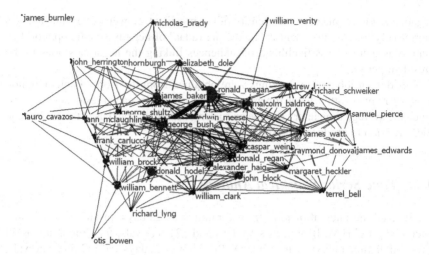

Fig. 3.1 Aggregate Reagan cabinet

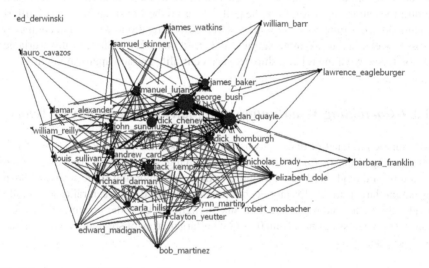

Fig. 3.2 Aggregate G.H.W. Bush cabinet

proportion of zero centrality time periods. Because centrality can be computed only on a connected network, this indicates that in these periods isolated pairs of cabinet members or isolated individuals were treated in the news stories within the observation window. This finding was confirmed by systematic visual examination of the senior Bush administration's zero centrality periods. Because the White House itself is the primary source of cabinet news it would appear that this recurring deviation from the norm may have been strategic, in that presidential-level political communication is unlikely left to chance. Across the series, G.H.W Bush is most similar

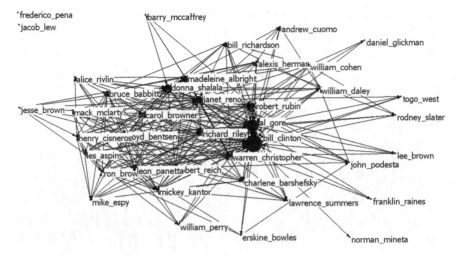

Fig. 3.3 Aggregate Clinton cabinet network

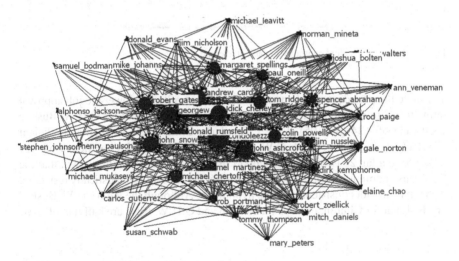

Fig. 3.4 Aggregate G.W. Bush cabinet network

to his cabinet members in centrality. Clinton stands out as generally being the most central compared to his cabinet.

3.3.1 Hypotheses Tests

The cross-correlations with differencing to remove serial autocorrelation based on +7 through −7 lags found that a lag of 1 produced the highest coefficient at −.13 ($p < .05$) for the ratio of president to cabinet centrality in relation to job approval.

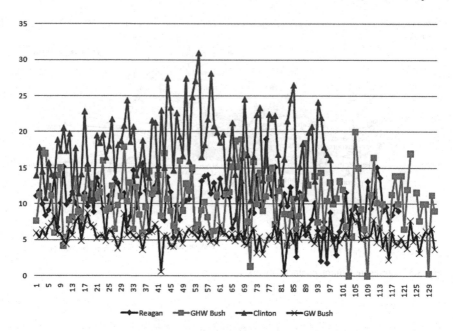

Fig. 3.5 Ratio of president centrality to cabinet average

The more the president stood apart in terms of centrality, the lower the job approval rating three time periods later. The same lag pattern was found for G.H.W. Bush, a coefficient of $-.34$ ($p < .05$) at lag 1. Similarly, Clinton data showed a coefficient of $-.16$ ($p < .05$), but at lag 4. G.W. Bush centrality ratio had a coefficient of $-.14$ ($p < .05$) at a lag 2. These results support hypothesis one. Hypothesis two, that the G.W. Bush administration would have a shorter lag, cannot be statistically tested but the results are not consistent with the hypothesis. Although the lag for G.W. Bush is one half that for Clinton, the lags for Reagan and G.H.W. Bush are half that of G.W. Bush.

3.4 Discussion

The findings support the hypothesis that as the president's centrality is closer to the average cabinet centrality, there is a positive association with job approval. For two presidents, Reagan and G.H.W. Bush, when the president's centrality drops closer to the average, by the next polling period job approval is higher. The same pattern occurs for the other two presidents but their lags are longer. For Clinton the lag is 4 periods and for G.W. Bush the lag is 2 time periods.

It was theorized that when the president stands above the rest of the cabinet in network centrality, negative press information is more likely to be associated with the president in the minds of members of the public and they will report lower presidential job approval ratings. The president identity is like a lightning rod absorbing the negative press sentiment. On the other hand, when the president's centrality is closer to that of the other cabinet members, he is less likely to be associated with negative press information, "flying below the radar" of public opinion processes. It is as if the negative press information fragments and diffuses into smaller bolts attached to other cabinet members. As the president is not being as directly connected with negative press content, job approval ratings increase.

The hypothesis about the shortening of the lag cycle associated with the Internet's shortening of the news cycle was not clearly supported by the evidence. While G.W. Bush's lag was one half that of Clinton's, both were longer than for the two prior presidents.

Nevertheless, studying only four administrations introduces problems of external validity. One would not want to generalize the findings of this study to the population of presidencies, certainly those that occurred prior to the establishment of the *New York Times* and *Washington Post* as elite political newspapers. Even if this were feasible, it would not be desirable given an assumption widely held by political observers that the introduction of television changed presidential politics, and now the observation that the Internet has changed presidential politics in yet other ways.

It is interesting to note, however, that for the two presidencies that took place before the Internet, the time lag is the same and is only one period long, while for the two presidencies during and after Internet development the lag is longer. While this may be mere coincidence, it suggests a possible hypothesis for future research that elite newspaper coverage, in the *New York Times* and *Washington Post*, takes longer to have an effect as alternative online news sources have proliferated. It would be useful to conduct a future study that would comparatively test the basic hypothesis examined here by mapping networks separately both in the elite press and in Internet content.

We sought to present an illustration of time series analysis of social networks obtained from data mining, yet used political communication theory to generate some hypotheses to add further meaningfulness to the analysis. The study is fruitful on three counts. One is that it reveals substantive variation that future research can address; second, it demonstrates that the WORDij 3.0-based methods produce useful variation; and, third, it offers a new model for political communication and presidential job approval.

When data mining for social networks, the representations one obtains are based on the nature of the source data and on the assumptions made for the operationalization of data extraction and the network representation. These are the networks as portrayed in the medium from which data is mined. Questions about the extent to which such networks compare to the "real" or "actual" network are misplaced, for there is no real or actual network that is independent of data collection and extraction procedures or the subjective impressions of the participants or observers of them. The latter may be the basis for an "inter-subjective" network, but this is as close as one could come to the actual network independent from the instrumentation extracting network data.

Rather than the reality of the networks, the key is the validity of the networks. Face validity is the first level of validity and least measurable, but when linking network representations to other data, such as to job approval and news sentiment in this study, predictive validity becomes relevant. Although external validity is limited because of studying only four administrations, the statistical results provide predictive validity for the investigation.

Some philosophers [3] argue that the media are a simulacrum with a completely self-contained representation of information that bears no correspondence to that outside of it. This is an extreme position that is invalidated by the fact that one can link media representations of such things as social networks among actors to data from outside the media system, in this study to Gallup job approval poll data. Such cross-system predictive validity is important to data mining for social networks as it is in any sort of social research. When extracting a social network from data mining one should move quickly to establish whether and how much predictive validity such constructions have, otherwise mining for "toy" networks is merely for analytical playmates. For example, some research has linked networks of message content from president's letters to stockholders to stock price performance [12, 36, 38]. In the present study, we illustrate not only a procedure for mining of social network data but we link these data over time to independently obtained side data of Gallup presidential approval polls through which the results of mining can be validated.

Work is underway to more fully automate social network mining to move beyond the use of a priori lists of actors to ontological categories of actors for which software can automatically add new actors.

Acknowledgments The authors are grateful for Rafal Radulski and his timely, efficient, and effective programming assistance and for his excellent communication skills. The authors are thankful for the insightful comments of two anonymous reviewers. This research is supported by National Science Foundation Grant 0527487, Human and Social Dynamics Program.

References

1. Adamic, L., and Glace, N. The political blogosphere and the 2004 U.S. election: Divided they blog. In *LinkKDD '05: Proceedings of the 3rd International Workshop on Link Discovery*, Chicago, IL, pp. 36–43, 2005.
2. Batagelj, V. Pajek: Program for large network analysis. *Connections,* 21(2):47, 1998.
3. Baudrillard, J. *Simulacra.* Translated by S.F. Glaser. Ann Arbor, MI: University of Michigan Press, 1994.
4. Bonacich, P., Factoring and weighting approaches to status scores and clique identification. *Journal of Mathematical Sociology,* 2:113–120, 1972.
5. Borgatti, S.P. NetDraw: Graph visualization software. Harvard, MA: Analytic Technologies, 2002.
6. Borgatti, S.P. Centrality and network flow. *Social Networks,* 27:55–71, 2005.
7. Borgatti, S.P., Everett, M.G., and Freeman, L.C. UCINET for windows: Software for social network analysis. Harvard, MA: Analytic Technologies, 2002.
8. Cepela, N., and Danowski, J.A. Automatic mapping of political networks of actors from large collections of news stories. In *Proceedings of the 1st ASONAM Conference,* Athens, Greece, 2009.

9. Cohen, J.E. The polls: The components of presidential favorability. *Presidential Studies Quarterly,* 30(1):169–177, 2000.
10. Dahl, R. A critique of the ruling-elite model. *American Political Science Review,* 52:463–469, 1961.
11. Danowski, J.A. A network-based content analysis methodology for computer-mediated communication: An illustration with a computer bulletin board. In M. Burgoon (ed.), *Communication Yearbook 5,* pp. 904–925. New Brunswick, NJ: Transaction Books, 1982.
12. Danowski, J.A. Organizational infographics and automated auditing: Using computers to unobtrusively gather and analyze communication. In G. Goldhaber and G. Barnett (eds.), *Handbook of Organizational Communication,* pp. 335–384, Norwood, NJ: Ablex, 1988.
13. Danowski, J.A. Network analysis of message content. In G. Barnett and W. Richards (eds), *Progress in Communication Sciences XII,* pp. 197–222, Norwood, NJ: Ablex, 1993a.
14. Danowski, J.A. WORDij: A word pair approach to information retrieval. In *Proceedings of the DARPA/NIST TREC Conference,* Washington, DC: National Institute of Standards and Technology, pp. 131–136, 1993b.
15. Danowski, J.A. WORDij 3.0 [computer program]. Chicago, IL: University of Illinois at Chicago, 2009a. http://WORDij.net
16. Danowski, J.A. Inferences from word networks in messages. In Krippendorff, K. and Bock, M.A (eds), *The Content Analysis Reader,* pp. 421–429, Thousand Oaks, CA: Sage Publications, 2009b.
17. Dezsö, Z., Almaas, E., Lukács, A., Rácz, B., Szakadát, I., and Barabási, A.L. Dynamics of information access on the web. *Physical Review E,* 73, 066132-1-066132-6, 2006.
18. Diesner, J. and Carley, K. *AutoMap 1.2: Extract, Analyze, Represent, and Compare Mental Models from Texts,* 2004. reports-archive.adm.cs.cmu.edu
19. Entman, R.M. Framing: Toward clarification of a fractured paradigm. *Journal of Communication,* 43(4):51–58, 1993.
20. Entman, R.M. Framing bias: Media in the distribution of power. *Journal of Communication,* 57:163–173, 2007.
21. Farrell, H. and Drezner, D.W. The power and politics of blogs. *Public Choice,* 134:15–30, 2008.
22. Fenno, R.F. *The President's Cabinet: An Analysis in the Period from Wilson to Eisenhower.* Cambridge, MA: Harvard University Press, 1959.
23. Freeman, L.C. A set of measures of centrality based on betweenness. *Sociometry,* 40(1): 35–41, 1977.
24. Galaskiewicz, J. The structure of community organizational networks. *Social Forces,* 57(4):1346–1364, 1979.
25. Gronke, P. and Newman, B. FDR to Clinton, Mueller to ?: A field essay on presidential approval. *Political Research Quarterly,* 56(4):501–512, 2000.
26. Hanneman, R.A. and Riddle, M. *Introduction to Social Network Methods.* Riverside, CA: University of California, 2005, Riverside (http://faculty.ucr.edu/~hanneman/)
27. Hunter, F. *Community Power Structure.* Chapel Hill: University of North Carolina Press, 1953.
28. Jones, S. Television news: Geographic and source biases, 1982–2004. *International Journal of Communication.* 2:223–250, 2008.
29. Katz, E., and Lazarsfeld, P. *Personal Influence.* New York, NY: Free Press, 1955.
30. Knoke, D. *Political Networks: The Structural Perspective.* Cambridge :Cambridge University Press, 1994.
31. Lazarsfeld, B., Berelson, B., and Gaudet, H. *The People's Choice.* New York, NY: Columbia University Press, 1948.
32. McCombs, M.E., and Shaw, D.L. The agenda-setting function of mass media, *The Public Opinion Quarterly,* 36(2):176–187, 1972.
33. Nicholson, S.P., Segura, G.M., and Woods, N.D. Presidential approval and the mixed blessing of divided government. *The Journal of Politics,* 64(3):701–720, 2002.

34. Polsby, N. *Community Power and Political Theory*. New Haven, CT: Yale University Press, 1963.
35. Rousseau, R., and Zhang, L. Betweenness centrality and Q-measures in directed valued networks. *Scientometrics,* 75(3):575–590, 2008.
36. Swales, Jr., G.S., and Yoon, Y. Applying artificial neural networks to investment analysis. *Financial Analysts Journal*, 48(5):78–80, 1992.
37. Tichy, N.M., Tushman, M., and Fombrun, C. Social network analysis for organizations. *The Academy of Management Review*, 4(4):507–519, 1979.
38. Zhai, Y., Hsu, A., and Halgamuge, K. Combining news and technical indicators in daily stock price trends prediction, In Liu et al. (eds), *ISNN 2007*, Part III, LNCS 4493, pp. 1087–1096. Berlin: Springer-Verlag Berlin Heidelberg.

Chapter 4
A Social Network-Based Recommender System (SNRS)

Jianming He and Wesley W. Chu

Abstract Social influence plays an important role in product marketing. However, it has rarely been considered in traditional recommender systems. In this chapter, we present a new paradigm of recommender systems which can utilize information in social networks, including user preferences, item's general acceptance, and influence from social friends. A probabilistic model is developed to make personalized recommendations from such information. We extract data from a real online social network, and our analysis of this large data set reveals that friends have a tendency to select the same items and give similar ratings. Experimental results on this data set show that our proposed system not only improves the prediction accuracy of recommender systems but also remedies the data sparsity and cold-start issues inherent in collaborative filtering. Furthermore, we propose to improve the performance of our system by applying semantic filtering of social networks and validate its improvement via a class project experiment. In this experiment we demonstrate how relevant friends can be selected for inference based on the semantics of friend relationships and finer-grained user ratings. Such technologies can be deployed by most content providers.

4.1 Introduction

In order to overcome information overload, recommender systems have become a key tool for providing users with personalized recommendations on items such as movies, music, books, news, and web pages. Intrigued by many practical applications, researchers have developed algorithms and systems over the last decade. Some of them have been commercialized by online venders such as Amazon.com, Netflix.com, and IMDb.com. These systems predict user preferences (often represented as numeric ratings) for new items based on the user's past ratings on other

J. He (✉)

Computer Science Department, University of California, Los Angeles, CA 90095, USA

e-mail: jmhek@cs.ucla.edu

N. Memon et al. (eds.), *Data Mining for Social Network Data*,
Annals of Information Systems 12, DOI 10.1007/978-1-4419-6287-4_4,
© Springer Science+Business Media, LLC 2010

items. There are typically two types of algorithms for recommender systems – *content-based methods* and *collaborative filtering*. Content-based methods measure the similarity of the recommended item (target item) to the ones that a target user (i.e., user who receives recommendations) likes or dislikes [22, 25, 30] based on item attributes. On the other hand, collaborative filtering finds users with tastes that are similar to the target user's based on their past ratings. Collaborative filtering will then make recommendations to the target user based on the opinions of those similar users [3, 5, 27].

Despite all of these efforts, recommender systems still face many challenging problems. First, there are demands for further improvements on the prediction accuracy of recommender systems. In October 2006, Netflix announced an open competition with the grand prize of $1,000,000 for the best algorithm that predicts user ratings for films (http://www.netflixprize.com). The improvement in the prediction accuracy can increase user satisfaction, which in turn leads to higher profits for those e-commerce web sites. Second, algorithms for recommender systems suffer from many issues. For example, in order to measure item similarity, content-based methods rely on explicit item descriptions. However, such descriptions may be difficult to obtain for items like ideas or opinions. Collaborative filtering has the*data sparsity* problem and the *cold-start* problem [1]. In contrast to the huge number of items in recommender systems, each user normally only rates a few. Therefore, the user/item rating matrix is typically very sparse. It is difficult for recommender systems to accurately measure user similarities from those limited number of reviews. A related problem is the cold-start problem. Even for a system that is not particularly sparse, when a user initially joins, the system has none or perhaps only a few reviews from this user. Therefore, the system cannot accurately interpret this user's preference.

To tackle those problems, two approaches have been proposed [3, 21, 23, 29]. The first approach is to condense the user/item rating matrix through dimensionality reduction techniques such as *singular value decomposition (SVD)* [3, 29]. By clustering users or items according to their latent structure, unrepresentative users or items can be discarded, and thus the user/item matrix becomes denser. However, these methods do not significantly improve the performance of recommender systems, and sometimes make the performance even worse.

The second approach is to "enrich" the user/item rating matrix by (1) introducing default ratings or implicit user ratings, e.g., the time spent on reading articles [23]; (2) using half-baked rating predictions from content-based methods [21]; or (3) exploiting transitive associations among users through their past transactions and feedback [12]. These methods improve the performance of recommender systems to some extent. In this chapter we try to solve these problems from a different perspective. In particular, we propose a new paradigm of recommender systems by utilizing information in social networks, especially that of *social influence*.

Traditional recommender systems do not take into consideration explicit social relations among users, yet the importance of social influence in product marketing has long been recognized [32, 36]. Intuitively, when we want to buy a product that is not familiar, we often consult with our friends who have already had experience with the product, since they are those that we can reach for immediate advice. When friends recommend a product to us, we also tend to accept the recommendation because their inputs are trustworthy. Many marketing strategies that have leveraged this aspect of human nature have achieved great success. One classic example is the Hotmail's free e-mail service. The marketing strategy of Hotmail is to attach a promotion message at the bottom of every outgoing e-mail: "Get your private, free e-mail at http://www.hotmail.com." People who receive the e-mail will sign up and then further propagate this promotion message. As a result, the number of Hotmail user accounts grew from 0 to 12 million in 18 months on only a $500,000 advertising budget – thereby out-performing many conventional marketing strategies [14]. Thus, social influences play a key role when people are making decisions of adopting products.

Additionally, the integration of social networks can theoretically improve the performance of current recommender systems. First, in terms of the prediction accuracy, the additional information about users and their friends obtained from social networks improves the understanding of user behaviors and ratings. Therefore, we can model and interpret user preferences more precisely, and thus improve the prediction accuracy. Second, with friend information in social networks, it is no longer necessary to find similar users by measuring their rating similarity, because the fact that two people are friends already indicates that they have things in common. Thus, the data sparsity problem can be alleviated. Finally, for the cold-start issue, even if a user has no past reviews, recommender system still can make recommendations to the user based on the preferences of his/her friends if it integrates with social networks. All of these intuitions and observations motivate us to design a new paradigm of recommender systems that can take advantage of information in social networks.

The recent emergence of online social networks (OSNs) gives us an opportunity to investigate the role of social influence in recommender systems. With the increasing popularity of Web 2.0, many OSNs, such as Myspace.com, Facebook.com, and Linkedin.com, have emerged. Members in those networks have their own personalized space where they not only publish their biographies, hobbies, interests, blogs, etc., but also list their friends. Friends or visitors can visit these personal spaces and leave comments. Note that in this chapter we define *friends* as any two users who are connected by an explicit social link. We define *immediate friends* as those friends who are just one hop away from each other in a social network graph, and *distant friends* as friends who are multiple hops away. OSNs provide platforms where people can place themselves on exhibit and maintain connections with friends. As OSNs continue to gain more popularity, the unprecedented amount of personal information and social relations improves social science research where it was once limited by a lack of data.

In our research, we are interested in the role of explicit social relations in recommender systems, such as how user preferences or ratings are correlated with those of friends, and how to use such correlations to design a better recommender system. In particular, we design an algorithm framework which makes recommendations based on user's own preferences, the general acceptance of the target item, and the opinions from social friends. We crawl a real online social network from Yelp.com and perform extensive analysis on this data set. Some of the key questions, such as whether or not friends tend to select the same item, and whether or not friends tend to give similar ratings, have been studied in this data set. We also use this data set to evaluate the performance of our proposed system on the prediction accuracy, data sparsity, and cold-start. The experimental results of our system show significant improvement against traditional collaborative filtering in all of those aspects. For example, the prediction accuracy has improved by 17.8% compared to traditional collaborative filtering. Furthermore, we propose to use the semantics of friend relationships and finer-grained user ratings to improve the prediction accuracy.

The remainder of the chapter is organized as follows. First, in Section 5.2 we give a background of traditional collaborative filtering algorithms. Then we formally propose a social network-based recommender system in Section 5.3. In Section 5.4 we introduce the data set that we crawled from Yelp and present some analytical studies on this data set. Following that, we evaluate the performance of the proposed system on the Yelp data set in Section 5.5. In Section 5.6 we propose to further improve the prediction accuracy of the system by applying semantic filtering of social networks and validate its improvement via a class experiment. In Section 5.7 we review related studies and conclude in Section 5.8.

4.2 Background

After the pioneering work in the Grouplens project in 1994 [27], collaborative filtering (CF) soon became one of the most popular algorithms in recommender systems. Many variations of this algorithm have also been proposed [2, 11, 13, 21, 35]. In this chapter we will use the traditional CF as one of the comparison methods. Therefore, the remainder of this section will focus on this algorithm.

The assumption of CF is that people who agree in the past tend to agree again in the future. Therefore, CF first finds users with taste similar to the target user's. CF will then make recommendations to the target user by predicting the target user's rating to the target item based on the ratings of his/her top-K similar users. User ratings are often represented by discrete values within a certain range, e.g., one to five. A one indicates an extreme dislike to the target item, while a five shows high praise. Let R_{UI} be the rating of the target user U on the target item I. Thus, R_{UI} is estimated as the weighted sum of the votes of similar users as follows.

$$R_{UI} = \overline{R_U} + Z \sum_{V \in \Psi} w(U, V) \times (R_{VI} - \overline{R_V}), \tag{4.1}$$

where $\overline{R_U}$ and $\overline{R_V}$ represent the average ratings of the target user U and every user V in U's neighborhood, Ψ, which consists of the top-K similar users of U. $w(U, V)$ is the weight between users U and V, and $Z = \frac{1}{\sum_V w(U,V)}$ is a normalizing constant to normalize total weight to one. Specifically, $w(U, V)$ can be defined using the Pearson correlation coefficient [27].

$$w(U, V) = \frac{\sum_I (R_{UI} - \overline{R_U})(R_{VI} - \overline{R_V})}{\sqrt{\sum_I (R_{UI} - \overline{R_U})^2 \sum_I (R_{VI} - \overline{R_V})^2}} \qquad (4.2)$$

where the summations over I are over the common items for which both user U and V have voted.

Other variations to this algorithm include different weighting techniques. For example, when two users have less than 50 co-rated items, [11] proposed to insert a significance weighting factor of $n/50$ to the original weight, where n is the number of co-rated items. As we can see, traditional collaborative filtering and its variations do not utilize the semantic friend relations among users in recommender systems; however, this is essential to the buying decisions of users. In the following sections, we are going to present a new paradigm of recommender systems which improves the performance of traditional recommender systems by using the information in social networks.

4.3 A Social Network-Based Recommender System

Before we introduce the system, let us first show a typical scenario. Angela wants to watch a movie on a weekend. Her favorite movies are dramas. From the Internet, she finds two movies particularly interesting, "Revolutionary Road" and "The Curious Case of Benjamin Button." These two movies are all highly rated in the message board at Yahoo Movies. Because she cannot decide which movie to watch, she calls her best friend Linda whom she often hangs out with. Linda has not viewed these two movies either, but she knew that one of her officemates had just watched "Revolutionary Road" and highly recommended it. So Linda suggests "Why don't we go to watch Revolutionary Road together?" Angela is certainly willing to take Linda's recommendation, and therefore has a fun night at the movies with her friend. If we review this scenario, we can see at least three factors that really contribute to the Angela's final decision. The first factor is Angela's own preference for drama movies. If Angela did not like drama movies, she would be less likely to pick something like "Revolutionary Road" to begin with. The second factor is the public reviews on these two movies. If these movies received horrible reviews, Angela would most likely lose interest and stop any further investigation. Finally, it is the recommendation from Angela's friend, Linda, that makes Angela finally choose "Revolutionary Road." Interestingly, Linda's opinion is also influenced by her officemate. If we recall the decisions that we make in our daily life, such as finding restaurants, buying a house, and looking for jobs, many of them are actually influenced by these three factors.

Figure 4.1 further illustrates how these three factors impact customers' final buying decisions. Intuitively, a customer's buying decision or rating is decided by both his/her own preference for similar items and his/her knowledge about the characteristics of the target item. A user's preference, such as Angela's interest in drama movies, is usually reflected from the user's past ratings to other similar items, e.g.,

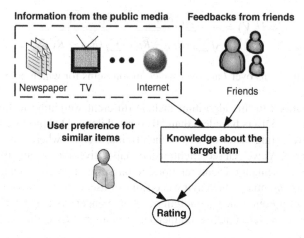

Fig. 4.1 The three factors that influence a customer's buying decision: user preference for similar items, information regarding the target item from the public media, and feedbacks from friends

the number of drama movies that Angela previously viewed and the average rating that Angela gave to those movies. Knowledge about the target item can be obtained from public media such as magazines, television, and the Internet. Meanwhile, the feedbacks from friends are another source of knowledge regarding the item, and they are often more trustworthy than advertisements. When a user starts considering the feedbacks from his/her friends, he/she is then influenced by his/her friends. Note that this influence is not limited to that from our immediate friends. Distant friends can also cast their influence indirectly to us; e.g., Angela was influenced by Linda's officemate in the previous scenario. Each one of these three factors has an impact on a user's final buying decision. If the impact from all of them is positive, it is very likely that the target user will select the item. On the contrary, if any has a negative influence, e.g., very low ratings in other user reviews, the chance that the target user will select the item will decrease. With such an understanding in mind, we are going to propose a social network-based recommender system *(SNRS)* in the following subsections. As we mentioned, social influences can come from not only immediate friends but also distant friends. The techniques for handling these types of influences are different. We shall begin with the *immediate friend inference*, in which we only consider influences from immediate friends. Then, in the *distant friend inference*, we will describe how we incorporate influences from distant friends via leveraging the immediate friend inference.

4.3.1 Immediate Friend Inference

We introduce the following naming conventions for the variables used in this chapter. We use capitalize letters to represent variables, and use capitalize and bold letters to represent the corresponding sets. The value for each variable or variable set is represented by the corresponding lowercase letter.

Formally, let us consider a social network as a graph $G = (U, E)$ in which U represents nodes (users) and E represents links (social relations). Each user U in U has a set of attributes A_U as well as immediate neighbors (friends) $N(U)$ such that if $V \in N(U)$, $(U, V) \in E$. The values of attributes A_U are represented as a_U. Moreover, a recommender system contains the records of users' ratings, which can be represented by a triple relation of $T = (U, I, R)$ in which U is the users in the social network G; I is the set of items (products or services), and each item I in I has a set of attributes A_I'. R stands for the ratings such that each R_{UI} in R is user U's rating on item I. R_{UI} has a numeric value k (e.g., $k \in \{1, 2, \dots 5\}$). Moreover, we define $I(U)$ as the set of items that user U has reviewed and refer to the set of reviewers of item I as $U(I)$. The goal of this recommender system is to predict $\Pr(R_{UI} = k \mid A' = a_I'$, $A = a_U$, $\{R_{VI} = r_{VI}: \forall V \in U(I) \cap N(U)\})$; i.e., the probability distribution of the target user U's rating on the target item I given the attribute values of item I, the attribute values of user U, and the ratings on item I rated by U's immediate friends. Once we obtain this distribution, R_{UI} is calculated as the expectation of the distribution. Items with high estimated ratings will be recommended to the target user, and users with high estimated ratings on the target item are the potential buyers.

In order to estimate $\Pr(R_{UI} = k \mid A' = a_I', A = a_U, \{R_{VI} = r_{VI}: \forall V \in U(I) \cap N(U)\})$, we adopt the naive Bayes assumption which assumes that the influences from item attribute values, user attribute values, and immediate friends' ratings are independent. Although this assumption simplifies the correlations among these variables, the naive Bayes model has been shown to be quite effective in many applications including textual document classification [16]. By making this assumption, the original conditional probability can be factorized as follows:

$$\Pr(R_{UI} = k | A' = a_I', A = a_U, \{R_{VI} = r_{VI} : \forall V \in U(I) \cap N(U)\})$$
$$= \frac{1}{Z} \Pr(R_{UI} = k | A' = a_I') \times \Pr(R_{UI} = k | A = a_U) \qquad (4.3)$$
$$\times \Pr(R_{UI} = k | \{R_{VI} = r_{VI} : \forall V \in U(I) \cap N(U)\})$$

First, $\Pr(R_U = k \mid A' = a_I',)$ is the conditional probability that the target user U will give a rating k to an item with the same attribute values as item I. This probability represents U's preference for items similar to I. Because this value depends on the attribute values of items rather than an individual item, we drop the subscript I in R_{UI} for simplification. Second, $\Pr(R_I = k \mid A = a_U)$ is the probability that the target item I will receive a rating value k from a reviewer whose attribute values are the same as U. This probability reflects the general acceptance of the target item I by users like U. For the same reason, because this value depends on the attribute values of users rather than a specific user, we drop the subscript U in R_{UI}. Finally, $\Pr(R_{UI} = k \mid \{R_{VI} = r_{VI}: \forall V \in U(I) \cap N(U)\})$ is the probability that the target user U gives a rating value k to the target item I given the ratings of U's immediate friends on item I. This is where we actually take social influences into consideration in our system. In addition, Z is a normalizing constant. We shall present the methods to estimate each of the factors in the following subsections.

4.3.1.1 User Preference

As we pointed out, $\Pr(R_U = k \mid A' = a_I')$ measures the target user U's preference for the items similar to item I. For example, if we want to know how high Angela will rate "Revolutionary Road," $\Pr(R_U = k \mid A' = a_I')$ gives us a hint of how likely it is that Angela will give a rating k to a drama movie which is also casted by Kate Winslet. To estimate this probability, we adopt the naive Bayes assumption again. We assume that the item attributes in A', e.g., category and cast, are independent of each other. Therefore, we have

$$
\begin{aligned}
\Pr(R_U = k | A' = a_I') &= \frac{\Pr(R_U = k) \times \Pr(A_1', A_2', \ldots, A_n' | R_U = k)}{\Pr(A_1', A_2', \ldots, A_n')} \\
&= \frac{\Pr(R_U = k) \times \prod_{j=1}^{j=n} \Pr(A_j' | R_U = k)}{\Pr(A'_1, A'_2, \ldots, A'_n)}, A' = \{A_1', A_2', \ldots, A_n'\}
\end{aligned}
\tag{4.4}
$$

where $\Pr(A'_1, A'_2, \ldots, A'_n)$ can be treated as a normalizing constant, $\Pr(R_U = k)$ is the prior probability that U gives a rating k, and $\Pr(A_j' | R_U = k)$ is the conditional probability that each item attribute A_j' in A' has a value a_j' given U rated k; e.g., $\Pr(\text{movie type} = \text{drama} | R_U = 4)$ is the probability that a movie will be a type of drama movie, given that U gives a rating 4. The last two probabilities can be estimated from counting the review ratings of the target user U. Specifically,

$$
\Pr(R_U = k) = \frac{|I(R_U = k)| + 1}{|I(U)| + n}, \text{ and}
\tag{4.5}
$$

$$
\Pr(A_j' = a_j' | R_U = k) = \frac{\left| I(A_j' = a_j', R_U = k) \right| + 1}{|I(R_U = k)| + m},
\tag{4.6}
$$

where $|I(U)|$ is the number of reviews of user U's in the training set, $|I(R_U = k)|$ is the number of reviews that user U gives a rating value k, and $|I(A_j' = a_j', R_U = k)|$ is the number of reviews that U gives a rating value k while attribute A_j' of the corresponding target item has a value a_j'. Notice that we insert an extra value 1 to the numerators in both equations, and add n, the range of review ratings to the denominator in Eq. (4.5), and m, the range of A_j''s values, to the denominator in Eq. (4.6). This method is also known as Laplace estimate, a well-known technique in estimating probabilities [7], especially on a small size of training samples. Because of Laplace estimate, "strong" probabilities, like 0 or 1, from direct probability computation can be avoided.

Moreover, in some cases when item attributes are not available, we can approximate $\Pr(R_U = k \mid A' = a_I')$ by the prior probability $\Pr(R_U = k)$. Even though $\Pr(R_U = k)$ does not contain information specific to certain item attributes, it does take into account U's general rating preference; e.g., if U is a generous person, he/she gives high ratings regardless of the items.

4.3.1.2 Item Acceptance

$\Pr(R_I = k \mid A = a_u)$ captures the general acceptance of item I from users like user U. For example, for a reviewer who is similar to Angela (e.g., the same gender and age), how likely is it that "Revolutionary Road" will receive a rating of 5 from her. Similar to the estimation in user preference, we use the naive Bayes assumption and assume user attributes are independent. Thus, we have

$$
\begin{aligned}
\Pr(R_I = k | A = a_U) &= \frac{\Pr(R_I = k) \times \Pr(A_1, A_2, \ldots, A_m | R_I = k)}{\Pr(A_1, A_2, \ldots, A_m)} \\
&= \frac{\Pr(R_I = k) \times \prod_{j=1}^{j=m} \Pr(A_j | R_I = k)}{\Pr(A_1, A_2, \ldots, A_m)}, A = \{A_1, A_2, \ldots, A_m\}
\end{aligned}
\tag{4.7}
$$

in which $\Pr(R_I = k)$ is the prior probability that the target item I receives a rating value k, and $\Pr(A_j \mid R_I = k)$ is the conditional probability that user attribute A_j of a reviewer has a value of a_j given item I receives a rating k from this reviewer. These two probabilities can be learned by counting the review ratings on the target item I in a manner similar to what we did in learning user preferences. When user attributes are not available, we use $\Pr(R_I = k)$, i.e., item I's general acceptance regardless of users, to approximate $\Pr(R_I = k \mid A = a_u)$. In addition, $\Pr(A_1, A_2, \ldots, A_m)$ in Eq. (4.7) is a normalizing constant.

4.3.1.3 Influence from Immediate Friends

Finally, $\Pr(R_{UI} = k \mid \{R_{VI} = r_{VI}: \forall V \in U(I) \cap N(U)\})$ is where SNRS utilizes the influences from immediate friends. To estimate this probability, SNRS learns the correlations between the target user U and each of his/her immediate friends V from the items that they both have rated previously, and then assume each pair of friends will behave consistently on reviewing the target item I too. Thus, U's rating can be estimated from r_{VI} according to the correlations. A common practice for learning such correlations is through estimating user similarities or coefficients, either based on user profiles or based user ratings. However, user correlations are often so delicate that they cannot be fully captured by a single similarity or coefficient value. It is even worse that most of those measures seem ad hoc. Different measures return different results and have different conclusions on whether or not a pair of users is really correlated [15]. To another extreme, user correlations can be also represented in a joint distribution table of U's and V's ratings on the same items that they have rated; i.e., $\Pr(R_{UI}, R_{VI}) \forall I \in I(U) \cap I(V)$. This table fully preserves the correlations between U's and V's ratings. However, in order to build such a distribution with accurate statistics, it requires a large number of training samples. For example, for ratings ranging from one to five, the joint distribution has 25 degrees of freedom, which is difficult to be estimated robustly with limited training samples. This is especially a problem for recommender systems, because in most of these systems, users only review a few items compared to the large amount of items available in the system, and the co-rated items between users are even less. Therefore, in this study, we use another approach to remedy the problems in both cases.

Friends are similar and give similar ratings. Our data analysis in Section 5.4 on a real online social network also shows that immediate friends tend to give more similar ratings than non-friends. Thus, for each pair of immediate friends U and V, we consider their ratings on the same item to be close with some error ε. That is,

$$R_{UI} = R_{VI} + \varepsilon, \qquad I \in I(U) \cap I(V), V \in N(U) \cap U(I) \tag{4.8}$$

From Eq. (4.8), we can see that error ε can be simulated from the histogram of U's and V's rating differences $H(R_{UI} - R_{VI}) \; \forall I \in I(U) \cap I(V)$. Thus, $H(R_{UI} - R_{VI})$ serves as the correlation measure between U and V. For rating ranges from one to five, $H(R_{UI} - R_{VI})$ is a distribution of nine values, i.e. from -4 to 4. Compared to similarity measures, it preserves more details in friends' review ratings. Compared to a joint distribution approach, it has fewer degrees of freedom.

Assuming U's and V's rating difference on the target item I is consistent with $H(R_{UI} - R_{VI})$. Therefore, when R_{VI} has a rating r_{VI} on the target item, the probability that R_{UI} has a value k is proportional to $H(k - r_{VI})$.

$$\Pr(R_{UI} = k | R_{VI} = r_{VI}) \propto H(k - r_{VI}). \tag{4.9}$$

For example, assume that both U and V rated the items as shown in Table 4.1. Given their ratings in the table, we want to predict U's possible ratings on item I_6 according to the correlation with V. From the previous ratings of U and V, we find out that two out of five times U's rating is the same as V's, and three out of five times U's rating is lower than V's by one. According to such a correlation, we predict that there is a 40% chance that R_{UI6} is 4 and 60% chance that R_{UI6} is 3.

Table 4.1 An example of predicting user rating from an immediate friend	U	V
I_1	5	5
I_2	3	4
I_3	4	4
I_4	2	3
I_5	4	5
I_6	?	4

The previous example illustrates how we utilize the correlation between the target user and one of his/her immediate friends. When the target user has more than one immediate friend who co-rates the target item, the influences from all of those friends can be incorporated in a product of normalized histograms of individual friend pairs.

$$\Pr(R_{UI} = k | \{R_{VI} = r_{VI} : \forall V \in U(I) \cap N(U)\} = \frac{1}{Z} \prod_V \frac{1}{Z_V} H(k - r_{VI}) \quad (4.10)$$

where Z_V is the normalizing constant for the histogram of each immediate friend pair, and Z is the normalizing constant for the overall product.

Once we obtain $\Pr(R_U = k \mid A' = a_I',)$, $\Pr(R_I = k \mid A = a_u)$, and $\Pr(R_{UI} = k \mid \{R_{VI} = r_{VI}: \forall V \in U(I) \cap N(U)\})$, the ultimate rating distribution of R_{UI}, under the factors of user preference, item's general acceptance, and the correlations with immediate friends, can be estimated from Eq. (3). R'_{UI}, the estimated value of R_{UI}, is the expectation of the distribution as shown in Eq. (11).

$$R'_{UI} = \sum_k k \times \Pr(R_{UI} = k | A' = a_I', A = a_U, \{R_{VI} = r_{VI} : \forall V \in U(I) \cap N(U)\}$$

$$(4.11)$$

4.3.2 Distant Friend Inference

In the previous section, we introduced the approach to predict the target user's rating on a target item from those of his/her immediate friends on the same item. However, in reality, most immediate friends of the target user may not have reviewed the target item, because there are a large number of items in recommender systems but users may only select a few of them. Therefore, the influences from those friends cannot be utilized in immediate friend inference, and it is even worse that the ratings of many users cannot be predicted because they have no immediate friends who co-rate the target item. To solve this problem, we propose a method to incorporate the influences from distant friends via extending immediate friend inference.

The idea of distant friend inference is intuitive. Even though V, an immediate friend of the target user U, has no rating on the target item, if V has his/her own immediate friends who rated the target item, we should be able to predict V's rating on the target item via the immediate friend inference, and then to predict U's rating based on the estimated rating of V's. This process conforms to real scenarios, such as Linda's officemate influences Linda who further influences Angela in our previous example. Followed by this intuition, we decide to apply an *iterative classification* method [17, 24, 31] for distant friend inference.

Iterative classification is an approximation technique for classifying relational entities. This method is based on the fact that relational entities are correlated with each other. Estimating the classification of an entity often depends on the estimations of classification of its neighbors. The improved classification of one entity will help to infer the related neighbors and vice versa. Unlike traditional data mining which assumes that data instances are independent and identically distributed (i.i.d.) samples, and classifies them one by one, iterative classification iteratively classifies all the entities in the testing set simultaneously because the classifications of those entities are correlated. Note that iterative classification is an approximation technique, because exact inference is computationally intractable unless the network structures have certain graph topologies such as sequences, trees, or networks with low tree width. Iterative classification has been used to classify company profiles [24], hypertext documents [17], and e-mails [6] with reasonable success in the previous research.

The algorithm for distant friend inference is shown in Table 4.2. This algorithm predicts the users' ratings on each target item at a time. The original iterative classification method classifies the whole network of users. However, since the number of users in social networks is usually large, we save the computation cost by limiting the inference to a user set N which includes the target users of the target item I and their corresponding immediate friends. In each iteration, we generate a random ordering O of the users in N. For each user U in O, if U has no immediate friend who belongs to $U(I)$, which is the set of users whose rating (either ground truth or estimated value) is observable, the estimation of R_{UI} will be skipped in this iteration. Otherwise, $\Pr(R_{UI} = k \mid A' = a_I', A = a_U, \{R_{VI} = r_{VI} : \forall V \in U(I) \cap N(U)\})$ will be estimated by immediate friend inference, and R'_{UI} is then obtained from Eq. (4.11). Because user rating is an integer value, in order to continue the iterative process we round R'_{UI} to a close integer value and insert into or update $U(I)$ with R'_{UI} if different. This entire process iterates M times or until no update occurs in the current iteration. In our experiment, the process usually converges within 10 iterations.

Table 4.2 Pseudo-code for distant friend inference

---

1. For each item I in the testing set do
2.   Select a set of users N for inference. N includes the target users of item I and their corresponding immediate friends.
3.   For iteration from 1 to M do
4.   Generate a random ordering, O, of users in N
5.   For each user U in O do
6.   If U has no immediate friend who exists in $U(I)$
7.   Continue
8.   Else
9.   Apply immediate friend inference
10. $R'_{UI} = \sum_k k * \Pr(R_{UI} = k \mid A = a_U, A' = a_I', \{R_{VI} = r_{VI} : \forall V \in U(I) \cap N(U)\})$
11.   Insert into or Update $U(I)$ with R'_{UI} if different
12.   End If
13.   End For
14.   If no updates in the current iteration
15.   Break
16.   End If
17.   End For
18.   Output the final predictions for the target users
19. End For

It is worth pointing out that after we compute $\Pr(R_{UI} = k \mid A' = a_I', A = a_U, \{R_{VI} = r_{VI} : \forall V \in U(I) \cap N(U)\})$, there are two other options for updating R'_{UI} besides rounding the expectation in distant friend inference. The first option is to select R'_{UI} with the value k such that it maximizes $\Pr(R_{UI} = k \mid A' = a_I', A = a_U,$

$\{R_{VI} = r_{VI} : \forall V \in U(I) \cap N(U)\}$). However, by doing so, we are actually throwing out clues of small probabilities at the same time. After many iterations, the errors caused by the greedy selection will be exacerbated. The target users are likely to be classified with the majority class. The other option is to directly use $\Pr(R_{UI} = k \mid A' = a'_I, A = a_U, \{R_{VI} = r_{VI} : \forall V \in U(I) \cap N(U)\})$ as soft evidence to classify other users. However, in our experiments, this approach does not return results as good as those of rounding the expectation.

4.4 Data set

In this section, we introduce the data set that we use for this research and present some interesting characteristics of this data set. Our data set is obtained from a real online social network Yelp.com. As one of the most popular web 2.0 web sites, Yelp provides users local search for restaurants, shopping, spas, nightlife, hotels, auto services, financial services, etc. Users that come to this site can either look for information from Yelp or make their own voices by writing reviews for some local commercial entities that they have experienced. Yelp provides a homepage for each local commercial entity. An example of a homepage for a restaurant at Yelp, "Yoshi's Sushi," is shown in Fig. 4.2a. On top of this homepage is a profile of this restaurant, which includes restaurant attributes such as category, location, hours, price range, parking information. In addition, this homepage contains a list of reviews of users who have visited this restaurant before. Each review comes with a numerical rating ranging from one to five stars. Five starts means the highest rating to this restaurant, and one star is the lowest rating.

Besides maintaining traditional features of recommender systems, Yelp provides social network features so that it can attract more users. Specifically, Yelp allows users to invite their friends to join Yelp or make new friends existing at Yelp. The friendship at Yelp is mutual relationship, which means that when a user adds another user as a friend, the first user will be automatically added as a friend of the second user. Yelp also provides a homepage for each of its users. Each user homepage contains basic personal information, all the reviews written by this user, and links to the friends that are explicitly identified by this user.

Since restaurant is the most popular category at Yelp, we picked restaurant as the problem domain. We crawled and parsed the homepages of all the Yelp restaurants in the Los Angeles area that registered before November 2007. We ended up with 4152 restaurants. By following the reviewers' links in the Yelp restaurant homepages, we also crawled the homepages of all these reviewers, which resulted in 9414 users. Based on the friend links in each user's homepage, we are able to identify friends from the crawled users, and thus reconstruct a social network. Note that the friends we collected for each user may only be a subset of the actual friends listed on his/her homepage. That is because we require every user in our data set to have a least one review in the crawled restaurants. In other words, the social network that we crawled focuses on dining.

Fig. 4.2 (a) The homepage of a Yelp restaurant "Yoshi's Sushi" and (b) the corresponding abstract graphical representation of Yoshi's Sushi in which each node represents a reviewer in the restaurant, and nodes are connected by explicit friend relations. The size of each node is proportional to the corresponding reviewer's rating on this restaurant

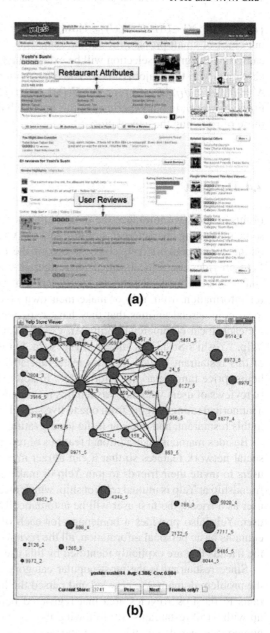

(a)

(b)

To illustrate users' ratings and their relationships, we built a graphical tool to represent each restaurant in our data set. Figure 4.2b shows the alternative view of "Yoshi's Sushi" in Fig. 4.2a. Each node represents a reviewer of the restaurant, and the size of the node represents the corresponding reviewer's rating on this restaurant.

Two nodes are connected if they claim each other as friends. Since friends in Yelp are mutual, the social network structure is an undirected graph. From Fig. 4.2b, we can see that nodes in this graph are highly connected, which means many friends are involved in writing reviews for "Yoshi's Sushi."

A preliminary study on this data set yields the following results. The total number of reviews in this data set is 55,801. Thus, each Yelp user on average writes 5.93 reviews and each restaurant on average has 13.44 reviews. In terms of friends, the average number of immediate friends of every user is 8.18. If we take a closer look at the relations between the number of users and the number of their immediate friends (as shown in Fig. 4.3a), we can see that it actually follows a *power-law distribution*; this means that most users have only a few immediate friends while a few users have a lot of immediate friends. A similar distribution also applies to the relations between the number of users and the number of reviews, as shown in Fig. 4.3b. Because most users on Yelp review only a few restaurants, we expect the data set to be extremely sparse. In fact, the sparsity of this data set, i.e., the percentage of user/item pairs whose ratings are unknown is 99.86%.

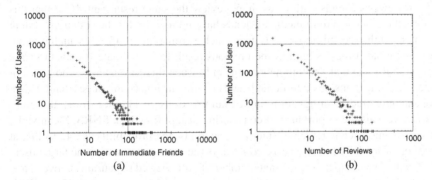

Fig. 4.3 (**a**) The number of users versus the number of immediate friends in the Yelp network and (**b**) the number of users versus the number of reviews both follow the power-law distribution

Furthermore, we perform the following analysis on this data set, particularly focusing on immediate friends' review correlation and rating correlation. Basically, we want to answer two questions: (1) whether or not friends tend to review the same restaurant and (2) whether or not friends tend to give ratings that are more similar than those from non-friends. Clearly, these two questions are essential to SNRS.

4.4.1 Review Correlations of Immediate Friends

Let us first study the correlation of immediate friends in reviewing the same restaurants. Specifically, we want to know if a user reviews a restaurant, what is the chance that at least one of his/her immediate friends has also reviewed the same restaurant? To answer this question, we count, for each user, the percentage of restaurants that has also being reviewed by at least one of his/her immediate friends.

The average percentage over all users in the data set is 18.6%. As a comparison, we calculate the same probability if assuming immediate friends review restaurants uniformly at random and independently. In a social network with n users, for a user with q immediate friends and a restaurant with m reviewers (including the current user), the chance that at least one of q immediate friends appears in m reviewers is,

$$1 - \frac{\binom{n-q-1}{m-1}}{\binom{n-1}{m-1}}.$$

We calculate this value for every user and every restaurant he/she reviewed. The average probability over all users is only 3.7%. Compared to 18.6% as observed in the data set, it is clear that immediate friends do not review restaurants randomly. There are certain correlations between friends.

We also extend the previous study by considering the probability that at least one of a reviewer's friends within two hops review the same restaurant. Note that this covers the cases where immediate friends have no reviews for the restaurant, but at least one of the second-hop friends does. Such a probability is 45.2%, which is about two and a half times as high as the previous result for immediate friends (18.6%). Since SNRS can make recommendations only when there are friends who have co-rated the same items, if we limit the friends within one hop (immediate friends), then we can only predict ratings for a limited number of users. In other words, this comparison reveals the importance of considering distant friends in SNRS. Meanwhile, if we assume friends review restaurants randomly, the probability is 34.2% that at least one friend, within two hops, co-reviews the same restaurant as the target user.

Finally, we compare the average number of co-reviewed restaurants between any two immediate friends and any two users on Yelp. The results are 0.85 and 0.03, respectively, which again illustrates the tendency that immediate friends co-review the same restaurants.

4.4.2 Rating Correlations of Immediate Friends

To show that whether immediate friends tend to give more similar ratings than non-friends, we compare the average rating differences (in absolute values) on the same restaurant between reviewers who are immediate friends and non-friends. We find that, for every restaurant in our data set, if two reviewers are immediate friends, their ratings on this restaurant differ by 0.88 on average with a deviation of 0.89. If they are not, their rating difference is 1.05 and the standard deviation is 0.98. This result clearly demonstrates that immediate friends, on average, give more similar ratings than non-friends.

In this section we presented some characteristics of our data set. The results on review correlations as well as rating correlations between immediate friends are critical in validating our assumptions in SNRS. In the next section, we are going to present a set of experiments to demonstrate the advantages of considering social network information in a recommender system.

4.5 Experiments

In the experiments we evaluate the performance of SNRS on the Yelp data set, focusing on the issues of the prediction accuracy, data sparsity, and cold-start, which are the main issues of current recommender systems. Additionally, we will study the role of distant friends in SNRS.

The following is the setting for our experiments. We used a restaurant's price range as the item attribute. Since there is no useful user attribute on Yelp, we substituted $\Pr(R_I = k \mid A = a_u)$ with $\Pr(R_I = k)$ when estimating item acceptance. Finally, we set a threshold to require every pair of immediate friends to have at least three co-rated restaurants. If they do not, we ignore their friend relationships.

4.5.1 Comparison Methods

As a comparison, we implemented the following methods along with SNRS.

Friend average (FA). To leverage the ratings of friends for inference, the most straightforward approach is to predict the ratings of the target users on the target items with the average ratings of their immediate friends on the same item. We therefore implemented this method as a baseline.

Weighted friends (WVF). Unlike treating immediate friends equally as in *FA*, *WVF* considers that every immediate friend has a different impact (or weight) on the target user. The more the impact from an immediate friend, the closer the target user's rating is to the rating of that friend. Thus, the probability of the target user's rating is proportional to the accumulated weight in each rating value.

$$\Pr(R_{UI} = k | \{R_{VI} = r_{VI} : \forall V \in N(U) \cap U(I)\}) = \frac{1}{Z} \sum_V w(U, V) \delta(k, r_{VI}) \quad (4.12)$$

in which z is a normalizing constant. $w(U, V)$ is the weight between U and V. In this experiment, we use the cosine similarity between U's and V's ratings as their weight. $\delta(k, r_{VI})$ is the delta function which returns one only when $r_{VI} = k$, and zero otherwise. WVF is essentially same as a relational-neighbor classifier [18] which performs really well on classifying relational data sets such as citations and movies.

Naive Bayes (NB). Social networks can be also modeled using Bayesian networks [10]. In this study, we implemented a special form of Bayesian networks, a naive Bayes classifier. Specifically, when predicting the rating of a target user U, the *NB* classifier assumes U's rating influences the ratings of U's immediate friends, and the ratings of U's immediate friends are independent of each other. Although with strong assumptions, *NB* classifiers have been widely used for probabilistic modeling and often result in surprisingly good results [16]. Therefore, we also included this method for comparison.

Given the ratings of the immediate friends on the target item I, we calculate the conditional probability $\Pr(R_{UI}| \{R_{VI}: \forall V \in N(U) \cap U(I)\})$ as follows:

$$\Pr(R_{UI} = k|\{R_{VI} = r_{VI} : \forall V \in N(U) \cap U(I)\})$$
$$= \frac{1}{Z} \Pr(R_U = k) \prod_V \Pr(R_V = r_{VI}|R_U = k) \qquad (4.13)$$

where $\Pr(R_U = k)$ is the prior rating distribution of the target user U, which can be estimated by counting the review ratings of U. $\Pr(R_V = r_{VI}| R_U = k)$ is the conditional probability that an immediate friend V's rating is equal to r_{VI} given U's rating is k. Because there are not enough samples to estimate these probabilities for every individual pair of immediate friends, we estimate these probabilities by counting the review ratings for all pairs of immediate friends in the data set. Moreover, Z is a normalizing constant. The estimated rating of the target user U is the rating value that has the maximum probability.

Collaborative filtering (CF). We implemented the standard collaborative filtering algorithm as we described in Section 5.2. The K value we used is 20.

4.5.2 Prediction Accuracy And Coverage

We carried out this experiment in a 10-fold cross-validation. The prediction accuracy was measured by the *mean absolute error* (MAE), which is defined as the average absolute deviation of predictions to the ground truth data over all the instances, i.e., target user/item pairs, in the testing set.

$$\text{MAE} = \frac{\sum_{U,I} |r_{UI} - r'_{UI}|}{L}, \qquad (4.14)$$

where L is the number of testing instances. The smaller the MAE, the better the inference.

Since SNRS, FA, WVF, and NB rely on friends' ratings on the target item in order to make predictions; thus, there is no prediction when the target user has no friends who have rated the item. Similarly, CF does not make predictions unless it finds similar users for the target user. Therefore, another metric that we study for each method is the *coverage*, which is defined as the percentage of the testing instances for which the method can make predictions.

The experimental results are listed in Table 4.3. From this table, we note that SNRS achieves the best performance in terms of MAE (0.718), while CF is the worst (0.871). SNRS improves the prediction accuracy of CF by 17.8%. The other methods that use the influences from friends also achieve better results than CF. Clearly, considering social influence does improve predictions in recommender systems. In terms of the coverage, the coverage of all these methods is relatively low;

Table 4.3 Comparison of the MAEs of the proposed social network-based recommender system (SNRS), collaborative filtering (CF), friend average (FA), weighted friends (WVF), and naive Bayes (NB) in a 10-fold cross-validation

	MAE	Coverage
SNRS	0.716	0.482
FA	0.814	0.228
WVF	0.808	0.228
NB	0.756	0.237
CF	0.871	0.552

e.g., none of these methods have the coverage better than 0.6. This is because the data set we have is extremely sparse, with a sparsity of 99.86%. However, among these methods, CF is the best. Because most of the time, CF is able to find similar users for the target user from all the other users in the training set. On the other hand, the coverage of the other methods is decided by whether there is a friend who has rated the item, and we pruned many friend relationships by setting a threshold of three co-rated items for each pair of friends. Therefore, the coverage of those methods is lower than CF. The coverage of FA, WVF, and NB is even lower than that of SNRS, because SNRS can still utilize the influence from distant friends even if immediate friends have not rated the restaurant, while the other methods cannot.

4.5.3 Data Sparsity

CF suffers from problems with sparse data. In this study, we want to evaluate the performance of SNRS at various levels of data sparsity. To do so, we randomly divided the whole user/item pairs in our data set into ten groups, and then randomly selected n sets as the testing set, and the rest as the training set. The value of n controls the sparsity of the data set. At each value of n, we repeated the experiment 100 times. The performance was measured by the average MAEs and the coverage.

Figure 4.4a compares the MAEs of SNRS and CF when the percentages of testing sets vary from 10 to 70%. Due to the high sparsity of the underlying Yelp data set, even when the percentage of testing set is 10%, the actual sparsity is as high as 99.87%. From Fig. 4.4a, we first observe that the MAEs of SNRS are consistently lower than those of the CF, which again shows that SNRS indeed outperforms CF. Second, the prediction accuracy of CF is greatly affected by data sparsity. For example, the MAEs of CF increase by 14.4% from 0.868 and 0.993 when the testing set is increased from 10 to 70% of the whole data set. Meanwhile, the MAEs of SNRS grow at a much slower pace. For instance, the MAEs of SNRS increase by only 2.8% from 0.716 to 0.736 under the same conditions.

Figure 4.4b compares the coverage of both methods. Unfortunately, the coverage of both methods severely drops as the training set becomes sparser. For example, the coverage of CF drops from 0.549 to 0.064 when the size of the testing set increases from 10 to 70%, and the coverage of SNRS decreases from 0.482 to 0.123 at the

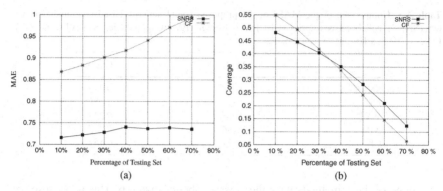

Fig. 4.4 Comparison of the (**a**) MAEs and the (**b**) coverage of SNRS and CF at different sizes of the testing set

same time. This decrease in the coverage is expected, as explained earlier, but the trend of these two methods also indicates their differences. CF performs better with a large training set, allowing it to find more similar users. When the training set becomes sparser, CF finds similar users from fewer candidates for each target user. The similarity obtained from each pair of users is less accurate because that there are fewer co-rated items between these users. Thus, both the prediction accuracy and the coverage of CF are adversely affected by the data sparsity. Meanwhile, the coverage of SNRS also decreases because there are fewer friends who have ratings on the target items as the data set becomes sparser. But the coverage of SNRS decreases with a slower pace compared to that of CF. Initially, CF has a better coverage than SNRS. However, the coverage of SNRS starts to exceed that of CF after the percentage of the testing set is above 30%. Such a change in the trend is because that some users can still be inferred since the influences from distant friends are able to propagate to them even when the data set is sparse. In Section 5.5.5, we will study the role of distant friends again. On the other hand, the prediction accuracy of SNRS is consistent at all levels of data sparsity. This is because friends are provided explicitly by social networks, and there is no need for SNRS to find similar users from the training set. Therefore, as long as there are friends who have reviewed the target item, SNRS can make accurate predictions.

4.5.4 Cold-Start

Cold-start is an extreme case of data sparsity where a new user has no reviews. In such a case, CF cannot make a recommendation to this new user since CF is not able to find similar users for him/her. SNRS cannot either if this new user has also no friends. However, in some cases of cold-start when a new user is invited by some existing users in the system, the initial friend relationships of this new user can still make the inference of SNRS possible. Even though there is no prior knowledge of the new user's own preference, SNRS can make recommendations to this new user based on the preferences of his/her friends. In this study, we simulated the latter case of cold-start by making the following experimental settings: (1) we did not use the target user's prior ratings in the training set; thus, there was no influence from user preference. We simply set the output from $\Pr(R_U = k \mid A' = a_I{}')$, as a uniform distribution. (2) Since we cannot learn the rating correlation between this new user and his/her friends, we directly used friends' rating distribution on the target item, $\Pr(\{R_{VI} = r_{VI} : \forall V \in U(I) \cap N(U)\})$, as the result from friend inference. (3) Except for the target user, the ratings of all other users were known.

We simulated cold-start for every user in the data set. The resulting MAE is 0.706 and the coverage is 0.691. This result demonstrates that even in cold-start, SNRS can still perform decently. The coverage of SNRS is high compared to that in the 10-fold cross-validation (0.422) because the ratings of every target user's friends are all observable in the setting of this experiment.

4.5.5 Role of Distant Friends

In this study we investigate the role of distant friends in SNRS. Specifically, we compared the performance of SNRS with and without distant friend inference in a 10-fold cross-validation. The experimental results are shown in Table 4.4. From these results, we can see that by considering the influences from distant friends, the coverage of SNRS is increased from 0.237 to 0.482, which is equivalent to a 103% improvement. However, the improvement is achieved at the cost of a slight reduction in the prediction accuracy. In our experiments, the MAE increases from 0.682 to 0.716, which is only a 5% difference. This is consistent with our intuition that the impact from distant friends is not as direct as from immediate friends, and certain errors will be inevitably introduced when considering distant friends. On the other hand, compared to the drastic gain in the coverage, the minor loss in precision is still acceptable.

Table 4.4 Comparison of the performance of SNRS with and without distant friend inference

	MAE	Coverage
With distant friend inference	0.716	0.482
Without distant friend inference	0.682	0.237

4.6 Semantic Filtering of Social Networks

In the previous section we showed that SNRS improves the prediction accuracy of recommender systems by utilizing information such as social influences in social networks. In this section, we shall discuss how to further improve the performance of SNRS by applying semantic filtering of social networks.

Although friends influence each other when selecting items, such influence is sensitive to the types of items. For example, two friends who have similar taste on CDs may not necessarily agree with each other in their choice of favorite restaurants. Therefore, to recommend restaurants, we should not consider friends who have common preferences only in music. In other words, to effectively use the social influence, an appropriate set of friends needs to be selected according to the type of target items, which is what we called semantic filtering of social networks. In fact, we considered this issue when we performed experiments on Yelp. Rather than considering all friends listed in user's profiles, we pruned a set of friends who had reviewed only a small number of common restaurants. For example, even though two real friends may have reviewed many common hotels on Yelp, they are not necessarily friends in SNRS unless they have enough reviews on common restaurants. However, this is still a poor man's version of semantic filtering, because even within the domain of restaurants, friends can be further grouped based on their opinions on different food categories, price range, restaurant environment, etc.

A better selection of relevant friends requires us to know in what aspects two friends influence each other. Unfortunately, such information is not available in most current OSNs. Some OSNs, such as Linkedin, ask how friends know each other, e.g., whether they were/are classmates or colleagues. Information like this definitely helps us understand friend relationships. However, it is still too general to bring a practical usage to recommender systems. Instead, the semantics that we really want to know from friend relationships should be more specific to the domain of interest. For example, in terms of dining, it would be better to know whether two friends are friends because they have a similar taste in food or a similar preference in the price of meals, etc. To obtain such information, the most direct solution is for content providers (e.g., Yelp) to explicitly ask users to rate their friends on those aspects. If that puts too much of a burden on users, an alternative is for content providers to collect finer-grained user ratings rather than overall ratings alone, and then implicitly deduce friend relationships from the semantics in those finer-grained ratings. The problem with overall ratings is that they encapsulate decision reasoning of users on many factors. For example, when a user gives a rating of 4 to a restaurant, it is not clear if the user really likes the taste, price, service, or environment of this restaurant. If content providers could ask users to rate on those factors, such finer-grained ratings would not only allow us to model user preference and item acceptance more precisely but also help us to know on which category two friends are in agreement or whether they influence each other. For instance, two friends may not give the same overall rating, but they might still agree on the quality of restaurant service.

In the following text, we describe an experiment that we designed to demonstrate how relevant friends can be selected for inference by obtaining the semantics in friend relationships and user ratings, and then validate its improvement on SNRS.

This experiment was to predict students' ratings for online articles. It was conducted as a class project assignment with 22 students. At the beginning of the experiment, we selected 20 online articles. These articles focus on three topics: the recent economic crisis, controversies in technologies such as stem cell research and file sharing, and controversies in culture like gay marriage. These articles all contain strong opinions expressed by the authors. We collected the demographic information of students, including gender, age, ethnicity, employment, and interests. We also asked them a set of questions related to the articles that we selected. For example, "Has the rise in unemployment affected you or someone in your family?" and "Given the current state of the economy, are you concerned about getting a job after you graduate?" After that we asked the students to review every article by giving four ratings (from 1 to 5) based on each of the following criteria: (1) Interestingness: Is the article interesting? (2) Agreement: How much do you agree with the author? (3) Writing: Is the article well written? and (4) Overall: Overall evaluation. The reason that we included the first three ratings is because they usually play important roles when we give an overall score to an article. Since most students did not know each other before the experiment, it would have been difficult to form a social network from their original relationships. We therefore decided to divide the students into groups and let them get to know each other by discussing the articles within the groups. Specifically, we divided the students into three groups twice. The first grouping was based on students' ethnicities, and the second grouping was based on students' responses to the survey questions. The goal of these groupings was to organize the students in such a way that the students in a group will more likely to be friends after the group discussions. During the discussions, every student needed to explain the reasons why he/she liked or disliked each article. Thus, the other group members were able to know more about the speaker. After the discussions, the students evaluated other group members (using ratings from 1 to 3) according to the following three aspects: (1) Do you have common interests on the articles? (2) Do you agree with his/her opinions on the articles? and (3) Do you have common judgments about the author's writing skill? In addition to evaluating group members, the students were allowed to revise their previous ratings to the articles if they had a new understanding of the articles due to the discussion.

Compared to the Yelp data set, there are mainly two changes in this data set. First, instead of having just an overall rating, each article now has three fine-grained ratings (interestingness, agreement, and writing) which, as mentioned earlier, provide the semantics of the overall rating. Second, friend relationships have semantics too. Rather than just knowing that two students are friends, we are now able to know whether it is because they have similar interests or similar opinions, etc. In the following experiment, we are going to compare the prediction accuracies of SNRS with and without the consideration of semantic filtering of social networks.

Similar to the experimental setup in Section 5.5.3, we randomly divided the student/article pairs into ten groups. We randomly selected n groups as the testing set, and the rest as the training set. For each value of n, we repeated the experiment 100 times. For each pair in the testing set, we predicted the target student's ratings on the target article by applying and not applying semantic filtering of social networks. When we applied semantic filtering to predict a particular rating, we only considered the ratings of the target user's friends in the corresponding category. For example, to predict the target article's interestingness, we selected the set of students whom the target student had rated as friends (with a rating of 3) in terms of having similar interests, and then used their ratings on interestingness for inference. Thus, the social networks used for predicting each category are different. On the other hand, without semantic filtering, we considered the ratings on interestingness from all the students whom the target user had rated as friends in any of the three aspects. We measured the average MAEs for predicting each rating of the article, and the corresponding MAEs in CF.

We show the results of predicting student ratings on the interestingness of the articles in Fig. 4.5a. From this figure, we observe two trends. First, regardless of semantic filtering or not, the MAEs of SNRS are persistent for different data sparsity, while the MAEs of CF dramatically increase as the data becomes sparser. This phenomenon is consistent with our findings on the Yelp data set in Section 5.5.3. Second, we find that, at any level of data sparsity, the MAEs of SNRS with semantic filtering are consistently lower than those of SNRS without semantic filtering as well as those of CF. This result demonstrates that semantic filtering does indeed improve the prediction accuracy of SNRS. In Fig. 4.5b–d, we plot the results of predicting ratings on the agreement and writing of the articles and overall ratings, respectively. We observe similar trends in these figures. Note that when predicting

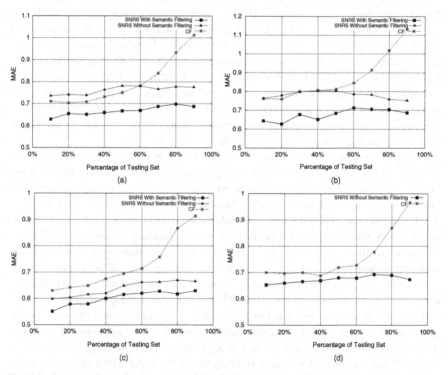

Fig. 4.5 Comparisons of the accuracies of CF and SNRS with and without semantic filtering on predicting student ratings on (**a**) interestingness, (**b**) agreement, (**c**) writing, and (**d**) overall aspects of the articles

the overall rating, we consider the overall ratings of all friends of a target student, which means there is no semantic filtering.

In this chapter we assume the reviews that users provide are real. However, in reality, there are always users who purposely provide false reviews to attack the adversaries or praise themselves, and traditional recommender systems have no control on them at all. On the other hand, SNRS is still able to detect and exclude those malicious users through reputation systems [19].

4.7 Related Work

Domings and Richardson proposed to mine customers' network values from a social network [8, 28]. The network value comes from the different potentials of customers to influence their social contacts to purchase the same products. Thus, the more people they can influence, the higher network value they have. Merchandisers can increase the expected lift in profit by sending advertisements only to those users who have high network values. Reference [8] estimates the conditional probability of whether a user will purchase a product given the adoption values of his/her friends, and marketing actions are tailored by using a relaxation labeling approach. Such a probability is modeled as a weighted sum of each user's internal probability of purchasing a product and an external effect from his/her friends [28]. The authors conduct simulation studies, first on a synthesized social network in [8], and then on Epinon.com, a review web site in [28].

There is also previous work on exploiting explicit user trust in recommender systems. Reference [9] presented a FilmTrust system which used explicit trust values between users as the weights in collaborative filtering. Similarly, [20] proposed a trust-aware recommender system which is also based on explicit trust values between users. They proposed a method for trust propagation in which the trust between distant friends is calculated by a linear decay model. Although these research efforts realized the importance of person-to-person influences in recommender systems, they are limited by the availability of prior knowledge of explicit trust values. These systems need to know not only who is trusting whom but also how much they trust each other. Thus, recommender systems that rely on explicit trust values cannot scale. In contrast, our system makes recommendations by using the correlations between friends, which can be viewed as implicit trust. We do not need to acquire trust values since they can be obtained from the rating correlations between friends. In addition to social influences, our system incorporates user's own attributes and the characteristics of items. These two factors are important for making target specific recommendations. Otherwise, recommender systems will simply suggest an item to a user whenever his/her trusted friend likes it.

Interestingly, [4] studied the factors that drive people's decision making and advice seeking through empirical studies and found out that the profile similarity and rating overlap of a recommender have a significant impact on a person's decision. In addition, [4] suggested that recommender systems support the social element of advice seeking through communication and explicit user matching functions.

Therefore, advice seekers can judge the validity and appropriateness of a recommendation. In Section 5.6 we proposed a recommender system design. In this design we think it is more important to consider the semantics in friend relationships when measuring their similarities based on user profiles and rating overlap.

More directly related work is found in [37]. Here, the authors proposed to combine social networks with recommender systems. They estimated the weights in collaborative filtering with an exponential function of the minimal distance of two users in a social network. This is, however, an over-simplified correlation between users. Distance has no semantic meaning of similarity, and two distant friends may still share common opinions. As noted by the authors, this approach does not work well. Reference [37] also proposed another approach to reduce the computational cost in recommender systems by limiting the candidate similar users within a user's social network neighbors. This approach actually will make the data sparsity problem of a recommender system even worse, because there are far less candidates for similar users than before.

4.8 Conclusions

Social networks provide an important source of information regarding users and their interactions. This is especially valuable to recommender systems. In this chapter we presented a social network-based recommender system (SNRS) which makes recommendations by considering a user's own preference, an item's general acceptance and influence from friends. In particular, we proposed to model the correlations between immediate friends with the histogram of friend's rating differences. The influences from distant friends are also considered in an iterative classification. In addition, we have collected data from a real online social network. The analysis on this data set reveals that friends have a tendency to review the same restaurants and give similar ratings. We compared the performance of SNRS with other methods, such as collaborative filtering (CF), friend average (FA), weighted friends (WVF), and naive Bayes (NB) with the same data set. In terms of the prediction accuracy, SNRS achieves the best result. It yields a 17.8% improvement compared to that of CF. In the sparsity test, SNRS returns consistently accurate predictions at different values of data sparsity. The coverage of SNRS decreases when the data is sparse but at a slower speed than CF. In the cold-start test, SNRS still performs well. We also studied the role of distant friends in SNRS and found that by considering the influences from distant friends, the coverage of SNRS can be significantly improved with only a minor reduction in the prediction accuracy. The performance of SNRS can be further improved by selecting relevant friends for inference, which can be achieved by collecting the semantics of the friend relationships or fine-grained user ratings. Such an approach can be adopted by current content providers.

Acknowledgments The authors would like to thank Professor Zhuowen Tu and Mr. Jiayan Jiang of UCLA for their stimulating discussions in statistical modeling of social networks.

References

1. Adomavicius, G. and Tuzhilin A. Toward the next generation of recommender systems: A survey of the state-of-the-art and possible extensions. *IEEE Transactions on Knowledge and Data Engineering*, 17(6):734–749, 2005.
2. Basu, C., Hirsh, H., and Cohen, W. Recommendation as classification: Using social and content-based information in recommendation. In *Recommender System Workshop'* 98. pp. 11–15, 1998.
3. Billsus, D. and Pazzani, M. Learning collaborative information filters. In *Proceedings of International Conference on Machine Learning*, Madison, WI, 1998.
4. Bonhard, P. and Sasse, M.A. "Knowing me, knowing you" – using profiles and social networking to improve recommender systems. *BT Technology Journal*, 24(3):84–98, July 2006.
5. Breese, J.S., Heckerman, D., and Kadie, C. Empirical analysis of predictive algorithms for collaborative filtering. In *Proceedings of the 14th Conference on Uncertainty in Artificial Intelligence*, Madison, WI, pp. 43–52, 1998.
6. Carvalho, V. and Cohen, W.W. On the collective classification of email speech acts. In *Proceedings of International ACM SIGIR conference on research and development in information retrieval*, pp. 345–352, 2005.
7. Chandra, B., Gupta, M., and Gupta, M.P. Robust approach for estimating probabilities in Naive-Bayes classifier. *In Pattern Recognition and Machine Intelligence*, 4815/2007:11–16, 2007
8. Domings, P. and Richardson, M. Mining the network value of customers. In *Proceedings of 7th ACM SIGKDD International Conference on Knowledge Discovery and Data Mining*, New York, NY: ACM Press, pp. 57–66, 2001.
9. Golbeck, J. Generating predictive movie recommendations from trust in social networks. In *Proceedings of the 4th International Conference on Trust Management*, Pisa, Italy, 2006.
10. He, J., Chu, W.W., and Liu, Z. Inferring privacy information from social networks. In *Proceedings of IEEE Intelligence and Security Informatics Conference (ISI 2006)*, San Diego, CA, May 2006.
11. Herlocker, J.L., Konstan, J.A., Borchers, A., and Riedl, J. An algorithmic framework for performing collaborative filtering. In *Proceedings of ACM SIGIR*, pp. 230–237, Berkley, USA, 1999.
12. Huang, Z., Chen, H., Zeng, D. Applying associative retrieval techniques to alleviate the sparsity problem in collaborative filtering. *ACM Transactions on Information Systems*, 22(1):116–142, 2004.
13. Jin, R., Chai, J.Y. and Si, L. An automatic weighting scheme for collaborative filtering. In *Proceedings of the 27th Annual International ACM SIGIR Conference on Research & Development on Information Retrieval (SIGIR04)*, New York, NY, 2004
14. Jurvetson, S. What exactly is viral marketing? *Red Herring*, 78:110–112, 2000.
15. Lathia, N., Hailes, S., and Capra, L. The effect of correlation coefficients on communities of recommenders. In *Proceedings of SAC'08*, Fortaleza, Ceará, Brazil, March 16–20, 2008.
16. Lowd, D. and Domingos, P. Naive bayes models for probability estimation. In *Proceedings of the 22nd International Conference on Machine Learning (ICML)*, Bonn, Germany: ACM Press, 2005.
17. Lu, Q. and Getoor, L. Link-based classification. In *Proceedings of the 20th International Conference on Machine Learning (ICML)*, Washington, DC, pp. 496–503, 2003.
18. Macskassy, S. and Provost, F. A simple relational classifier. In *Proceedings of the KDD-2003 Workshop on Multirelational Data Mining*, Washington, DC, 2003.
19. Marti, S. and Garcia-Molina, H. Taxonomy of trust: Categorizing P2P reputation systems. *Computer Networks*, 50(4):472–484, 2006.

20. Massa, P. and Avesani, P. Trust-aware collaborative filtering for recommender systems. In *Proceedings of Federated Int. Conference On The Move to Meaningful Internet: CoopIS, DOA, ODBASE*, pp. 492–508, 2004.

21. Melville, P., Mooney, R.J., and Nagarajan, R. Content-boosted collaborative filtering for improved recommendations. In *Proceedings of the 18th National Conference on Artificial Intelligence (AAAI-2002)*, Edmonton, Canada, pp. 187–192, July 2002.

22. Mooney, R.J. and Roy, L. Content-based book recommending using learning for text categorization. In *Proceeding of ACM SIGIR'99 Workshop Recommender Systems: Algorithms and Evaluation*, Berkley, CA, 1999.

23. Morita, M. and Shinoda, Y. Information filtering based on user behavior analysis and best match text retrieval. In *Proceedings of the 7th Annual Information ACM SIGIR Conference on Research and Development in Information Retrieval*, Dublin, Ireland, pp. 272–281, 1994.

24. Neville, J. and Jensen, D. Iterative classification in relational data. In *Proceedings of the Workshop on Learning Statistical Models from Relational Data at the 17th National Conference on Artificial Intelligence (AAAI)*, Austin, Texas, pp. 13–20, 2000.

25. Pazzani, M. and Billsus, D. Learning and revising user profiles: The identification of interesting web sites. *Machine Learning*, 27:313–331, 1997.

26. Pazzani, M. A framework for collaborative, content-based, and demographic filtering. *Artificial Intelligence Review*, 13:393–408, 1999.

27. Resnick, P., Iakovou, N., Sushak, M., Bergstrom, P., and Riedl, J. GroupLens: An open architecture for collaborative filtering of netnews. In *Proceedings of 1994 Computer Supported Cooperative Work Conference*, Chapel Hill, NC, 1994.

28. Richardson, M. and Domingos, P. Mining knowledge-sharing sites for viral marketing. In *Proceedings of 8th ACM SIGKDD International Conference on Knowledge Discovery and Data Mining*, New York, NY: ACM Press, pp. 61–70, 2002.

29. Sarwar, B., Karypis, G., Konstain, J., and Riedl, J. Application of dimensionality reduction in recommender systems – a case study. In *Proceedings of ACM WebKDD Workshop*, Boston, MA, 2000.

30. Sarwar, B., Karypis, G., Konstan, J., and Riedl, J. Item-based collaborative filtering recommendation algorithms. In *Proceedings of 10th International WWW Conference*, New York, NY, 2001.

31. Sen, P. and Getoor, L. Empirical comparison of approximate inference algorithms for networked data. *ICML Workshop on Open Problems in Statistical Relational Learning*, Pittsburgh, PA, 2006.

32. Subramani, M. R. and Rajagopalan, B. Knowledge-sharing and influence in online social networks via viral marketing. *Communications of the ACM*, 46(12):300–307, 2003.

33. Taskar, B., Abbeel, P., and Koller, D. Discriminative probabilistic models for relational data. In *Proceedings of the 18th Conference on Uncertainty in Artificial Intelligence (UAI)*, Edmonton, AB, pp. 485–492, 2002.

34. Ungar, L.H. and Foster, D.P. Clustering methods for collaborative filtering. In *Workshop on Recommender Systems at the 15th National Conference on Artificial Intelligence*, Madison, WI, 1998.

35. Wang, J., Vires, A.P., Reinders, M.J.T. Unifying user-based and item-based collaborative filtering approaches by similarity fusion. In *Proceedings of the 29th Annual International ACM SIGIR Conference on Research & Development on Information Retrieval (SIGIR06)*, August 6–11, 2006.

36. Yang, S. and Allenby, G.M. Modeling interdependent consumer preferences. *Journal of Marketing Research*, 40:282–294, 2003.

37. Zheng, R., Provost, F., and Ghose, A. Social network collaborative filtering: preliminary results. In *Proceedings of the 9th Workshop on eBusiness (WEB2007)*, Montreal, December 2007.

Chapter 5
Network Analysis of US Air Transportation Network

Guangying Hua, Yingjie Sun, and Dominique Haughton

Abstract There has been a considerable growth in interest in network analysis. Air transportation networks are regarded as complex networks which are full of dynamics and complexity. This study focuses on the US air transportation network, which is one of the most diverse and dynamic transportation networks in the world. All of the data are drawn from the US Bureau of Transportation Statistics (BTS). The topology features show that the network is a scale-free small-world network; the degree distribution follows a truncated power law. The network also confirms the 9/11 impact on the US air travel industry. A discrete dynamic model is constructed to investigate the evolution of the network. Our analysis offers direct confirmation for the existence of preferential attachment in the air transportation network. We conclude that both an aging effect and preferential attachment are the two mechanisms driving the network evolution.

5.1 Introduction

Many biological, economic, and social systems are best described by networks [1]. The range of applications using network research has grown exponentially. Researchers from different fields try to understand the topological features of these real networks and their network growth and evolution mechanisms [2, 3]. Many different networks have some common properties. Watts and Strogatz showed that many real networks exhibit small-world properties rather than totally random or fully connected ones [4]. Small-world networks have two main characteristics: a high clustering coefficient and a low shortest path distance [2]. Most nodes in the network can be reached by a very small number of steps. In small-world networks, if the distribution of degree follows a power-law distribution, then the network is

G. Hua (✉)
Department of Mathematical Sciences, Bentley University, 175 Forest Street, Waltham, MA 02452, USA
e-mail: ghua@bentley.edu

N. Memon et al. (eds.), *Data Mining for Social Network Data*,
Annals of Information Systems 12, DOI 10.1007/978-1-4419-6287-4_5,
© Springer Science+Business Media, LLC 2010

also a scale-free network. The mechanism behind a small-world network is growth and preferential attachment [2]. The growth indicates that the network continuously expands with the increase of new nodes and new links, while the preferential attachment states that highly connected nodes have a higher probability of acquiring new links.

The range of application of network analysis has expanded to many areas, such as social networks, transportation systems, communication networks, bioinformatics. Air transportation networks are regarded as complex networks full of dynamics and complexity. Examining them will not only help us understand the features and dynamics of these networks but also their importance to society since they play a very important role in a country's infrastructure. Research has been conducted on the topology of air transportation networks in different countries [5–8]. These different air transportation networks not only show small-world properties but also exhibit some different properties. In the worldwide transportation network, there is a different relationship among degree and betweenness; the most connected cities are not necessarily the most central ones [6]. Both the Chinese and Indian airport networks display a truncated power-law degree distribution [7, 8]. In this study, we focus on the US air transportation network, which is one of the most diverse and dynamic transportation networks in the world. We examine the network topological features and the evolution of the network by considering the change in the number of passengers and in the nature of connections over time. We show that the US air transportation network has different topological features compared to the worldwide air transportation network and that of other countries. To trace the evolution of the US air transportation network, we also model the growth of links among cities based on preferential attachment. Our results show that both an aging effect and preferential attachment influence the network evolution.

This chapter is organized as follows. Section 5.2 provides a brief overview of network analysis. The US air transportation network data are described in Section 5.3. We also present an exploratory network analysis to show the topological features of the network and the dramatic impact of 9/11 on the network in this section. Section 5.4 presents network dynamics which are modeled on the basis of preferential attachment and aging effect. This chapter concludes with a discussion of the network properties and evolution.

5.2 Network Analysis Foundation

5.2.1 Network Foundation

The methodological body of network analysis is frequently applied to different fields, ranging from physics, computer science, economics to social science. Network analysis in a variety of different areas may have some differences in notation and have some fundamental differences in how to approach network analysis research questions [3, 9]. Despite these differences, they all share a common mathematical foundation, graph theory. In graph theory, a network is denoted as

$G = (V, E)$, where V is the set of nodes, while E is the set of links among those nodes [9]. If two nodes are joined by a link, they are adjacent and we call them neighbors. We write $E = \{(u, v)|u, v \in V\}$. The links between nodes represent relations among nodes, which can be undirected or directed. In a directed network, each link has an origin and destination. The meaning of nodes varies in different networks. In social science, nodes can represent people or organizations, and the links between them are always referred to as ties. In a transportation network, each node can represent a city. The relationship among the node varies accordingly. For example, friendship or kinship is common in social network analysis [10], while the information flow is the link in an email communication network [11].

In the real world, many different systems such as genetic networks or the World Wide Web are best described as networks with a complex topology [1]. A common property of many large networks is that the degrees of nodes follow a scale-free power-law distribution [2]. Besides this topological feature of networks, the dynamic of networks is driven by growth and preferential attachment [2]. Preferential attachment has become a paradigm to explain the structure and evolution of complex network. It states that the probability that a node i will connect to a new node j is proportional to the current degree of node i, so that $P(k_i) = \frac{k_i}{\Sigma_j k_j}$ where k_i is the degree of node j. The degree of node i indicates the number of connections of node i to its neighbors. Thus, a node with a higher degree has a higher probability to connect to new nodes when the network grows. As mechanisms driving the evolution of many complex networks, growth and preferential attachment have been identified and modeled in many real networks, such as online social networks [12], networks of biotechnology firms [13], protein networks [14], financial network [15], and transportation networks [5, 6, 16].

5.2.2 Network Properties

In this section, we give definitions for a few essential concepts used in the chapter.

5.2.2.1 Average Shortest Path (Distance)

When we consider the paths between a pair of nodes, there are probably many differing path lengths. A shortest path is referred to as a geodesic. The distance between two nodes is defined as the length of a geodesic between them. The average shortest path is the average of the smallest distance between pairs of nodes. The average shortest path measures the network distance of a distributed network and shows how well a network is connected.

5.2.2.2 Degree

The degree is a measure of node centrality in the network. It indicates the number of connections that a given node has. For a given node, its neighbors are those nodes which have a direct link with it. The degree for a node k is the number of its neighbors. The degree defined here includes in and out degrees. The network degree centralization measures how centralized the degree of the whole network is. This measure reaches its maximum value of 1 with a star graph and reaches its minimum value of 0 with a circle graph where all nodes have the same degree.

5.2.2.3 Betweeness

Betweeness is proposed by Freeman and measures the extent to which a particular node lies "between" the other nodes in the graph [17]. This centrality index indicates the number of shortest paths going through a given node. The interaction between two nonadjacent nodes might depend on the other nodes that lie on the paths between the two. A node with relatively low degree may play the role of an intermediary in the network and so might be central to the network. A higher betweenness implies that the node lies between many of the nodes via their shortest paths and thus has great influence over what flows in the network.

5.2.2.4 Clustering Coefficient

The clustering coefficient measures the strength of sub-group formation and the density of the network. The clusters are defined as a group of nodes within which the connections are dense but between which they are sparser. Clusters reflect a tendency for neighbors of a given node to be connected. Clustering coefficients can be used to uncover clusters in the network. The clustering coefficient was introduced by Watts and Strogatz [4] and is defined as the probability that a node's neighbors are all connected with each other. For an undirected network, it can be written as follows:

$$C_i = \frac{2E_i}{k_i(k_i - 1)}$$

where k_i is the degree of node i and E_i is the total number of links among node i's neighbors. Note that in an undirected network, if the degree of node i is k_i, there are $\frac{k_i(k_i-1)}{2}$ links among node i's neighbors if the graph is complete. The clustering coefficient reflects to what extent a node's neighbors are also neighbors, and thus measures how well connected the neighborhood of the node is. If the neighborhood is fully connected, $E_i = \frac{k_i(k_i-1)}{2}$, the clustering coefficient is 1 and a value close to 0 means that there are hardly any connections in the neighborhood. The average cluster coefficient is defined as $C = \frac{\sum_{i=i}^{n} C_i}{n}$ and shows the tendency of the network to form clusters. Optimal networks are characterized by a high average cluster coefficient and a low average shortest path; such networks are designated as small-world networks [4].

5.3 The US Air Transportation Network Analysis

5.3.1 The US Air Transportation Network Data

This study focuses on the US air transportation market; all of the data are drawn from the US Bureau of Transportation Statistics (BTS). Each airline is required to submit their transportation schedule to BTS every quarter; this constitutes the data source for the database T100 of BTS. The data cover 18 years from 1990 to 2007. There are different tables recording the air transportation information from different perspectives. The table we used is that from the T100 segment data. There are two types of data in T100: market data and segment data. Market data are data from a passenger's perspective and contain the origin and destination airport on a passenger's itinerary. Segment data are based on flight information and record every flight's origin and destination airport information, passenger totals, seats, and cargo information. Each segment reported in T100 segment is unique, distinctly defined by air carriers and type of equipment flown [18]. In the air transportation network, we are interested in the connection between cities, so we focus on T100 segment data. Within the T100 segment data, we only look at US carriers which compose the US airline industry and dominate the US air travel network.

A passenger's itinerary usually consists of one or more flight segments. Each flight segment involves a nonstop flight between two airports. In our study, we focus on cities instead of airports. Each node represents a city, and a link between cities means that there are nonstop flights between them. The total number of passengers between any two cities is the weight of this link. We use a graph G to represent the US air transportation network, $G = (V, E)$, where V is a set of nodes representing cities and E is a set of links representing the nonstop flight connections between the nodes. The adjacency matrix for the graph shows it is almost symmetric, which means there are always back and forth flights between two cities. Therefore, the network we analyze is undirected.

Once the data were extracted from BTS, some preprocessing was performed. The database has much redundant information; for example, looking at nonstop flights from Boston to Chicago, we see that there are several records with different passenger numbers, so we group them all together based on year and the city pair (in this example Boston, Chicago). The records in which the origin and destination city are the same were excluded since they do not represent the migration of people.

5.3.2 Network Topological Properties

We select the 2007 network data (most recent data in our database) as an example to show the topological properties of the US air transportation network. As we will see, our analysis shows that the US air transportation network exhibits small-world network properties. There are 1372 cities in the 2007 network data and 14,181 connections among them. The total density of the network is 0.015, which indicates the whole network is far from fully connected. The shortest path length L between any two nodes is defined as the minimum number of cities that have to be passed through to get from the given node to the destination. The average shortest path length shows how well a network is connected. Most airports can be connected within two flights. The average distance among cities is 3.23, and compared to the network size N, this number is very small. The most distant nodes are between Ophir Airport (OPH) in Alaska and Jackson Carroll Airport (KJK) in Kentucky, where the distance is 8.

The average clustering coefficient for the 2007 network is .5341, which means that the airport network is relatively well connected, considering the large number N of nodes. The network degree centralization is 0.2559, which means the air transportation network is far from a star graph; instead it is closer to a circle graph. In our network, the degree of a city measures how many cities are connected with it through nonstop flights. The average degree of the network is 8 and Atlanta International Airport has the maximum degree 371. There are large differences in the degrees among nodes, but the degree distribution shows some pattern, as we now discuss.

A degree power-law distribution is defined as follows: $P(K > k) \propto k^{-\alpha}$, where α is the power-law exponent, k is the degree. Figure 5.1 displays the function $P(k)$ of the degree k in a log–log plot. We cannot fit the data with a single line, which means that the degree distribution does not follow a scale-free power-law distribution. However, the data show a two-regime power-law distribution with two different exponents, with a turning point at degree k_0 around 145.

$$P(K > k) \sim \begin{cases} k^{\alpha_1}, for\, k \le k_c \\ k^{\alpha_2}, for\, k > k_c \end{cases}$$

$\alpha_1 = .6931$ and $\alpha_2 = 2.4759$. As the exponent increases from α_1 to α_2, the tail of the cumulative degree distribution decays faster than a power law would. This is consistent with the findings related to the worldwide air transportation network [6]. A similar property was found for the Chinese air transportation network [7].

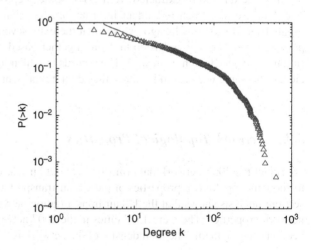

Fig. 5.1 Graph of $P(k)$ for the 2007 network

For the air transportation network, a city with a high betweenness means that the city is central to the transportation network since there are quite a few connections between pairs of cities which have to pass through this city to make the connection. We calculated the betweenness with the software Pajek for each node and then compared it with the degree [19]. There is a correlation between betweenness and degree; betweeness tends to increase with the degree. However, the geographical location can influence the correlation between degree and betweenness. Some cities have very high betweenness but relatively small degrees. For example, the city of Anchorage in Alaska has the highest betweenness .2620, but its degree 165 is not very high. The special geographical position of Anchorage enables it to serve as a bridge, since many local cities in Alaska connect to the continental United States through Anchorage.

5.3.3 9/11 Impact on the Aviation Industry

The US aviation industry has evolved since the early twentieth century. The deregulation in 1978 lowered the entry barrier for new airlines. The competition became very severe and more and more airline companies strove to survive. A hub and spoke network was developed, which lowered the cost of transportation and operations for airlines. At the same time, there was a dramatic increase in the number of passengers in the 1990s. Even though airlines experienced ups and downs in their profits, the air transportation network had maintained a steady development until the tragic events of September 11, 2001 (9/11). Since then, the aviation industry has been transformed dramatically; Delta, United, US Airways, and Northwest Airlines all declared bankruptcy following the tragedy. The year 2001 was a turning point for the aviation industry, when a massive restructuring occurred. Bhadra and Texter discussed the large losses of the airline industry in 2001 [18]. As we will see, our network data also confirm the impact of this tragedy on the air transportation network.

Our yearly network analysis shows that from 1990 to 2007, some new patterns have arisen in the air transportation network. The number of passengers steadily increased except during 2001 and 2002 as shown in Fig. 5.2. We then scrutinize the total number of passengers per month as shown in Fig. 5.3. We found that the total number of passengers for the first 8 months increased by 0.33% from 2000 to 2001, but the total number of passengers for the last 4 months decreased by 22.04%. The profitability of the aviation industry heavily relies on the number of passengers. The decrease in the number of passengers, especially business travelers, made airline companies face a much greater challenge. The dramatic change in passenger numbers strongly shows the large impact of 9/11 on the US air travel industry.

Accordingly the number of cities in the network held relatively steady except for a big jump from 2001 to 2002 as shown in Fig. 5.4, which implies that the network structure dramatically changed at that time. To interpret the sudden increase in the total number of nodes in 2002, we analyzed the total number of carriers per month.

Fig. 5.2 Total number of
passengers per year

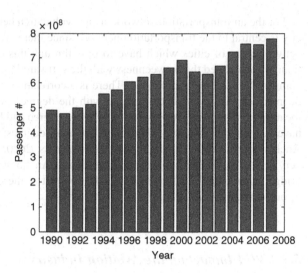

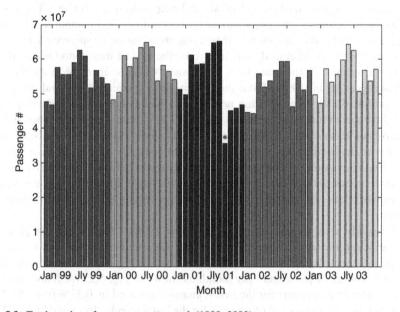

Fig. 5.3 Total number of passengers per month (1999–2003)

We found that in January 2002, 26 new airlines were added to the T100 segment
record and that 25 of them are from Alaska. In October 2002, another 41 new airlines
were added nationwide. From 2001 to 2002, the number of nodes increased from
691 to 1283. The sudden increase of the number of small airlines in Alaska and of
airlines nationwide explained the big jump in the number of nodes from 2001 to
2002.

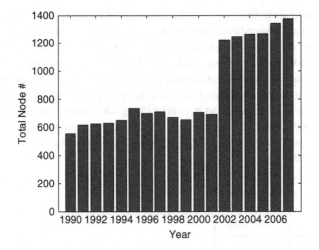

Fig. 5.4 Total number of nodes per year

Fig. 5.5 Total number of
links per year

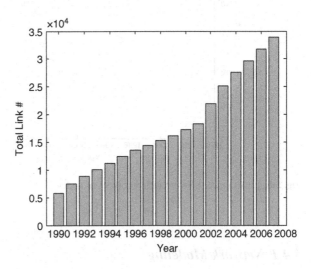

Figure 5.5 displays the number of links per year from 1990 to 2007. Unlike
the big change of the number of nodes and passengers, the number of links in the
network has increased steadily, albeit more sharply after 2001.

5.4 Network Dynamics

We have shown that the US air transportation network is not steady. It changes every
year with new added cities, new flight routes among cities, and with passenger numbers going up and down each year. However, the network still falls into the category

of a small-world scale-free network. Barabasi and Albert explain two mechanisms which can drive a power-law distribution: growth and preferential attachment [2]. In this section, we discuss the evolution of the network. In existing research which attempts to model the topological evolution of networks, a very important assumption is that of the preferential attachment; in which highly connected nodes increase their connectivity faster than their less connected peers [20]. Preferential attachment has been shown to arise in airport networks [5, 6]. Our analysis shows that only the number of connections has displayed a steady increase within the past 18 years. However, we can observe in Fig. 5.6 a big jump in links between new added nodes from 2001 to 2002.

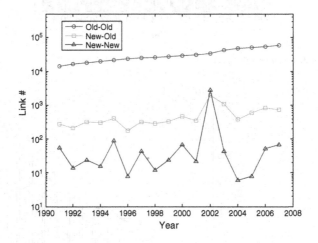

Fig. 5.6 Link number between different types of nodes

5.4.1 Network Modeling

In this section, we propose the model the evolution of the network as explained below and displayed graphically in Fig. 5.7.

At time T_i there are n nodes in the network $V(T_i) = \{v_1, v_2,...,v_n\}$. At time T_{i+1} m new nodes $V_{new}(T_{i+1}) = \{v_{n+1}, v_{n+2}, \ldots, v_{n+m}\}$ are added to the network. The set $V(T_i)$ is defined as the set of old nodes at time T_{i+1}, i.e., $V_{old}(T_{i+1}) = V(T_i)$. Therefore we have $V(T_{i+1}) = V_{old}(T_{i+1}) \bigcup V_{new}(T_{i+1}) = \{v_1, v_2, \ldots, v_n + m\}$.

The preferential attachment hypothesis states that the rate with which a node with $\varepsilon(T_i)$ links at time T_i acquires new links at times T_{i+1} depends on $\varepsilon(T_i)$. . In our case the evolution dynamics of the air transportation network can be modeled as in [20]:$\varepsilon(T_{i+1}) - \varepsilon(T_i) = \tau(\varepsilon(T_i)) = \varepsilon(T_i)^\alpha$, where r is a function of the degree of the old node at time T_i.

Fig. 5.7 Diagram of the network evolution model

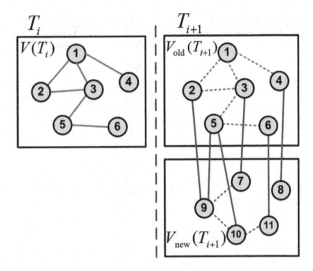

Since we analyze yearly network data, we have $\Delta T = T_{i+1} - T_i = 1$. Considering the characteristics of the air transportation network, we determine the rate r in the above equation numerically. In order to calculate the rate, we study the new links established between the old nodes and newly added nodes $\{V_{\text{old}}(T_{i+1}), V_{\text{new}}(T_{i+1})\}$ at time and the links established between the old nodes $\{V_{\text{old}}(T_{i+1}), V_{\text{old}}(T_{i+1})\}$. The change in the number of links between old nodes also shows how the network would self-organize without new nodes. The solid lines in Fig. 5.7 represent the definition of the above links. As shown in Fig. 5.6, the number of links between new nodes $\{V_{\text{new}}(T_{i+1}), V_{\text{new}}(T_{i+1})\}$ is much smaller than for the links of type old–new or old–old, except for the year 2002, and the new links established between the old nodes are dominant. When plotting the histogram (graph omitted here) of the number of new links acquired by nodes with degree $\varepsilon(T_i)$, we see that the histogram displays a long tail, so we use the median to estimate $r(\varepsilon(T_i))$ at each degree. We then fit the median for all different connections to a power function. The network exhibits significant fluctuations, particularly for nodes with large degrees.

For each year from 1991 to 2007, we fit a power function as in Figs. 5.8 and 5.9, yielding $\alpha = .46 \pm .07$, as shown in Fig. 5.10. For rates with, the degree distribution follows a stretched exponential [21].

5.4.2 Network Aging Effect

The aging effect of the network implies that even a very highly connected node will stop acquiring new links after a given time. The node is still part of the network and contributes to network statistics while it no longer receives new links. Therefore, the aging of the nodes limits the effect of preferential attachment on the growth of the network [22].

Fig. 5.8 Preferential
attachment rate in 1991

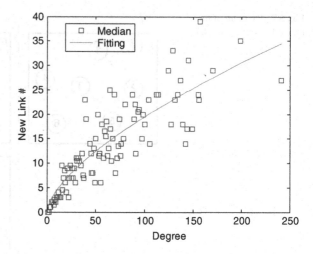

Fig. 5.9 Preferential
attachment rate in 2007

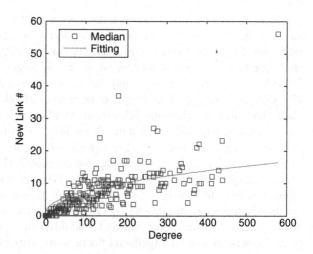

For the network aging effect analysis, we focus on the newly added nodes in the air transportation network and study the growth behavior of new nodes. We find that most of the new nodes show that the capability for continuously acquiring new links will decay as the age of the nodes increases. The aging effect of the network is modeled as: $n(t) = n_0 \, e^{-t/\tau}$ where $n(t)$ is the number of new nodes showing a link increment and is a time constant. Here is the age of the new nodes in the network. If a node is added in the network at time T_i then the age of the node at time T_j is defined as $t = T_j - T_i$. In Fig. 5.11, we plot the histogram of the number of new nodes showing a link increment at different ages. The total number of new nodes is 1342, which is n ($t = 0$). At age $t = 1$, 1015 new nodes continue to acquire new links; however, only 103 new nodes show link increment at age 10. We fit the occurrences of new nodes showing a link increment to the above exponential equation and find

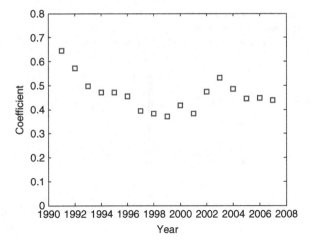

Fig. 5.10 Preferential attachment analysis

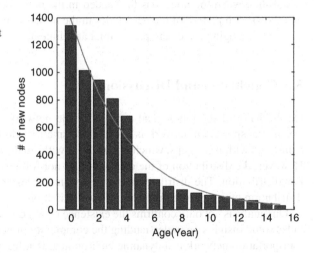

Fig. 5.11 Histogram of new nodes showing link increment

that τ is about 4 years. As shown in Fig. 5.11, the exponential decay model can fit the real data very well.

We define the number of links established by the new node i at age j as $l_{ij}(l_{ij} > 0)$. Figure 5.12 plots the median of the l_{ij} for all new nodes which acquire new links at different ages j. Most of the nodes show an aging effect after they were added to the network and their capacity to acquire new links decreases as age increases. When 80% of the new nodes stop acquiring new links after age 5 as shown in Fig. 5.11, the median of the new link in Fig. 5.12 begins to increase. Therefore the growth of the network shows two regimes: for most of the new nodes especially those with a smaller number of links, the aging effect is dominant; while for those with a larger number of links, the effect of preferential attachment is dominant. The growth mode of the new nodes depends on the initial condition, which is the number of links

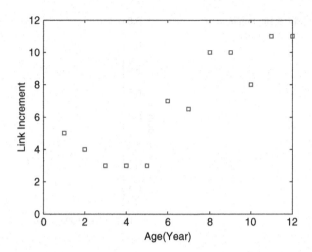

Fig. 5.12 Link increment distribution of new nodes

established when the node was first added in the network. Therefore we conclude that the growth pattern of the new nodes in the network results from a combination of a network aging effect and preferential attachment.

5.5 Conclusion and Discussion

On the basis of the topological analysis of the network, we have shown that the US air transportation network is a scale-free small-world network. Most cities are connected within six steps, which is consistent with small-world network properties. However, the distribution of the degree k does not follow a strict scale-free power-law distribution. The distribution of k decays much faster. Thus, we fit the degree distribution with a two-regime power-law distribution.

Our analysis not only confirms the existence of scale-free properties but also provides some insights on understanding the complexity of network dynamics. The air transportation network is a dynamic environment that has number of variants [18]. The growth of the air transportation network is influenced not only by its dynamics but also by social, economic, and political factors. Air transportation patterns are strongly correlated with socioeconomic factors such as population density and economic development [5]. The US air transportation network shows that a geographical factor plays an important role in deciding the betweenness of cities. In addition, the attack of 9/11 dramatically destabilized the whole air transportation network.

A discrete dynamics model is constructed to investigate the evolution pattern of the network. Our analysis confirms the existence of preferential attachment in the US air transportation network. The growth rate follows a stretched power law ($\alpha < 1$), which indicate the existence of sublinear attachment [21]. Our study also indicates that the aging effect has an impact on the growth of new nodes in the network. Based on our data, the time constant is about 4 years. We conclude that both an aging effect and preferential attachment are the two mechanisms driving the evolution of new nodes in the US air transportation network.

References

1. Dorogovtsev, S.N. and Mendes, J.F.F. *Evolution of Networks: From Biological Nets to the Internet and WWW*. Oxford: Oxford University Press, 2003.
2. Barabasi, A.L. and Albert, R. Emergence of scaling in random networks. *Science*, 286: 509–512, 1999.
3. Borgatti, S.P., Mehra, A., Brass, D.J., and Labianca, G. Network analysis in the social sciences. *Science*, 323:892–895, 2009.
4. Watts, D.J. and Strogatz, S.H. Collective dynamics of 'small-world' networks. *Nature*, 393:409–410, 1998.
5. Guimera, R. et al. The worldwide air transportation network: Anomalous centrality, community structure, and cities' global roles. In *Proceedings of the National Academy of Sciences*, 102:7794–7799, 2005.
6. Guimerá, R. and Amaral, L. Modeling the world-wide airport network. *The European Physical Journal B – Condensed Matter*, 38:381–385, 2004.
7. Li, W. and Cai, X. Statistical analysis of airport network of China. *Physical Review*, 69:046106, 2004.
8. Bagler, G. Analysis of the airport network of India as a complex weighted network. *Physical A: Statistical Mechanics and its Applications*, 387:2972, 2008.
9. Brandes, U. and Erlebach, T. *Network Analysis: Methodological Foundations*. New York, NY: Springer, 2005.
10. Hanneman, R.A. and Riddle, M. *Introduction to Social Network Methods*. Riverside, CA: University of California, 2005.
11. Bird, C., Gourley, A., and Swaminathan, A. Mining email social networks, *MSR'06*, Shanghai, China, 2006.
12. Mislove, A., Koppula,H.S., Gummadi, K.P., Druschel, P., and Bhattacharjee, B. Growth of the flickr social network, *ACM SIGCOMM Workshop on Online Social Networks*, Seattle, WA, USA, 2008.
13. Gay, B. and Dousset, B. Innovation and network structural dynamics: Study of the alliance network of a major sector of the biotechnology industry. *Research Policy*, 34:1457–1475, Dec. 2005.
14. Eisenberg, E. and Levanon, E.Y. Preferential attachment in the protein network evolution. *Physical Review Letters*, 91:138701, 2003.
15. Boginski, V., Butenko, S., and Pardalos, P.M. Statistical analysis of financial networks. *Computational Statistics & Data Analysis*, 48:431–443, 2005.
16. Huber, H. Inside the mechanics of network development: How competition and strategy reorganize Europe air traffic. *Journal of Air Transportation*, 11:64–86, 2006.
17. Wasserman, S. and Faust, K. *Social Network Analysis: Methods and Application*. Cambridge: Cambridge University Press, 1994.
18. Bhadra, D. and Texter, P. Airline networks: An econometric framework to analyze domestic U.S. air travel. *Journal of Transportation and Statistics*, 7:87–102, 2004.
19. de Nooy, W., Mrvar, A., and Batagelj, V. *Exploratory Social Network Analysis with Pajek*. Cambridge: Cambridge University Press, 2005.
20. Jeong, H., Néda, Z., and Barabási, A.L. Measuring preferential attachment in evolving networks. *Europhysics Letters*, 61:567–572, 2003.
21. Krapivsky, P.L., Redner, S., and Leyvraz, F. Connectivity of growing random networks. *Physical Review Letters*, 85:4629, 2000.
22. Amaral, L.A.N. et al. Classes of small-world networks, In *Proceedings of the National Academy of Sciences of the United States of America*, 97:11149–11152, Oct. 2000.

Chapter 6
Identifying High-Status Nodes in Knowledge Networks

Siddharth Kaza and Hsinchun Chen

Abstract The status of a node in a social network plays an important part in determining evolution of the network around it. High-status nodes in knowledge networks are likely to attract more links and influence the use of knowledge by nodes connected directly or indirectly to them. In this study, we model knowledge flow within an innovative organization and contend that it exhibits unique characteristics not incorporated in most social network measures designed to determine node status. Based on the model, we propose the use of a new measure based on team identification and random walks to determine status in knowledge networks. Using data obtained on collaborative patent networks, we find that the new measure performs better than others in identifying high-status inventors.

6.1 Introduction

The status of a node in a social network can determine its evolution and influence other nodes linked directly or indirectly to it. In knowledge networks – defined here as social networks with individuals sharing knowledge with each other while being connected through collaborative links – the status of individuals can influence the evolution of knowledge and the innovation resulting from it. Innovation has been described as a problem-solving process where the solutions are discovered via the search novel recombination of existing knowledge [12, 24]. Organizations have a choice in selecting knowledge that is recombined to produce new innovations. The selection of knowledge for recombination is influenced by the status of inventors in an organization's internal knowledge network [29, 41, 45]. Organizations (and inventors within) attach more value and recombine knowledge of high-status inventors.

S. Kaza (✉)
Department of Computer and Information Sciences, Towson University, Towson, MD, USA
e-mail: skaza@towson.edu

N. Memon et al. (eds.), *Data Mining for Social Network Data*,
Annals of Information Systems 12, DOI 10.1007/978-1-4419-6287-4_6,
© Springer Science+Business Media, LLC 2010

Various social network measures have been used to establish the status of inventors in knowledge networks [30, 34, 40, 43]. However, the measures make implicit assumptions about the flow of knowledge within an organization. For instance, the widely used betweenness centrality measure [15] assumes that knowledge flows along shortest paths. Often these assumptions are not valid for modeling knowledge flow, and establishing the status of inventors based on these measures may lead to misleading results.

In this chapter, we determine the inventor status in intra-organizational knowledge network and study its effect on the selection of knowledge that is recombined to produce innovation. We focus on intra-organization networks since recombination of internal knowledge helps establish competitive advantage for a longer time [11, 38]. We model the flow of knowledge within a research focused organization and contend that it exhibits unique characteristics not incorporated in most social network measures. Using the model, we also propose a new measure based on random walks and team identification and use it to examine innovation selection in a large organization.

In particular, we explore the following research questions: How can we effectively model the flow of knowledge within an intra-organizational knowledge network? How can we establish the status of an individual in a collaborative knowledge network? How does the status of an inventor in a knowledge network affect innovation evolution?

The rest of this chapter is organized as follows: Section 6.2 presents the literature review and background and Section 6.3 describes the research design and testbed. Section 6.4 presents the experimental results and discussion. Section 6.5 concludes and proposes future directions.

6.2 Literature Review

6.2.1 Social Network Measures

Various measures to quantify characteristics of social networks have been proposed in the literature [3, 47]. Small-world measures (clustering coefficient and average shortest path length) are used to examine the structure of the whole network. The clustering coefficient shows the tendency of individuals to cluster together to form cliques. The average shortest path length shows that even though a network may be large, most individuals are located within a few steps from each other. However, in this section, we focus on measures that are used to identify high-status nodes in a network (these measures are usually known as centrality or prestige measures). As mentioned before, these high-status individuals may influence the evolution of innovation in an organization.

Several measures of node centrality have been developed including degree centrality, closeness, betweenness, information centrality, and influence measures [6, 39]. These measures are not independent of the dynamic processes that unfold within a network [17] and make different implicit assumptions about the path of knowledge flow in a network. For instance, Freeman's betweenness centrality assumes that knowledge flows along shortest paths in the network [15]. However, many studies use these measures without regard to the implicit assumptions made by them. This might lead to poor results or a wrong interpretation of the network phenomenon under study [6]. Thus, it is necessary to model the assumptions pertinent to the network under study prior to selecting the centrality measure.

Based on analysis of previous studies [6, 13, 46], we contend that there are three primary requirements for a measure to correctly identify high-status nodes in a knowledge network of inventor collaborations. These are as follows:

Account for Diversity of knowledge (D): This implies that a high-status inventor is likely to receive diverse knowledge from different parts of the network. In SNA theory, this is best represented by betweenness measures. Betweenness is a measure of the influence a node has on the spread of information through the network [31]. The higher the betweenness, the more frequently a node is likely to receive information from disjoint parts of a network. This is important as the recombination of diverse knowledge from disjoint parts of the network is likely to lead to more innovation [13, 46].

Random diffusion (R): This implies that the measure should assume that knowledge does not select a preferred path (like the shortest path) of travel through a network. This does not necessarily imply that all paths (of all lengths) are equally important. It has been shown that shorter paths may be important in transferring certain kinds of knowledge [19].

Parallel duplication (P): This implies that multiple copies of the same knowledge can exist in a network. Thus, when given a choice in the path of travel, knowledge can travel on multiple paths at once [6]. For instance, knowledge is transferred to multiple individuals during team presentations. This assumption is especially important in this study since we are studying inventors within organizations where they are likely to be organized in project teams.

Table 6.1 reviews important centrality measures and classifies them according to these requirements. As shown in the table, none of the measures satisfy all the requirements to model information flow. For instance, Freeman's betweenness measure [15] does not take into account the duplication of knowledge. Bonacich's power [5] accounts for random diffusion and parallel duplication; however, it is not a betweenness measure and thus does not consider diversity of knowledge. Newman's random walk betweenness [31] assumes D and R, however, does not contain a parallel duplication component. A comprehensive discussion of these centrality measures and their assumptions is provided by Borgatti [6]. We propose a measure based on Newman's random walk betweenness centrality to model knowledge flow in the collaboration networks studied here. A team identification component is added to the measure that assumes parallel duplication of knowledge within teams in an organization. Details of the proposed measure are presented in the research design. We believe that the proposed measure satisfies all three requirements for knowledge flow and better identifies high-status inventors.

Table 6.1 Centrality measures and their knowledge flow assumptions

Measure	Intuition/formulation	Knowledge flow assumption	Requirement
Closeness centrality [15]	Sum of geodesic distances from all other nodes	Shortest path, no parallel duplication	
Betweenness centrality [15]	Number of times that a node is on the shortest path between two nodes	Shortest path, no parallel duplication	D
Degree centrality [15]	Node is central if it has a high degree	One-link paths, parallel duplication	P
Bonacich power [5]	Node is central to the extent that it is connected to other central nodes	Random diffusion, parallel duplication	R P
Information centrality [44]	Harmonic mean of lengths of paths ending at a node	Random diffusion, no parallel duplication	R
Flow betweenness [16]	Flow through a node when a maximum amount of flow travels between source and target	Defined path, parallel duplication	D P
Structural holes [9]	Non-redundancy of a node's neighbors and the links between them (usually one-link neighborhood)	One-link paths, parallel duplication	D P
Random walk centrality [33]	Speed at which a random walk reaches a target node	Random diffusion, no parallel duplication	R
Random walk betweenness centrality [31]	Number of times a random walk between a source and target passes through a node	Random diffusion, no parallel duplication	D R

6.2.2 Innovation and Knowledge Networks

Innovation has been described in the literature as a problem-solving process wherein solutions are discovered via the search and recombination of existing knowledge [12, 21, 24]. During this process, each organization is faced with a decision to select existing knowledge that is recombined to produce new innovative artifacts. As the recombination process proceeds, a focal innovation emerges that other innovations build upon [29, 35, 38] . In order to understand innovation evolution, it is necessary to identify the factors leading to the selection of a focal innovation. It has been shown that individuals and organizations do not select innovations just by their technical merits [13, 35], other factors like the expertise of inventors, scope of the innovation, and number of other innovations in the same field play an important role in the selection process. Inventors also select the focal innovation based on the status of the innovation's inventors in the knowledge network [29, 41]. One way to establish the status of an inventor is to use social network measures.

Various studies (Table 6.2) have focused on the status of inventors and innovation selection. Singh [41] found that the degree centrality of an inventor did not have a significant effect on the impact of his/her innovation. Podolny & Stuart [35] found that inventor status did not have a significant positive impact on the selection of their innovation. They also found that the status of other related innovators in the network had a positive association on the impact of the focal innovation. However, both these studies used degree to establish status which may not be an accurate representation of inventor status in a knowledge network and thus may not give the right results. Singh [40] found that as shortest path length between inventors increased, they were less likely to cite each other. The study acknowledged that the presence of multiple paths between inventors may have different effects. Nerkar & Paruchuri [29] found that Bonacich power of an inventor had a significant positive impact on the selection of his/her innovation. We used the same statistical technique as their study; however, we proposed a new measure better suited to the problem domain.

Table 6.2 Studies using node-level measures

	Network extent	Measures	Aim/result
[7]	Inter-org.	Shortest path	Study the geographic diffusion of innovation
[34]	Inter-org.	Degree centrality	Effect of collaboration on IT innovation. Result: Close collaborations lead to evolutionary innovation
[41]	Inter-org.	Degree centrality and extensions	Impact of collaboration on innovation selection and future productivity
[4]	Both	Degree centrality	Impact of managerial network on innovation. Result: higher degree leads to higher innovation
[29]	Intra-org.	Bonacich power, structural holes	Impact of inventor positions on innovation selection
[40]	Both	Shortest paths	Effect of shortest path on innovation selection
[2]	Inter-org.	Node degree, structural holes	Effect of measures on the organization's innovative output. Result: degree – positive, structural holes – negative
[35]	Inter-org.	Degree centrality	Study the factors that determine innovation selection

6.3 Research Design and Testbed

Figure 6.1 shows the research design and process used to acquire data, extract knowledge networks, develop the network measures, and statistically evaluate the effect of network measures on innovation selection.

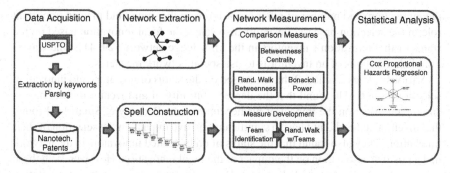

Fig. 6.1 Research design and process

6.3.1 Data Acquisition

This study used nanotechnology-related patents from the United States Patent and Trademark Office (USPTO). This is because patents are considered to be excellent indicators of innovation in organizations [23, 29]. We selected nanotechnology as it is an innovative field that promises fundamental changes to a wide variety of research domains [10]. The patents were limited to the nanotechnology field by using a keyword search on the full text of the patent (for details see Huang, Chen, Chen, and Roco [22]). Each patent document was downloaded using a web spider and parsed to extract information on assignee organization, inventors, issue and application dates, citation, and other fields. Table 6.3 shows the statistics of the patents obtained. The testbed in this study included the top organization by the number of inventors (International Business Machines – IBM). Large organizations are usually in business for a longer period of time and tend to have more established knowledge networks and better developed internal knowledge. This is important in this study as an organization with a quality internal knowledge base is likely to specialize in a certain area and recombine its own knowledge to produce innovations.

Table 6.3 Key statistics of nanotechnology patents extracted from USPTO

Date range	1976–2006
Patents	97,562
Assignee institutions (organizations)	26,304
Inventors (individuals)	189,045

6.3.2 Network Extraction

A knowledge network based on common affiliations was extracted for inventors in IBM. In the network, each node was represented by an inventor and two inventors were linked to each other if they were listed on the same patent. Such a network reflects strong associations as inventors listed on the same patent are likely to have intense collaboration while working on that innovation. Such an observed collaboration marks the beginning of a strong tie that lasts beyond the collaboration date [1, 40].

6.3.3 Spell Construction

A spell divides the life of a patent (from issue date till the end of the dataset) into time periods. Each time period is used as a data point to determine the effect of various variables on the citation (or no citation) of the patent in that spell. In line with prior research [29, 35], spells of up to 1 year were created for each patent. The first spell began at issue date and ended either at the close of the same year or at the citation date if the patent is cited within that year. The next spell began at the start of the year – if the previous spell ended at the previous year or at the citation date – if the previous spell ended in a citation.

Figure 6.2 shows an example of the spells created for a patent which was granted on 1/16/01 and cited three times on 6/14/01, 8/24/01, and 6/17/02.

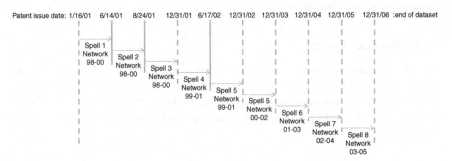

Fig. 6.2 Example spells for a patent in the dataset
Note: The *solid line* denotes that the spell ended with a citation, the *dashed line* denotes that the spell ended with no citation. The next spell begins the day after the previous spell ends. The network indicates the time span of the knowledge network that was used for computing measures for that spell

The strategy of dividing time into spells effectively measures the effect of network measures of individuals who coauthored that patent on the citation of a patent through its entire life. The measures were computed on the basis of the network 3 years prior to the spell. That is, only inventors who had applied for patents in the 3 years prior to the spell were considered to be part of the network for that spell. This is in line with previous research that shows that inventors are productive for 3–5 years [36]. We found support for this with the median productive life span of an inventor being 3–5 years in our dataset.

6.3.4 Network Measurement

In this section, we describe the social network measures that were used to determine the status of inventors in the network. Based on previous studies [29, 35] three measures were selected for comparison: betweenness centrality, Bonacich power, random walk centrality. We also proposed a new measure called random walk w/teams which is likely to suit this problem domain more than other measures.

6.3.4.1 Betweenness Centrality

This is a well-known and widely used betweenness measure proposed by Freeman [15]. Intuitively, BC of node k is defined as the fraction of times that a node i needs the node k in order to reach node j via the shortest path. BC for a node k is calculated as [6]:

$$\sum_{\substack{i \\ i \neq j \neq k}} \sum_{j} \frac{g_{ikj}}{g_{ij}}$$

where g_{ij} is the number of geodesic paths from i to j and g_{ikj} is the number of these geodesics that pass through k.

6.3.4.2 Bonacich Power

The BP measure suggests that a node is important to the extent that it is connected to other important nodes. The importance of a node emerges recursively from the pattern of connections among all the inventors (this concept is similar to the PageRank [8] algorithm). Details on the implementation of the measure can be found in Bonacich [5].

6.3.4.3 Random Walk Betweenness (RW)

RW is a relatively new measure that includes contributions from all paths between nodes to calculate betweenness [31]. RW for node k is equal to the number of times a random walk from i to j passes through k – averaged over all i and j. Thus, the measure includes paths that may not be optimal, though shorter paths still contribute more to the score. Details on the method can be found in Newman [31]. The measure also assumes that on each step during the random walk, information passes from the current node to one adjacent node (i.e., no parallel duplication). However, this assumption may not hold in knowledge networks of the kind studied here. Diffusion of information may happen in parallel within teams and follow a random walk outside them.

Random Walk with Teams (RWT)

Organizations generally have teams of inventors working together on projects. The communication levels within these project teams are much higher as compared to between teams [20]. We contend that there is close to parallel duplication of knowledge within teams, i.e., if one member of a team receives knowledge that is pertinent to the project, then all members of the team have access to it. With this assumption, we propose to add team identification to the RW measure to address the issue of parallel duplication.

Team identification: Figure 6.3a shows a schematic of the assumed flow of knowledge within an organization with three teams. The circles in the figure indicate teams of inventors. The dashed arrows indicate parallel information duplication (within teams). The solid arrows indicate random walks between teams. As can be seen in the figure, we assume that knowledge diffuses in a parallel fashion within teams and flows through random walks outside them. In order to use this phenomenon to establish the status of inventors, we need to identify teams within an organization. There are several algorithms to identify communities or teams in social networks, Fortunato [14] gives a comprehensive survey. Selecting an algorithm is a trade-off between computational times and accuracy; however, there have been few comprehensive comparisons of the algorithms on real-world networks. In addition, the choice of algorithms may also be defined by the network being studied; some algorithms may provide better results with certain kinds of networks. Our choice of an algorithm for this study was based on three factors: (1) computational time was not a consideration since the networks were not large, (2) we wanted to select an algorithm that was known to be accurate enough to show that teams mattered in these networks, and (3) we needed an algorithm that had been used extensively on real-world intra-organizational networks. We selected the widely used community identification algorithm proposed by Girvan and Newman [18] to identify teams in the collaboration network. The algorithm identifies cohesive communities using an iterative edge removal strategy based on betweenness measures. It has been shown to be superior to other community detection techniques [32] specially in scientific collaboration networks. Another recent comparative study [26] showed that the algorithm had a satisfactorily high accuracy of close to 90%.

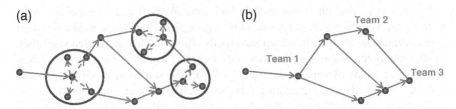

Fig. 6.3 (**a**) Flow of knowledge within an organization with teams (**b**) network after teams are identified and collapsed

Network collapse: Once teams are identified, the network is collapsed with each team replaced by a single composite node. Essentially, the composite "team" node is structurally equivalent [27] to the combination of all the individual nodes in that it preserves the connections between the teams members and individuals outside. Thus, in Fig. 6.3a each of the large circles containing team members would be collapsed into a single node, the resulting nodes and connections are shown in Fig. 6.3b.

Weak component identification: Once the network is collapsed, all the connected components in the network are identified and the measure is calculated for each component separately. This is different from some previous studies that use only the largest component in the network to calculate measures. This is important since different divisions of an organization may have self-contained groups of inventors and calculating measures for the largest component would ignore smaller groups.

RW betweenness calculation: Random walk betweenness (using the Newman [31] procedure for RW) scores are calculated for each node in each component of the collapsed network. Thus, the RWT measure calculated the RW betweenness score for entire teams taken as one node and single inventors who are not part of any teams. For statistical analysis, every individual in a team received the same RWT score. We believe that these new RWT scores will explain innovation diffusion better and identify individuals whose knowledge is valued for recombination within an organization.

6.3.5 Statistical Analysis

We used patent citation data for statistical analysis since citation leaves a trail of how a patent builds upon previous innovations. Unlike in academic papers, patent citations are not likely to be superfluous [40, 42]. An intra-organizational citation of a patent is a choice made by the organization (and individuals within) to build on knowledge contained in the patent. In this study, we aim to ascertain if the network position of an inventor influences this selection process. Thus, the dependent variable is the citation of a patent by inventors other than those involved in its creation.

Cox proportional hazard models were used to study the effects of network measures on patent citation (other models including Weibull and Exponential were tested; however, they were not found to be a good fit). The models used a repeated event hazard rate analysis to incorporate spells. These models were used since they incorporate both censored and uncensored cases, i.e., whether or not the patent was cited. Three kinds of variables were included in the statistical model: dependent variable: patent citation; explanatory variables: each of the social network measures; and control variables: factors (other than network measures) that effect patent citations. Since multiple inventors may be assignees on the same patent, a maximum of the social network scores among all the inventors for that patent was used as an independent variable.

Based on various previous studies, the following control variables were included:

- Calendar age: This controls for improvements in technology since the start of the dataset [35]. As databases and information retrieval techniques improve, patents are easier to find and cite.
- Patent age: A patent is more likely to be cited if it has been around longer.

- Patent age squared: As the age of a patent increases, it may be outdated and less likely to be cited.
- Scope of a patent: The USPTO uses a technology classification system where a patent is classified into one or more technology classes. Studies have used the number of classes to represent the breadth of a patent that has an effect on the patent's impact [25]. We include this variable as the number of USPTO technological classes the patent is classified into.
- Number of claims: The number of claims indicates the value of a patent and the technological spaces it occupies or protects [25].
- Age of prior art: Patents that build on old knowledge have different citation patterns than new ones [28]. This is calculated as the median of the difference between grant year of the focal patent and that of the references cited within that patent.
- Self-citation: A self-citation indicates confidence of an individual on his/her work. This may encourage other individuals to cite that work [29]. This is operationalized as a categorical variable which is "1" if patent has been self-cited before spell and "0" otherwise.
- Number of patent references/number of academic references: Patents that cite more prior art may have a different influence than others. They may be in technologically crowded classes and have a different influence as compared to other patents [12].
- Team size: One patent can have multiple inventors. When determining the effect of social network measures on the citation of a patent, we used the maximum of the measures among all the inventors of that patent. Including team size as a control variable accounts for effects of all inventors on the patent [29] since a heterogeneity in team members can lead to differences in the influence of a patent [37].
- International presence of an inventor: Knowledge flows across international boundaries are different [41] and may affect the citation of a patent. This is operationalized as a variable that is set to "1" if any inventor on patent is outside the USA and "0" otherwise.
- Time to grant: A patent that is granted immediately may be uncontroversial and simple. A complex patent may take time to get approved. This might affect citation rates [29].
- Technological effects: This controls for the difference in patenting across technological areas. Certain technological areas may cite a larger number of prior patents than others. This is operationalized as dummy variables for the top 20 classes (with ties retained) each organization patents in.

Based on the results obtained by previous node-level studies and the assumptions for knowledge flow in a network, four hypotheses were examined in this study with each in its own independent model. Each hypothesis tested the effect of an inventor's status (as established by a network measure) on the likelihood of his/her knowledge being selected by other inventors. These are summarized in Table 6.4.

Table 6.4 Hypotheses tested

	Measure	Effect
H1	Betweenness centrality	No effect
H2	Bonacich power	No effect
H3	Random walk	No effect
H4	Random walk w/teams (proposed)	Positive effect

6.4 Experimental Results and Discussion

In this section, we show the results of the Cox proportional hazards analysis. Five models were constructed for IBM – one for control variables only (Model 0) and the others including one of the four measures (Model 1–4) along with the control variables. These models were constructed as described in Section 3.5. The correlation matrix (Table 6.5) shows that all correlations except those between some network measures are low and do not pose multi-collinearity problems. The high correlations between some network measures do not cause problems since each regression model contains only one measure.

Table 6.6 shows the results for all four Cox regression models for IBM. The first column lists all the network measures and control variables. Each model (from Model 1 to Model 4) contained one network measure. As can be seen in Model 0, the likelihood of a patent being cited decreased (i.e., the hazard ratio <1.0) with an increase in patent age and time to grant. This may be because as a patent increases in age, its contents become less relevant in a fast moving field like nanotechnology. The likelihood of patent citation increased with an increase in calendar age. The reason behind this may be the better availability of information retrieval technology and databases which make it easier to find a patent and cite it. The likelihood also increased with an increase in the claim count and academic references. As mentioned before, the claims are the number of "spaces" occupied by the patent. More the spaces occupied, more likely the patent will be cited [25]. Self-citation indicates, among other things, the confidence that an inventor has on his/her own patents. The model shows that the more an inventor self-cites, the more likely others are to cite his/her patents. The significance of these control variables generally persisted across all models.

Model 1 shows that the BC score of inventors was found to have an insignificant effect on the citation of their patents. Thus, the measure does not adequately explain the effect of inventor status on the selection of his/her knowledge for innovation. As discussed before, BC is based on the assumption that knowledge flows along shortest paths that may not suit this problem domain. Random walk [31] was also found to be insignificant (Model 2). This may be because even though the RW measure incorporates random diffusion and is a betweenness measure, it does not incorporate the influence of teams. Individuals between teams draw knowledge from diverse communities and the RW w/teams measure is likely to perform better in this problem domain.

Table 6.5 Correlation matrix

	(1)	(2)	(3)	(4)	(5)	(6)	(7)	(8)	(9)	(10)	(11)	(12)	(13)
(1) Random walk w/teams	1												
(2) Bonacich power	0.1040*	1											
(3) Random walk	0.4907*	0.2199*	1										
(4) Freeman betweenness	0.4094*	0.0084	0.7748*	1									
(5) Class scope	-0.0412*	-0.0364*	-0.0535*	-0.021	1								
(6) Prior age	-0.0673*	-0.0256	-0.0444*	-0.0167	0.0127	1							
(7) Patent refs.	0.0193	0.0506*	0.0319*	-0.0656*	-0.0255	0.0698*	1						
(8) Academic refs.	0.0745*	0.0104	0.0770*	0.1023*	-0.0523*	-0.0677*	0.0724*	1					
(9) Team size	0.1450*	0.1045*	0.2076*	-0.0365	-0.0296	-0.0529*	0.1958*	0.1209*	1				
(10) International presence	0.0592*	0.0123	0.0633*	0.1427*	-0.014	0.0553*	-0.2207*	0.0365*	-0.1036*	1			
(11) Time to grant	-0.022	0.0295	-0.0252	-0.0797*	-0.0370*	0.1610*	0.1936*	0.0178	0.1119*	0.0008	1		
(12) Claim count	0.0522*	0.0229	0.0573*	-0.0178	-0.0058	-0.0259	0.1016*	0.0905*	0.0590*	-0.0992*	0.0074	1	
(13) Self-cited	0.1503*	0.0231	0.2581*	0.2434*	-0.0621*	0.0007	0.0278	0.1207*	0.1094*	0.0670*	-0.0415*	0.0285	1

Note: All correlation values above 0.05 are significant at $p < 0.05$ (*)

Table 6.6 Cox regression results

	Model 0	Model 1	Model 2	Model 3	Model 4
Bet. centrality		1.3995			
Random walk			1.1211		
Bonacich power				0.9977**	
RW w/teams					1.8700*
Patent age	0.9981**	0.9998	0.9998**	0.9998*	0.9998**
Calendar age	1.3132*	1.5295	1.2942	1.4152	1.5933
Class scope	1 class*	1 class*	1 class*	1 class*	1 class*
Prior age	0.9999	0.9997*	0.9999	0.9999	0.9999
Patent refs.	1.0012	1.0113	1.0012	1.0014	1.0015
Acad. refs.	1.0205*	1.0172**	1.0204*	1.0204*	1.0200*
Team size	0.9780	1.01567	0.975	0.9798	0.9695
International	1.2651	1.5459*	1.2593	1.2863	1.2544
Time to grant	0.9996**	1.0001	0.9996**	0.9996**	0.9996**
Claim count	1.0131**	1.0088	1.0131**	1.0129**	1.0128**
Self-cited	1.5362*	1.8402*	1.5178*	1.5383*	1.4987*
Tech. effects	20 classes**	26 classes**	22 classes**	22 classes**	22 classes**

Note: $*p < 0.05$, $**p < 0.10$

The Bonacich power of an inventor was found to be significant in Model 3. The measure has also been found to be significant by prior studies [29]. This implies that an inventor's knowledge is perceived to be more important (and cited) if he/she is connected to other important inventors. However, the absolute effect of the BP measure is very small since the hazard ratio is close to 1.0. A hazard ratio of 1.0 indicates that the variable does not increase or decrease the likelihood of a patent citation.

As can be seen from the table (Model 4), the random walk w/teams measure had a significant positive association with the citation of a patent. A unit increase in the RWT score of an inventor associated with a patent increases the likelihood of the patent being cited by 87%. This shows that the position of the inventor in a network positively effects the selection of his/her knowledge for recombination. There are three components to the RWT measure that may have contributed to its significance. First, the focus on diversity of knowledge which implies that knowledge of inventors who have high betweenness scores is perceived to be valuable by an organization. Inventors with high betweenness are also likely to obtain knowledge from multiple disparate communities that may increase their innovative potential. Second, random diffusion is an important part of the RWT measure and this may have contributed to its positive significance. This is because information may not necessarily flow through shortest paths in a knowledge network (as shown by the insignificance of Freeman's betweenness centrality). A third factor is parallel diffusion; the RWT measure takes into consideration that knowledge can diffuse within a team from one individual to multiple individuals. These three assumptions in the RWT measure make it better suited to explain inventor status in the collaboration networks we study here.

6.5 Conclusions

In this study, we examined the role of inventor status in knowledge networks on the selection of knowledge that is recombined to produce innovation in the nanotechnology field. A new network measure based on random walks and team identification (RWT) was proposed to model knowledge flow within an inventor collaboration network. Using empirical methods, it was found that inventor status as measured by RWT had a significant positive relationship with the likelihood that his/her knowledge would be selected for recombination. We believe that the new measure in addition to modeling knowledge flow in a scientific collaboration network will help better understand how innovation evolves within organizations.

In future studies, we plan to test other important social network prestige measures like Burt's Structural Hole measures and information measures like flow centrality to test their effect on innovation selection and compare them to the proposed measure. In addition, we will examine the effects of collapsing the teams on other prestige measures. In doing so, we plan to conduct a similar study on multiple large organizations both individually and combined to a larger dataset to provide more validity to our results.

Acknowledgments This research was supported in part by "NanoMap: Mapping Nanotechnology Development," NSF, Grant #0533749 and the Faculty Development and Research Committee of Towson University. Portions of this chapter were presented in the Hawaii International Conference on System Sciences (HICSS-42) in 2009.

References

1. Agrawal, A., Cockburn, I.M., and McHale, J. Gone but not forgotten: Knowledge flows, labor mobility, and enduring social relationships. *Journal of Economic Geography,* 6:571–591, 2006.
2. Ahuja, G. Collaboration networks, structural holes, and innovation: A longitudinal study. *Administrative Science Quarterly*, 45(3):425–455, 2000.
3. Albert, R. and Barabasi, A.-L. Statistical mechanics of complex networks. *Reviews of Modern Physics*, 74(1):49, 2002.
4. Bell, G.G. Clusters, networks, and firm innovativeness. *Strategic Management Journal*, 26:287–295, 2005.
5. Bonacich, P. Power and centrality: A family of measures. *American Journal of Sociology*, 92(5):1170–1182, 1987.
6. Borgatti, S.P. Centrality and network flow. *Social Networks*, 27:55–71, 2005.
7. Breschi, S. and Lissoni, F. (2006). "Cross-firm" inventors and social networks: Local knowledge spillovers revisited. *Annales d'Economie et de Statistique*, pp. 79–80.
8. Brin, S. and Page, L. The anatomy of a large-scale hypertextual web search engine. *Computer Networks*, 30(1–7):107–117, 1998.
9. Burt, R. *Structural Holes: The Social Structure of Competition*. Cambridge, MA: Harvard University Press, 1992.
10. Chen, H., Roco, M.C., Li, X., and Lin, Y. Trends in Nanotechnology Patents. *Nature Nanotechnology*, 3(3):123–125, 2008.
11. Chesbrough, H.W. and Tece, D.J. When is virtual virtuous? organizing for innovation. *Harvard Business Review*, 74(1):65–74, 1996.

12. Fleming, L. Recombinant uncertainty in technological research. *Management Science*, 47(1):117–132, 2001.
13. Fleming, L., King, C., and Juda, A. Small worlds and regional innovation, 18(6):2007.
14. Fortunato, S. Community detection in graphs, 2009 (Publication no. arXiv:0906.0612v1). from arXiv.org:
15. Freeman, L.C. Centrality in social networks: Conceptual clarification. *Social Networks*, 1:215–239, 1979.
16. Freeman, L.C., Borgatti, S.P., and White, D.R. Centrality in valued graphs: A measure of betweenness based on network flow. *Social Networks*, 13:141–154, 1991.
17. Friedkin, N.E. Theoretical foundations for centrality measures. *American Journal of Sociology*, 96:1478–1504, 1991.
18. Girvan, M., and Newman, M.E.J. Community structure in social and biological networks. *Proceedings of the National Academy of Sciences*, 99(12):7821–7826, 2002.
19. Hansen, M.T. The search-transfer problem: The role of weak ties in sharing knowledge across organization subunits. *Administrative Science Quarterly*, 44:82–111, 1999.
20. Hansen, M.T. Knowledge networks: Explaining effective knowledge sharing in multiunit companies. *Organization Science*, 13(3):232–248, 2002.
21. Henderson, R.M., and Cockburn, I. Measuring competence: Exploring firm effects in pharmaceutical research. *Strategic Management Journal*, 15:63–84, 1994.
22. Huang, Z., Chen, H., Chen, Z.-K., and Roco, M.C. International nanotechnology development in 2003: Country, institution, and technology field analysis based on USPTO patent database. *Journal of Nanoparticle Research*, 6:325–354, 2004.
23. Jaffe, A.B., and Trajtenberg, M. *Patents, Citations, and Innovations: A Window on the Knowledge Economy*. Cambridge, MA: MIT Press, 2002.
24. Kogut, B., and Zander, U. Knowledge of the firm, combinative capabilities, and the replication of technology. *Organization Science*, 3(3):383–397, 1992.
25. Lanjouw, J.O. and Schankerman, M. Characteristics of patent litigation: A window of competition. *Journal Law and Economics*, 38:463–495, 2001.
26. Leon, D., Albert, D.-G., Jordi, D., and Alex, A. Comparing community structure identification. *Journal of Statistical Mechanics*, (9):8, 2005.
27. Lorrain, F. and White, H.C. Structural equivalence of individuals in social networks. *Journal of Mathematical Sociology*, 1(January), 49–80, 1971.
28. Nerkar, A. Old is gold? the value of temporal exploration in the creation of new knowledge. *Management Science*, 49(2):211–229, 2003.
29. Nerkar, A. and Paruchuri, S. Evolution of R&D capabilities: The role of knowledge networks within a firm. *Management Science*, 51(5):771–785, 2005.
30. Newman, M.E.J. Who is the best connected scientist? a study of scientific coauthorship networks. In E. Ben-Naim, H. Frauenfelder and Z. Toroczkai (eds), *Complex Networks*, pp. 337–370. Berlin: Springer, 2004.
31. Newman, M.E.J. A measure of betweenness centrality based on random walks. *Social Networks*, 27:39–54, 2005.
32. Newman, M.E.J. and Girvan, M. Finding and evaluating community structure in networks. *Physical Review E*, 69:026113, 2004.
33. Noh, J.D. and Rieger, H. Stability of shortest paths in complex networks with random edge weights. *Physical Review E*, 66:066127, 2002.
34. Patrakosol, B. and Olson, D.L. How interfirm collaboration benefits IT innovation. *Information & Management*, 44:53–62, 2007.
35. Podolny, J.M. and Stuart, T.E. A role-based ecology of technological change. *The American Journal of Sociology*, 100(5):1224–1260, 1995.

36. Rappa, M.A., and Garud, R. Modeling contribution spans of scientists in a field: The case of cochlear implants. *R&D Management*, 22(4):337–348, 1992.
37. Reagans, R. and Zuckerman, E.W. Networks, diversity, and productivity: The social capital of corporate R&D teams. *Organization Science*, 12(4):502–517, 2001.
38. Rosenkopf, L., and Nerkar, A. Beyond local search: Boundary-spanning, exploration and impact in the optical disc industry. *Strategic Management Journal*, 22:287–306, 2001.
39. Scott, J. *Social Network Analysis: A Handbook* (2nd ed.). London: Sage, 2000.
40. Singh, J. Collaborative networks as determinants of knowledge diffusion patterns. *Management Science*, 51(5):756–770, 2005.
41. Singh, J. External collaboration, social networks and knowledge creation: Evidence from Scientific Publications. *Paper presented at the Danish Research Unit of Industrial Dynamics Summer Conference 2007*, Denmark, 2007.
42. Sorenson, O., Rivkin, J.W., and Fleming, L. Complexity, networks and knowledge flow. *Paper presented at the DRUID Tenth Anniversary Summer Conference*, Copenhagen, Denmark, 2005.
43. Sorenson, O. and Stuart, T.E. Syndication networks and the spatial diffusion of venture capital investments. *American Journal of Sociology*, 106:1546–1588, 2001.
44. Stephenson, K.A. and Zelen, M. Rethinking centrality: Methods and examples. *Social Networks*, 11:1–37, 1989.
45. Tsai, W.P. Knowledge transfer in intraorganizational networks: Effects of network position and absorptive capacity on business unit innovation and performance. *Academy of Management Journal*, 41(4):996–1004, 2001.
46. Uzzi, B. and Spiro, J. Collaborations and creativity: The small world problem. *American Journal of Sociology*, 111(2):447–504, 2005.
47. Wasserman, S. and Faust, K. *Social Network Analysis: Methods and Applications*. New York, NY: Cambridge University Press, 1994.

Chapter 7
Modularity for Bipartite Networks

Tsuyoshi Murata

Abstract Several real-world data are represented as bipartite networks composed
of two types of vertices, such as paper–author networks and event–attendee networks. Discovering communities from such bipartite networks is important for
finding similar items and for understanding overall network structures. In order to
evaluate the quality of divisions of normal (unipartite) networks, Newman's modularity is widely used. Recently, modularities for bipartite networks are proposed
by Guimera and Barber. These bipartite modularities are, however, not sufficient for
evaluating the degree of correspondence between communities of different vertex
types, which is often important for understanding the characteristics of the communities. For example, close-knit paper communities and author communities indicate
that their research topics are relatively focused rather than loose-knit communities. This chapter proposes a new bipartite modularity for evaluating community
extraction from bipartite networks. Experimental results show that our new bipartite modularity is appropriate for discovering close-knit communities, and it is also
useful for characterizing the communities.

7.1 Introduction

Various kinds of real-world relations can be represented as networks, such as
citations of papers and friendships of SNS (Social Networking Service) users.
Discovering communities from networks is important for understanding their overall structures and for finding similar items. Community discovery attracts many
researchers from physics, computer science, and sociology.

In general, social networks can be divided into the following categories:
(1) direct connection between persons (such as MySpace or Twitter) and (2)

T. Murata (✉)

Department of Computer Science, Graduate School of Information Science and Engineering,
Tokyo Institute of Technology, W8-59 2-12-1 Ookayama, Meguro, Tokyo, 152-8552 Japan
e-mail: murata@cs.titech.ac.jp

N. Memon et al. (eds.), *Data Mining for Social Network Data*,
Annals of Information Systems 12, DOI 10.1007/978-1-4419-6287-4_7,

indirect connection through different types of entities (such as film co-starring or paper co-authoring). We call the former "homogeneous networks," and the latter "heterogeneous networks." There are bipartite, tripartite, and n-partite networks as the examples of such heterogeneous networks. As the first step for processing heterogeneous networks, we focus on bipartite networks composed of two types of vertices.

Newman's modularity [10] is widely used for evaluating the quality of divisions of normal (unipartite) networks. Modularity is a scalar value that measures the density of edges inside communities as compared to edges between communities. As the strategy for finding communities from given networks, modularity optimization is often employed. Modularity is, however, appropriate only for homogeneous networks that are composed of one type of vertices (such as SNS users in the above example). In real-world situations, there are many bipartite networks that are composed of two types of vertices, such as paper–author networks and movie–actor networks (Fig. 7.1). Modularity is not appropriate for community extraction from such bipartite networks since there are no edges that connect the vertices of the same type.

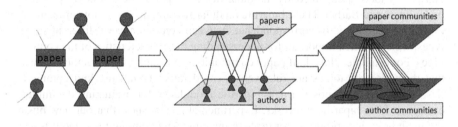

Fig. 7.1 Discovering communities from bipartite networks

Recently, modularities for bipartite networks are proposed by Guimera [7] and Barber [1]. Guimera extends the definition of Newman's modularity to bipartite networks, but his bipartite modularity takes the connectivities of only one vertex type into consideration. Barber defines another bipartite modularity by putting constraints to the null model of modularity, but his bipartitioning-based method is based on an assumption that the number of communities has to be specified in advance.

In order to understand the overall structure of bipartite networks, correspondence of the communities of different vertex types is often more important rather than the quality of communities of each vertex type. In the case of analyzing communities of paper–author bipartite networks, for example, close-knit paper communities and author communities indicate that their research topics are relatively focused. This is because the number of authors who contribute to the papers is limited rather than loose-knit communities. Both of the previous bipartite modularities are not sufficient for measuring the degree of correspondence between communities of different types.

This chapter proposes a new bipartite modularity for community extraction from bipartite networks. As far as the author knows, this is the first attempt for measuring the correspondence between communities of different vertex types. Experimental results using artificial network data show that our new bipartite modularity is a straightforward extension of Newman's modularity. By optimizing our bipartite modularity, we can find communities that are appropriate also for Guimera's bipartite modularity. Another experiments using real bipartite network data show that our new modularity is useful for characterizing discovered communities.

7.2 Modularity and Bipartite Modularities

The definition of Newman's modularity [10] is reviewed as the basis of the following discussion. Bipartite modularities proposed by Guimera [7] and Barber [1] are also described, followed by the explanation of related research on bipartite networks.

7.2.1 Modularity

Modularity is a quantitative measurement for the quality of a particular division of a network. Let us consider a particular division of a network into k communities. Let us suppose M is the number of edges in a network, V is a set of all vertices in the network, and V_l and V_m are the communities. $A(i,j)$ is an adjacency matrix of the network whose (i,j) element is equal to 1 if there is an edge between vertices i and j, and is equal to 0 otherwise. Then we can define e_{lm}, the fraction of all edges in the network that connect vertices in community l to vertices in community m:

$$e_{lm} = \frac{1}{2M} \sum_{i \in V_l} \sum_{j \in V_m} A(i,j)$$

We further define a $k \times k$ symmetric matrix E composed of e_{ij} as its (i,j) element, and its row sums a_i:

$$a_i = \sum_j e_{ij} = \frac{1}{2M} \sum_{i \in V_l} \sum_{j \in V} A(i,j)$$

In a network in which edges fall between vertices without regard for the communities they belong to, we would have $e_{ij} = a_i a_j$. Therefore modularity is defined as follows:

$$Q = \sum_i \left(e_{ii} - a_i^2 \right)$$

Modularity measures the fraction of the edges in the network that connect vertices within the same community minus the expected value of the same quantity in a network with the same community divisions but random connection between vertices. If the number of edges inside communities is no better than random, we will get $Q = 0$. Values approaching the maximum ($Q = 1$) indicate strong community structures. There are many related work regarding modularity. Clauset [3] proposes fast modularity algorithm for efficient search for network divisions of high modularity. Newman [9] proposes a spectral algorithm for improving the quality of network division. Blondel [2] attempts community extraction from large-scale networks. Danon [4] attempts the comparison of several network division methods. Fortunato [6] clarifies resolution limits of modularity-based network division methods.

7.2.2 Guimera's Bipartite Modularity

A community is characterized by larger density of intracommunity edges than that of intercommunity edges. However, bipartite networks are different from unipartite networks in that vertices of the same type are not directly connected. For this reason, density of intracommunity edges has to be redefined for bipartite networks. Guimera's bipartite modularity [7] is defined as the cumulative deviation from the random expectation of the number of Y-vertices in which two vertices of type X are expected to be together:

$$M_B = \sum_{s=1}^{N_M} \left\{ \frac{\sum_{i \neq j \in s} c_{ij}}{\sum_a m_a(m_a - 1)} - \frac{\sum_{i \neq j \in s} t_i t_j}{(\sum_a m_a)^2} \right\} \tag{7.1}$$

where s is a X-vertex community; N_M is the number of X-vertex communities; a is a Y-vertex; m_a is the number of edges that are connected to a; c_{ij} is the number of the Y-vertex communities in which vertices i and j are connected; and t_i and t_j are the total numbers of Y-vertices to which vertices i and j are connected, respectively.

As you can see, two vertex types are not treated symmetrically in the definition above. Guimera's bipartite modularity focuses on the connectivities of only one vertex type (via the vertices of the other type). It is therefore not sufficient for representing the connectivities of the other vertex type, which can be defined as follows:

$$M'_B = \sum_{a=1}^{N'_M} \left\{ \frac{\sum_{i \neq j \in a} c_{ij}}{\sum_s m_s(m_s - 1)} - \frac{\sum_{i \neq j \in a} t_i t_j}{(\sum_s m_s)^2} \right\} \tag{7.2}$$

In order to measure the connectivities of both vertex types, both M_B and M'_B have to be used.

7.2.3 Barber's Bipartite Modularity

Modularity is a deviation from null model, and bipartite networks have specific constraints that should be reflected in the null model. Barber [1] takes the constraints into consideration and formalizes bipartite modularity using modularity matrix. Since there is no edge between the vertices of same type, the adjacency matrix of a bipartite network is as follows:

$$\mathbf{A} = \begin{bmatrix} \mathbf{O}_{p \times p} & \tilde{\mathbf{A}}_{p \times q} \\ (\tilde{\mathbf{A}}^{\mathrm{T}})_{q \times p} & \mathbf{O}_{q \times q} \end{bmatrix},$$

where $\mathbf{O}_{i \times j}$ is the all-zero matrix with i rows and j columns. Probabilities in the null model that an edge exists between vertices i and j are represented as follows:

$$\mathbf{P} = \begin{bmatrix} \mathbf{O}_{p \times p} & \tilde{\mathbf{P}}_{p \times q} \\ (\tilde{\mathbf{P}}^{\mathrm{T}})_{q \times p} & \mathbf{O}_{q \times q} \end{bmatrix},$$

Then bipartite modularity can be defined as follows:

$$Q = \frac{1}{m} \sum_{i=1}^{p} \sum_{j=1}^{q} (\tilde{A}_{ij} - \tilde{P}_{ij}) \delta(g_i, g_{j+p}).$$

where g_i is the community that vertex i is assigned to, and δ_{ij} is the Kronecker's delta. This definition implicitly indicates that the numbers of communities of both types are equal. In order to optimize the bipartite modularity, repetitive bipartitioning is employed. Since the number of communities has to be specified in advance, search for appropriate number of communities is required.

The weaknesses of Barber's bipartite modularity are as follows: (1) the number of communities has to be searched in advance and (2) the numbers of communities of both vertex types have to be equal. Both weaknesses come from the bipartitioning method he employs. The first weakness is fatal for practical community extraction since the search for the number of communities is computationally expensive. The second weakness is also fatal for dividing real networks since the numbers of communities of both vertex types are often imbalanced.

7.2.4 Research on Bipartite Networks

Sun [11] proposes algorithms for computing the neighborhood of the vertices of bipartite networks using random walk with restarts and network partitioning. Algorithms for identifying abnormal vertices are also proposed, and their effectiveness and efficiency are confirmed by the experiments on several real data sets. Zhou [13] proposes a framework for co-ranking authors and documents in heterogeneous networks. The framework is based on coupling two random walks that separately rank authors and documents. As a result of the coupling, both document ranking and author ranking are improved since both ranking depend on each other in a mutually reinforcing way. Zhou [14] proposes a method for projecting bipartite networks to weighted homogeneous networks. Bipartite networks are regarded as resource allocation processes between X-vertices and Y-vertices. Initially assigned weights on X-vertices are propagated to Y-vertices and then back to X-vertices in order to obtain weighted homogeneous networks. Although the goals of these research are different from ours, these research put stress on the importance of processing bipartite networks appropriately.

7.3 Our New Bipartite Modularity

In order to overcome the weaknesses of previous bipartite modularities, the constraint of one-to-one correspondence between communities of both types is removed in our definition of bipartite modularity. One X-vertex community may correspond to many Y-vertices communities and vice versa.

Suppose a bipartite network is composed of X-vertices $\{x_0, x_1, ...\}$ and Y-vertices $\{y_0, y_1, ...\}$, and y_i is connected to both x_j and x_k. Projection is often used as a naive approach for transforming bipartite networks into unipartite networks. Projection is a transformation of such $x_j - y_i - x_k$ connection into $x_j - x_k$ connection so that a network composed of only X-vertices is obtained. However, projection loses information about the correspondence between X-vertex communities and Y-vertex communities, which is often quite valuable for characterizing the communities.

Let us suppose that communities of papers and communities of authors are discovered from a paper–author network. If there is one-to-one correspondence between a paper community and an author community, it shows that the topics of the papers attract only limited authors (Fig. 7.2). On the other hand, if there is one-to-many correspondence between a paper community and author communities, it shows that the topics of the papers attract several communities of authors (Fig. 7.3).

Fig. 7.2 One-to-one correspondence between communities

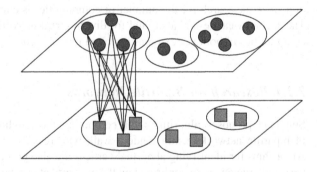

Newman's modularity is not appropriate for evaluating community extraction from bipartite networks. Let us suppose that a bipartite network composed of X-vertices and Y-vertices is given, and both X-vertex communities and Y-vertex communities are specified. Since a bipartite network does not have any direct edge between X-vertices (and between Y-vertices), $e_{ii} = 0$ for each X-vertex

Fig. 7.3 One-to-many
correspondence between
communities

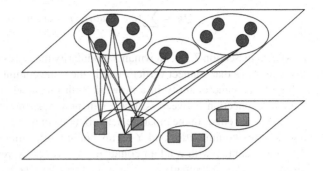

(Y-vertex) community V_i, so its modularity is quite low. For example, modularity
of the division of the bipartite network shown in Fig. 7.4 is -0.14.

Our definition of bipartite modularity is as follows. Let us suppose that M is the
number of edges in a bipartite network, and V is a set of all vertices in the bipartite network. Consider a particular division of the bipartite network into X-vertex
communities and Y-vertex communities, and the numbers of the communities are
L^+ and L^-, respectively. V^+ and V^- are the sets of the communities of X-vertices
and Y-vertices, and V_l^+ and V_m^- are the individual communities that belong to the
sets ($V^+ = \{V_1^+, ..., V_{L^+}^+\}$, $V^- = \{V_1^-, ..., V_{L^-}^-\}$). $A(i,j)$ is an adjacency matrix of the
network whose (i,j) element is equal to 1 if vertices i and j are connected and is
equal to 0 otherwise.

Under the condition that the vertices of V_l and V_m are different types (which
means $(V_l \in V^+ \wedge V_m \in V^-) \vee (V_l \in V^- \wedge V_m \in V^+)$), we can define e_{lm} (the
fraction of all edges that connect vertices in V_l to vertices in V_m) and a_i (its row
sums) just the same as those in Section 7.2.1.

$$e_{lm} = \frac{1}{2M} \sum_{i \in V_l} \sum_{j \in V_m} A(i,j)$$

$$a_i = \sum_j e_{ij} = \frac{1}{2M} \sum_{i \in V_l} \sum_{j \in V} A(i,j)$$

As in the case of homogeneous networks, if edge connections are made at random,
we would have $e_{ij} = a_i a_j$. Our new bipartite modularity Q_B is defined as follows:

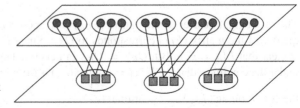

Fig. 7.4 An example of the
division of a bipartite network

$$Q_B = \sum_i (e_{ij} - a_i a_j), \quad j = \underset{k}{\operatorname{argmax}}(e_{ik})$$

As shown in Section 7.2.1, Newman's modularity measures the fraction of the edges in the network that connect vertices within the same community minus the expected value of the same quantity in a network with the same community divisions but random connection between vertices. Our new bipartite modularity measures the fraction of the edges in the bipartite network that connect vertices of the corresponding X-vertex communities and Y-vertex communities minus the expected value of the same quantity with random connections between X-vertices and Y-vertices. If given network is not bipartite, you can see that $Q_B = Q$, which means that our new bipartite modularity is a straightforward generalization of original modularity.

If the connection between X-vertices and Y-vertices is no better than random, we will get $Q_B = 0$. High Q_B value indicates strong community structure in a bipartite network. Our new bipartite modularity of the network shown in Fig. 7.4 is 0.66. If you take a closer look at the expression of Q_B, you will find that the value is the sum of bipartite modularities of different directions ($V^+ \rightarrow V^-$ and $V^- \rightarrow V^+$). Q_B can be divided as follows:

$$Q_{B\pm} = \sum_{i \in V^+} (e_{ij} - a_i a_j), \quad j = \underset{k \in V^-}{\operatorname{argmax}}(e_{ik})$$

$$Q_{B\mp} = \sum_{i \in V^-} (e_{ij} - a_i a_j), \quad j = \underset{k \in V^+}{\operatorname{argmax}}(e_{ik})$$

$$Q_B = Q_{B\pm} + Q_{B\mp}$$

$Q_{B\pm}$ is the bipartite modularity for $V^+ \rightarrow V^-$ direction, and $Q_{B\mp}$ is the bipartite modularity for $V^- \rightarrow V^+$ direction. In the example shown in Fig. 7.4, $Q_{B\pm} = 0.41$ and $Q_{B\mp} = 0.25$, which means that downward connections are relatively focused rather than upward connections.

The matrix E composed of e_{ij} as its (i,j) element is represented as follows if rows and columns are reordered appropriately.

$$\begin{pmatrix} 0 & \cdots & 0 & e_{1,L^++1} & \cdots & e_{1,L^++L^-} \\ \vdots & \ddots & \vdots & \vdots & \ddots & \vdots \\ 0 & \cdots & 0 & e_{L^+,L^++1} & \cdots & e_{L^+,L^++L^-} \\ e_{L^++1,1} & \cdots & e_{L^++1,L^+} & 0 & \cdots & 0 \\ \vdots & \ddots & \vdots & \vdots & \ddots & \vdots \\ e_{L^++L^-,1} & \cdots & e_{L^++L^-,L^+} & 0 & \cdots & 0 \end{pmatrix}$$

The upper right quarter of the matrix (E_{UR}) corresponds to $Q_{B\pm}$, and the lower left quarter of the matrix (E_{LL}) corresponds to $Q_{B\mp}$. Since E is a symmetric matrix, it is clear that $E_{UR}^T = E_{LL}$. But $Q_{B\pm} \neq Q_{B\mp}$ in general. This is because a set of (i,j) under the condition that $i \in V^+, j = \underset{k \in V^-}{\operatorname{argmax}}(e_{ik})$ is different from a set of (i,j) under the condition that $i \in V^-, j = \underset{k \in V^+}{\operatorname{argmax}}(e_{ik})$.

When two upper left communities in Fig. 7.4 are merged, Q_B increases to 0.67. But if all upper communities are merged into one community, Q_B decreases to 0.35. By maximizing our new bipartite modularity, unobvious community structure will be obtained from bipartite networks.

7.4 Experiments

7.4.1 Artificial Four-Community Networks

In order to clarify the properties of our bipartite modularity, modularity and bipartite modularity are compared in the following experiment. Networks with known community structure are used to see whether our bipartite modularity has abilities of detecting their structures.

We have generated many networks with 128 vertices, divided into four communities of 32 vertices each. Edges are placed independently at random with probability p_{in} for an edge to fall between vertices in the same community and p_{out} to fall between vertices in different communities ($p_{in} + p_{out} = 1$). Such artificial network data are used by Newman [10] and Danon [4]. Figure 7.5 illustrates an example of the networks. Figure 7.6 shows the average values of modularity and our bipartite modularity of 100 artificial networks.

Fig. 7.5 A network with four communities

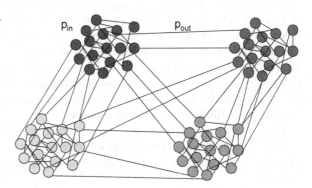

You can see from the figure that modularity and our bipartite modularity are the same for networks of high p_{in}. This is obvious from the definition of bipartite modularity. For the networks with high p_{in}, diagonal elements of matrix E are the biggest among all elements in the same row ($\forall j \; e_{ii} \geq e_{ij}$). Therefore $j = \underset{k}{\operatorname{argmax}}(e_{ik}) = i$ and $Q_B = Q$.

For networks of smaller $p_{in}(p_{in} < p_{out})$, diagonal elements of matrix E are *not* the biggest ($\exists j \; e_{ii} \leq e_{ij}$) and their modularities are below zero. On the other hand, bipartite modularities of the networks are positive because $j = \underset{k}{\operatorname{argmax}}(e_{ik})$ is set to the community that is densely connected with community i.

Fig. 7.6 Modularity and
bipartite modularity of
four-community networks

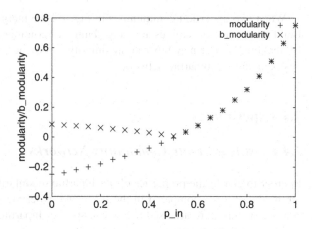

The above networks are not bipartite because four communities are connected
to each other. For the next experiment, we have generated bipartite networks with
128 vertices, divided into four communities of 32 vertices each. Edges are placed
independently at random with probability p_{in} for an edge to fall between vertices in
the same community, p_{same} to fall between vertices in the communities of same
type of vertices, and p_{diff1} and p_{diff2} to fall between vertices in the communities of different types of vertices ($p_{in} + p_{same} + p_{diff1} + p_{diff2} = 1$). Suppose
there are two communities for each type of vertices. p_{in} and p_{same} are set to zero
because there are no edges between vertices of the same type in bipartite networks.
Figure 7.7 illustrates an example of such networks. Networks with various p_{diff1} and
$p_{diff2}(p_{diff1} + p_{diff2} = 1)$ are generated and their modularity and bipartite modularity are calculated. Figure 7.8 shows the average values of modularity and bipartite
modularity of 100 artificial bipartite networks.

Figure 7.8 shows that original modularity is not appropriate for bipartite networks
because there is no edge between vertices of the same type. Bipartite modularity is
effective for detecting the existence of community structures for bipartite networks,

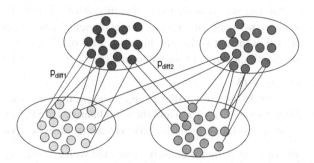

Fig. 7.7 Bipartite network
with four communities

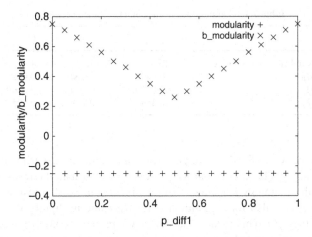

Fig. 7.8 Modularity and bipartite modularity for bipartite networks

and it also shows the degree of correspondence between communities of different types of vertices. In the case of networks with $p_{diff1} = 1$ or $p_{diff2} = 1$, there are complete one-to-one correspondence between communities of different types of vertices, and the values of bipartite modularity are the highest.

7.4.2 Southern Women Data Set

As an example for comparing different bipartite modularities, the following experiments are performed using southern women data set collected around Mississippi during the 1930 as part of an extensive study of class and race in the Deep South. The data set describes the participation of 18 women in 14 social events. The women and social events constitute a bipartite network whose vertices are women and social events, and whose edges are the participation in the events.

Experiments of network divisions by the following strategies are performed : (1) optimization of Guimera's bipartite modularity (M_B), (2) optimization of Guimera's bipartite modularity for the other vertex type (M'_B), and (3) optimization of our new bipartite modularity (Q_B). In addition (4) results of Barber's BRIM algorithm are also discussed later.

As an initial state of the network division, each woman/event is assigned to its own community. Then greedy searches for the optimization of bipartite modularities ((1), (2), (3)) are performed by merging a pair of women/event communities. The results of network divisions by the above strategies are shown in Table 7.1. Each row of Table 7.1 shows the number of discovered communities, values of M_B, M'_B, and Q_B, respectively. Each column shows the strategies (1), (2), and (3), respectively. Although communities are surely obtained with strategy (1), its division is good only for Guimera's bipartite modularity for one vertex type. Strategy (2) does

Table 7.1 Communities from southern women network

	(1)	(2)	(3)
Number of communities	13	32	4
M_B	0.140	0.000	0.0025
M_B'	−0.00797	0.000	0.0109
Q_B	0.354	0.138	0.575

not work for network division. We performed an additional experiment that combines the strategies (1) and (2), but its result is not better than the result of strategy (1). The result of strategy (3) shows that the obtained network division is good for Q_B, of course, and also for M_B', although its M_B value is slightly worse than the result of strategy (1). This means that our new bipartite modularity is appropriate for obtaining good network divisions from the viewpoint of connectivities of both vertex types, as well as the degree of correspondence between the communities of different types, which is our main objective.

According to Barber's paper, strategy (4) (optimization of Barber's bipartite modularity) results in the discovery of coarse division composed of only two communities. He claims that his method succeeds in discovering the "best" network division that matches the research results by sociologists. But the best division is obtained as the results of 500,000 trials from random community assignment as its initial state. Another weakness of Barber's approach is that the number of communities has to be specified in advance, as we mentioned previously.

7.4.3 Scotland Corporate Interlock Network

The next experiment is performed using a network of corporate interlocks in Scotland. It is a bipartite network composed of 136 directors and 108 firms. Three hundred fifty-eight edges represent memberships of the boards of directors for Scottish firms during 1904–1905.

The results of optimizing the following bipartite modularities are shown in Table 7.2: (1) Guimera's bipartite modularity (M_B), (2) Guimera's bipartite modularity for the other vertex type (M_B'), and (3) our new bipartite modularity (Q_B).

Table 7.2 Communities of scotland corporate interlock network

	(1)	(2)	(3)
Number of communities	26	29	10
M_B	0.612	0.613	0.521
M_B'	0.427	0.433	0.332
Q_B	0.593	0.628	0.762

The results show that communities obtained by the optimization of Guimera's bipartite modularity is much more than those obtained by the optimization of our bipartite modularity. This is just the same as the results shown in Table 7.1. The strategy of optimizing our bipartite modularity favors larger communities.

The experiment of optimizing Barber's bipartite modularity is also performed. The number of obtained communities is 34 (17 director communities and 17 firm communities). Barber's method is based on an assumption that there is one-to-one correspondence between communities of both vertex types. Since the assumption is not satisfied for the detected communities shown in Table 7.2, it is not appropriate to compare the values of Barber's bipartite modularity in Table 7.2.

7.4.4 Real Online Social Networks

Our bipartite modularity is also used for real-world networks. We have generated bipartite social networks composed of users and boards from the data of Yahoo! Chiebukuro (Japanese Yahoo! Answers, http://chiebukuro.yahoo.co.jp). The site is one of the most popular question–answering forums in Japan. The network of Yahoo! Chiebukuro is summarized in Table 7.3. Since the network is huge, community extraction by the optimization of bipartite modularity is computationally intractable. So we employ the following projection-based network division for the sake of convenience. From the above bipartite network, user communities and board communities are discovered by (1) projecting the bipartite network into unipartite networks (user network and board network) and (2) applying Clauset's fast modularity algorithm [3] for finding network divisions of high modularities. Both user communities and board communities are extracted from the networks. Newman's modularity (Q) and our bipartite modularity (Q_B) of the network division are -0.1021 and 0.2919, respectively.

Table 7.3 Statistics of the network of Yahoo! chiebukuro

Number of vertices	246,849
Number of edges	357,834
Average degree	2.89921
Clustering coefficient	0
Average path length	7.7587

Our bipartite modularity is for evaluating divisions of a bipartite network. In addition to that, bipartite modularity of each community (Q_{B_i}) can be used for measuring the degree of "close knitness" to the communities of the other vertex type. Figure 7.9 shows a distribution of bipartite modularity Q_{B_i} (X-axis) and the sizes (Y-axis) of discovered communities. Communities of upper half of the figure (more than 15,000 vertices) are board communities. Their bipartite modularities are high except the one located at middle left position. This community is like the one in Fig. 7.3: the main topics of the community (such as "entertainment and hobby" and "health and fashion") attract many users and thus its bipartite modularity is low. On

Fig. 7.9 Bipartite
modularities and the sizes of
communities

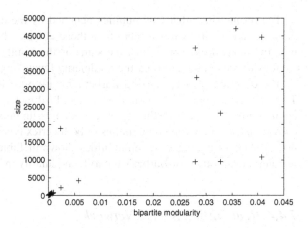

the other hand, other communities of high bipartite modularity are relatively focused
(such as "child care," "mental health," and "cars"), like the one in Fig. 7.2.

7.5 Conclusion

A new measurement for community extraction from bipartite networks is proposed
in this chapter. Previous attempts for defining bipartite modularity are not sufficient.
Guimera's bipartite modularity takes the connectivities of only one vertex type into
account. Barber's approach is unrealistic because the number of communities has
to be searched for his repetitive bipartitioning. Our new bipartite modularity is a
straightforward generalization of Newman's modularity. Experimental results show
that our bipartite modularity is appropriate for discovering communities that correspond to the communities of the other vertex type. In addition to that, our bipartite
modularity for each community represents the degree of correspondence to the communities of the other type of vertices, which can be used for characterizing the
communities.

Biclustering algorithms [5, 8, 12] also aim at finding division of incident matrices. These algorithms are mainly for the purpose of bioinformatics and document
clustering. One of the weaknesses of most of these algorithms is that the algorithms
do not scale to large networks. As described in Section 7.4.4, we calculated our
bipartite modularity for each of the communities that are already discovered from
large-scale social networks. But the discovery by the optimization of bipartite modularity is not an easy task for large-scale networks. Guimera and Barber also use
small bipartite networks for their experiments. Finding the divisions of high bipartite modularity from large-scale networks by modularity optimization is another
challenging research topic, which is left for our future work.

Our bipartite modularity proposed in this chapter is the first step for intelligent
processing of real heterogeneous networks. There are several bipartite, tripartite, and

n-partite networks in the Web. Social tagging systems can be represented as tripartite networks composed of three types of vertices (users, URLs, and tags). Discovering and evaluating communities of such heterogeneous networks is one of the important and challenging topics of Web mining.

Acknowledgments The author would like to thank Mr. Makoto Okamoto, Prof. Kikuo Maekawa (The National Institute for Japanese Language), and Prof. Sadaoki Furui (Tokyo Institute of Technology) for allowing us to use the data of Yahoo! Chiebukuro.

References

1. Barber, M.J. Modularity and community detection in bipartite networks. arXiv 0707.1616v3: 1–11, 2007.
2. Blondel, V.D., Guillaume, J.L., Lambiotte, and R., Lefebvre, E. Fast unfolding of community hierarchies in large networks. arXiv 0803.0476v1: 1–6, 2008.
3. Clauset, A., Newman, M.E.J., and Moore, C. Finding community structure in very large networks. *Physical Review E*, 70(066111): 1–6, 2004.
4. Danon, L., Diaz-Guilera, A., Duch, J., and Arenas, A. Comparing community structure identification. *Journal of Statistical Mechanics*, P09008: 1–10, 2005.
5. Dhillon, I.S. Co-clustering documents and words using bipartite spectral graph partitioning. In *Proceedings of the 7th ACM SIGKDD International Conference on Knowledge Discovery and Data Mining*, San Francisco, CA, pp. 269–274, 2001.
6. Fortunato, S. and Barthelemy, M. Resolution limit in community detection. In *Proceedings of the National Academy of Sciences of the United States of America*, 104(1): 36–41, 2007.
7. Guimera, R., Sales-Pardo, M., and Amaral, L.A.N. Module identification in bipartite and directed networks. *Physical Review*, 76(036102): 1–8, 2007.
8. Madeira, S.C. and Oliveira, A.L. Biclustering algorithms for biological data analysis: A survey. *IEEE/ACM Transactions on Computational Biology and Bioinformatics*, 1(1): 24–45, 2004.
9. Newman, M.E.J. Modularity and community structure in networks. In *Proceedings of the National Academy of Sciences of the United States of America*, 103: 8577–8582, 2006.
10. Newman, M.E.J. and Girvan, M. Finding and evaluating community structure in networks. *Physical Review E*, 69(026113): 1–15, 2004.
11. Sun, J., Qu, H., Chakrabarti, D., and Faloutsos, C. Neighborhood formation and anomaly detection in bipartite graphs. In *Proceedings of the 5th IEEE International Conference on Data Mining*, Houston, TX, pp. 418–425, 2005.
12. Tanay, A., Sharan, R., and Shamir, R. Discovering statistically significant biclusters in gene expression data. *Bioinformatics*, 18(Suppl.1): S136–S144, 2002.
13. Zhou, D., Orshanskiy, S.A., Zha, H., and Giles, C.L. Co-ranking authors and documents in a heterogeneous network. In *Proceedings of the 7th IEEE International Conference on Data Mining*, Omaha, NE, pp. 739–744, 2007.
14. Zhou, T., Ren, J., Medo, M., and Zhang, Y.C. Bipartite network projection and personal recommendation. *Physical Review E*, 76(046115): 1–7, 2007.

Chapter 8
ONDOCS: Ordering Nodes to Detect Overlapping Community Structure

Jiyang Chen, Osmar R. Zaïane, Jörg Sander, and Randy Goebel

Abstract Finding communities is an important task for the discovery of underlying structures in social networks. While existing approaches give interesting results, they typically neglect the fact that communities may overlap, with some hub nodes participating in multiple communities. Similarly, most methods cannot deal with outliers, which are nodes that belong to no germane communities. The definition of community is still vague and the criterion to locate hubs or outliers varies. Existing approaches usually require guidance in this regard, specified as input parameters, e.g., the number of communities in the network, without much intuition. Here we present a general community definition and a list of requirements for a community mining metric. We review advantages and disadvantages of existing metrics and propose our new metric to quantify the relation between nodes in a social network. We then use the new metric to build a visual data mining system, which first helps the user to achieve appropriate parameter selection by observing initial data visualizations, then detects overlapping community structure from the network while also excluding outliers. Experimental results verify the scalability and accuracy of our approach on real data networks and show its advantages over existing methods that also consider overlaps. An empirical evaluation of our metric demonstrates superior performance over previous measures.

8.1 Introduction

Many data sets of scientific interest can be modeled as networks, which consist of sets of nodes representing entities, connected by edges representing various relations between these entities. For example, the World Wide Web (WWW) can be viewed as a very large graph where nodes represent web pages and edges represent hyperlinks between pages. In social networks, nodes typically represent individuals

O.R. Zaïane (✉)
Department of Computing Science, University of Alberta, Edmonton, AB, Canada T6G 2E8
e-mail: zaiane@cs.ualberta.ca

N. Memon et al. (eds.), *Data Mining for Social Network Data*,
Annals of Information Systems 12, DOI 10.1007/978-1-4419-6287-4_8,
© Springer Science+Business Media, LLC 2010

and edges indicate relationships, e.g., in a tele-communication network, each node is a phone number and edges represent the fact that two nodes communicated. In such networks, the ability to detect closely related entity groups, i.e., communities, can be of significant practical importance. For instance, the fact that web pages in the same community might focus on related topics can be used to help page ranking and recommendation. Social network communities can be used to understand implicit network structures, e.g., organization structures, academic collaborations, or usage pattern in tele-communication networks.

In recent years, there has been a surge of research interests on finding communities in networks. A community (or *cluster*) can be seen as a subgraph such that the density of edges within the subgraph is greater than the density of edges between its nodes and nodes outside it [12]. Existing community detection approaches, such as spectral clustering [27] and modularity-based [24] and density-based methods [32], achieve good results for some data sets and have proposed various metrics to measure the similarity between social entities. However, all of them implicitly define communities based on metrics which measure only partial aspects of the social network; thus existing community definitions can only identify specific types of communities. A new metric is needed to more thoroughly quantify the relation between two social entities.

Recent studies have also revealed that network models of many real-world phenomena exhibit an overlapping community structure, i.e., a node can belong to more than one community, which is hard to take into account with classical graph clustering methods where every vertex of the graph belongs to exactly one community [26]. This is especially true for social networks, where individuals can connect to several groups in the network as *hubs*. Furthermore, in real networks we also have another node category, which belongs to no community, i.e., *outliers*. Therefore, a typical social network consists of communities, hubs, and outliers. It is essential for community discovery methods to identify nodes in these three categories, since the isolation of hubs, and outliers can be crucial for many applications. Unfortunately, a precise description of what a *community* really is has not yet been explicitly articulated. Moreover, the definition would be different across various domains or even across different networks of the same domain. Therefore, most proposed approaches [12, 13, 19, 26, 32] for overlapping community detection require the user to describe the communities they are looking for by giving parameters, e.g., community size, density range, the number of communities. However, appropriate parameters are usually extremely hard to determine without tedious and repeated testing. Moreover, arbitrary parameters may over-restrain the space in which communities are found and lead to inaccurate results. Overall, if the real value of community identification is to be achieved, we want tools that form the basis for community mining, so that useful and interesting structure emerges without too much parameter estimation required.

In this chapter, we first define social network communities with a list of requirements for a community mining metric, based on observations of social network characteristics. After reviewing the advantages and disadvantages of existing metrics, we propose the *R (Relation)* metric to measure the similarity between any pair of entities in a social network, then show its advantages by comparison with existing metrics. We then propose our approach ONDOCS (ordering nodes to detect overlapping community structure). Our visual data mining approach first generates preliminary visualizations of the network in question by ordering nodes based on their reachability scores (RS) to help the user understand the network structure in order to choose appropriate parameters. Selected parameters are then used to extract communities, hubs, and outliers from the network. We offer the following contributions in this chapter:

- A new metric R to quantify the relation between entities.
- A visual data mining approach to assist the user in finding appropriate parameters to describe the communities they are looking for.
- A scalable and efficient method to discover communities, hubs, and outliers in social networks.

The rest of the chapter is organized as follows. We discuss related work in Section 8.2. Section 8.3 introduces our community definition and reviews existing metrics. We present our R metric and the ONDOCS approach in Section 8.4 and report experimental results in Section 8.5, followed by conclusions in Section 8.6.

8.2 Related Work

8.2.1 Community Mining

The problem of finding communities in social networks has been studied for decades in many fields, including computer science, sociology, and physics. Originally, graph partitioning methods [9, 27, 28] were applied, but researchers soon realized that the condition for graph partitioning methods to be valid is that the number or the sizes of the communities into which the networks are divided should be fixed, which is not true for community mining. Various benefit functions have been proposed to solve the problem, such as *normalized cut* [28] and *min-max cut* [9], but they are still biased in favor of divisions into equal-sized parts and thus still suffer from the same drawbacks that make graph partitioning inappropriate for community detection. Recently, many quality metrics for community structure have been proposed [22, 24, 32]. Among them, modularity Q has been proved to be the most accurate [8] and has been pursued by many researchers [7, 10, 14, 22, 23, 31]. While all previous works focus on clique communities (defined in Section 8.3.1) and apply hierarchical methods, Xu et al. [32] propose the density-based SCAN algorithm to detect transitive communities (also defined in Section 8.3.1) and locate hubs and outliers in networks. However, all those metrics focus only on one type of community and do not consider a general community definition, not the whole picture of community mining in social networks, thus none of them satisfy all of the requirements listed in Section 8.3.

8.2.2 Overlapping Community Structure Detection

In general, there are two ways to detect overlapping community structure in a network. One natural idea is to first globally partition the network and then locally expand the discovered communities to locate overlapping components. Wei et al. [30] partition the network using the spectral clustering method and then locally expand to optimize a variation of the Modularity Q measure [24]. For overlapping community discovery in a name-entity network, Li et al. [18] generate community cores by merging triangles (3-clique) so that one vertex can be part of different communities if it belongs to several cliques. Similarly, Baumes et al. [5] initialize community cores using the Link Aggregate (LA) algorithm and then refine the peripheries by an Iterative Scan (IS) procedure. Another mainstream research direction for this problem is based on fuzzy clustering. Zhang et al. [35] combine modularity and a fuzzy c-means clustering algorithm to identify overlapping communities. Nepusz et al. [19] propose a similarity function based on membership and solve the fuzzy community detection problem as a constrained optimization problem. Recently, Palla et al. [26] propose the CFinder system to partition complex networks to k-clique communities, where k is a given parameter as clique size. Gregory proposes the CONGA algorithm [12] based on the betweenness score [24] and later extends it to the CONGO algorithm to improve the scalability [13]. He also shows that CONGO provides the same level of performance as CFinder, on synthetic networks. While all of the above methods successfully detect overlapping community structure, some major problems exist. Most methods do not consider outliers, which belong to no communities, thus many outliers would be classified as community members, i.e., they force outliers into existing clusters. Additionally, the fact that they intentionally focus on overlapping community structure makes them find or force overlap even for data without such structure. More importantly, not only many approaches require parameters that are difficult to determine but also their results are very sensitive to parameter settings, e.g., number of communities [12, 35], community density [18, 26], or size of a local community region [13].

8.2.3 Visual Data Mining

Most community mining approaches apply data mining algorithms, e.g., agglomerative hierarchical clustering for a bottom-up merge or partitional clustering for a top-down split. Having noted that community mining is also a data mining process, we believe that the idea of visual data mining could be helpful in the mining process, both to guide the mining toward goals and to better understand the results, since visualization and interaction capabilities enable the user to incorporate domain knowledge to finding communities in social networks. Generally speaking, the areas of data mining and information visualization offer various techniques which effectively complement one another supporting the discovery of patterns in data. Whereas traditional (algorithmic) techniques are analyzing the data automatically, information visualization techniques can leverage the data mining process from an orthogonal direction, by providing a platform for understanding the data and generating hypotheses about the data based on human capabilities such as domain knowledge, perception, and creativity [4]. In the past few years, visualization techniques have been specifically designed to support human involvement in the data mining process. For example, Ankerst et al. [2] propose an interactive decision tree classifier based on a multidimensional visualization of the training data. They later extend the work [3] to include categorical attributes to interactively build decision trees and thus support a much broader range of applications. Similar visual data mining ideas are also applied in [15, 29] to help users determine parameters for decision tree construction and classification rule discovery.

8.3 Preliminaries

In this section, we propose a definition for network communities and provide a list of requirements for a good measure for community detection. We discuss two existing measures based on those requirements.

8.3.1 Community Definition

Recent research has proposed community detection methods in two different ways based on various motivations and similarity measures. First, hierarchical methods [22, 24] tend to find communities *globally* so that nodes, which are more densely connected to nodes in the same community than outside nodes, are grouped together; second, density-based approaches [32] classify nodes into communities based on their *local* structure, i.e., nodes are in the same community if they share many neighbors. In experiments, these two approaches typically yield noticeably different results on the same data sets. They actually target two different kinds of communities. On the one hand, hierarchical methods partition networks by greedily maximizing an objective function, which increases for pairs of connected nodes that are in the same community and decreases for pairs of disconnected nodes also in the same community. Their methods favor communities where every node connects to everyone else in the same community, which we call *Clique Communities* (Fig. 8.1a). On the other hand, density-based approaches expand communities from nodes that are structurally dense, i.e., have enough neighbors, judged by appropriate parameters. Therefore, these approaches do not consider global properties but only the local network structure. They find communities where nodes may not directly connect to many others in the same community but are indirectly connected to every other node via some connections, which we call *Transitive Communities* (Fig. 8.1b). The difference between these two strategies is analogous to hierarchical-based and density-based methods in the data clustering field [34].

Fig. 8.1 Examples for clique
community and transitive
community

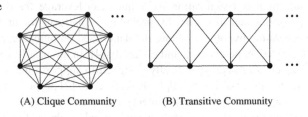

(A) Clique Community   (B) Transitive Community

While existing methods implicitly describe specific types of communities based
on their metrics and algorithms without clearly defining them, we give a general definition for social network communities based on the observations highlighted above:
*A community is a network partition such that entities within the same community
share some common trait or proximity, judged by some defined entity similarity or
relationship metric.*

No matter how communities are defined, there are two major issues for community mining that remain to be addressed. First, each pair of nodes should be
measured by their similarity or relationship; second, pairs with high similarity or
strong relationship should be put in the same community. Although it is the algorithm (hierarchical or density-based) that decides the community type to be found
(clique or transitive), a good similarity metric is vital for both clique and transitive
community structure detection. We present the requirements of a good metric in the
following section.

8.3.2 Requirements for a Good Community Mining Metric

It is easy to confuse graph partitioning with community mining since these two
lines of research are really addressing the same question, which can be described
as dividing vertices of a network into some number of groups. There are, however,
important differences between network characteristics of the two camps that make
quite distinct approaches and metrics desirable. For instance, in social network community mining, the relation between two nodes is asymmetric. (Take MySpace.com
as an example: user A might list user B as one of his best friends while he is not even
in the friend list of user B.) Thus, existing measures and approaches that are shown
to be effective for some graph partitioning may not fit for community mining, since
they do not take these differences into consideration. In the following, we propose
a list of requirements, which we believe should be satisfied by a good metric for
community mining.

1. *A metric should measure the similarity between every pair of nodes.*
   A similarity score between two nodes is required for all algorithms to decide
   whether to put these two nodes into one community or not. The metric should
   be able to measure all pairs, connected or disconnected. Metrics, which do not

consider disconnected pairs of nodes, may be able to find some community structure, but they naively assume that disconnected pairs should not be in the same community.

2. *A metric should reflect not only similarity but also dissimilarity.*
   In other words, the metric not only measures whether two nodes should be in the same community but also measures whether they should not be in the same community. For instance, the metric should provide a means to solve a disagreement while merging a node n in a community when some existing nodes relate to n and others do not.

3. *A metric should consider the asymmetric nature between pairs.*
   The pair asymmetry in social networks means that $Relation(i \rightarrow j) \neq Relation$ $(j \rightarrow i)$, e.g., consider people pair (i,j) where i has many friends and is j's only friend, i is much more important to j than j is to i. For undirected graphs, where the similarity measure is usually required to be symmetric, the asymmetric nature between the node pairs should still be considered.

4. *An overlapping community metric should handle both hubs and outliers.*
   We think there are three kinds of nodes in a social network: hubs (nodes that have many connections and can be seen as community overlaps), outliers (nodes that have very few connections and do not belong to any community), and normal nodes (nodes that have some connections and belong to a community). The influences of hubs and outliers to community discovery have to be minimized by the metric.

8.3.3 Existing Metrics for Community Detection

Newman et al. proposed the modularity Q as a quality measure of a particular division of a network [24]. For a social network with k communities, the modularity is defined as $Q = \sum_{c=1}^{k} \left[\frac{e_c}{m} - \left(\frac{d_c}{2m} \right)^2 \right]$ where m is the number of edges in the network, e_c is the number of edges between nodes within community c, and d_c is the sum of the degrees of the nodes in community c. The modularity Q measures the fraction of the edges in the network that connect vertices of the same community, i.e., within-community edges, minus the expected value of the same quantity in a network with the same community division but with random connections between the vertices. Q can be transformed as a sum of similarity scores for all node pairs [7, 23]:

$$Q = \sum Q_{ij} = \sum_{i,j} \left(\frac{A_{ij}}{2m} - \frac{d_i}{2m} * \frac{d_j}{2m} \right) \tag{8.1}$$

where $A_{ij} = 1$ if nodes i and j are connected, 0 otherwise, d_i, d_j are the degree of nodes i and j, m is the edge number. Note that $Q_{ij} = 2 * \left(\frac{A_{ij}}{2m} - \frac{d_i}{2m} * \frac{d_j}{2m} \right)$ since each pair (i, j) is calculated twice in the sum as (i, j) and (j, i). Also, note that Q_{ij} represents the difference between the probability of the event $i \leftrightarrow j$ (*nodes i* *and j are connected*) in the given graph structure $\left(P(i \leftrightarrow j) = \frac{A_{ij}}{m}\right)$ and that in a random model with the same number of vertices, edges, and degrees $\left(P(i \leftrightarrow j) = 2 * \frac{d_i}{2m} * \frac{d_j}{2m}\right)$. (See [23, 24] for details.)

The modularity Q provides a similarity score for all pairs of nodes. Whether the score is positive or negative depends on whether two nodes are connected or not, which reflects both similarity and dissimilarity. By taking the global information (the total edge number m) into consideration in the score calculation such that the higher degree the nodes have the lower score the pair gets, modularity handles the influence from hub nodes. However, the measure neglects the asymmetric nature between pairs in social networks by assuming $P(i \rightarrow j) = P(j \rightarrow i)$. Moreover, the method fails to handle outliers. Since outliers have small degrees and can achieve high scores given the formula, they are usually inaccurately merged first into a community by hierarchical algorithms.

Recently, Xu et al. [32] proposed another similarity measure S:

$$S_{ij} = \frac{|N_i \cap N_j|}{\sqrt{|N_i| * |N_j|}} \tag{8.2}$$

where N_i is the neighborhood of node i, including i itself and all nodes connecting to i. This metric normalizes the number of common neighbors by the geometric mean of the two neighborhoods' sizes in order to compare the neighborhood structure of the two vertices in question.

The S metric considers the local structure of compared nodes (the common neighbor number) as well as their local attributes (the sizes of both neighborhoods), thus it minimizes the score for both hubs and outliers. However, this metric does not measure dissimilarity, e.g., the score will be zero if two nodes share no neighbors, disregarding the network structure, and it fails to include pair asymmetry as well. Although this metric is easy to be extended for all pairs of nodes, it was originally proposed for connected pairs only. Additionally, even though the S metric considers the neighborhood size of the two nodes in question, it neglects the degrees of other nodes in the neighborhood, i.e., every node in the neighborhood is weighted equally as 1 disregarding whether it is a hub, an outlier, or a normal node.

We have summarized two state-of-the-art similarity metrics for community mining and analyze their advantages and disadvantages (see Table 8.1). While they

Table 8.1 Comparing community mining metrics

| Metric | Metric requirements | | | |
	All pairs	Similarity and dissimilarity	Asymmetry	Hub and outlier
Q	All	Yes	No	Only hub
S	Connected	No	No	Both
R	All	Yes	Yes	Both

successfully find communities for some data sets, they do not satisfy all given requirements and thus need to be improved.

8.4 Our ONDOCS Approach

In this section, we first present our characterization of the relation between nodes, then introduce the algorithm to generate network visualizations, and then show how to detect overlapping community structure based on observed parameters.

8.4.1 Relationship Definition

Originally, ONDOCS is inspired by the OPTICS algorithm proposed by Ankerst et al. [1], where points are ordered for data clustering. However, unlike their clustering approach, we do not have a distance measure between nodes, so we need to define a new node relationship. The existing community metrics reviewed in Section 8.3 are designed to find optimal communities of a specific type, i.e., Q for clique communities and S for transitive communities, which means they focus only on partial aspects of network structure. We think that comparing the community structure to a random model, in which nodes are randomly connected in a network, is a practicable way to quantify node relations. The intuition is that community structure can be identified as that which is non-random; so developing a measure with a notion of random connections should help identify non-random structure. The neighborhood around any two nodes in question is also important in assessing their relationship. Therefore we proposed a new measure R to combine these two aspects, defined as follows:

$$R(i,j) = \frac{R(i \to j) + R(j \to i)}{2} = \frac{\sum_{x \in N_j} r(i,x) + \sum_{x \in N_i} r(x,j)}{2} \tag{8.3}$$

where N_i is the neighborhood of node i, including i itself and all nodes that connect to i. The similarity between nodes i and j is defined as the average of $R(i \to j)$, representing the relationship from i to j's neighborhood, and $R(j \to i)$, representing relationship from j to i's neighborhood. $R(i \to j)$ is defined as the sum of relation scores r between i and all nodes in j's neighborhood, similarly for $R(j \to i)$ with respect to j and i's neighborhood. Next, in order to quantify the relation $r(i,j)$ between nodes i and j, we compare the probability of the event that i and j are connected in the original graph G to a random model, where we only keep the same node number n and node degrees $k_1, \ldots, k_n$ and leave the rest random. In such a random model, it is obvious that the probability of a node i having a connection to any other node is $P(i) = \frac{k_i}{n-1}$. Here we assume G is undirected so that the events of i connecting to j and j connecting to i are equivalent, thus the probability of i and j being connected is the maximum of $P(i)$ and $P(j)$:

$$P(i \leftrightarrow j) = \max(P(i \to j), P(j \to i)) = \max(P(i), P(j)) = \frac{\max(k_i, k_j)}{n-1} \qquad (8.4)$$

Now we define the relation score $r(i, j)$ between nodes i and j:

$$r(i, j) = A_{ij} - \frac{\max(k_i, k_j)}{n-1} \qquad (8.5)$$

where $A_{ij} = 1$ if nodes i and j are connected in G, 0 otherwise. Here we omit directed graphs since that is a straightforward extension. The proposed metric R, r, and the random model are justified in the next section.

8.4.1.1 Analyzing the R Measure

We evaluate our R metric using the requirements listed in Section 8.3. First, R assesses similarity for both connected and disconnected pairs of nodes. Two nodes are measured by the relation between them and their neighborhoods. Second, while the relation score r between each pair will be positive for connected pairs and negative for disconnected ones, R in Eq. 8.3 considers all pairs within the local neighborhood so that the R score represents an overall similarity, therefore $R(i, j)$ can be positive even if $r(i, j)$ is not. Similarly, $R(i, j)$ can be negative even if $r(i, j)$ is not. Third, the R metric is divided into two parts: $R(i \to j)$ and $R(j \to i)$, each of which represents the similarity between one node and the other's neighborhood. The asymmetric characteristic of social networks is thus considered. Finally, the influence from hubs *or* outliers to other nodes is minimized. Hubs have big degrees which lead to large $\frac{\max(k_i, k_j)}{n-1}$ and small r scores. Outliers have small neighborhoods so R is small since there are few pairs to contribute in the sum. Therefore, as shown in Table 8.1, the R metric satisfies all requirements for a good community mining measure.

We now justify the formula for the relation score r and the random model presented in Section 8.4.1. Recall that the intuition behind the r score is to compare the probability of the event E, *that two nodes i and j are connected*, in the original graph structure with the probability of the same event in a random model, which has the same node number and degrees. Only if the probability of having these two nodes connected in the random model is low does the fact that they are indeed connected show us strong relationship. Since the probability of E in the original graph is simply 1 or 0 given the network structure, we only need to answer the following question: *In an undirected graph G with n nodes, degrees $k_1, \ldots, k_n$, and the rest random, what is the probability of event E?* In this model, it is obvious that the probability of the event A, i connecting to j, equals $\frac{k_i}{n-1}$ and the probability of the event B, j connecting to i, equals $\frac{k_j}{n-1}$. However, either A or B confirms E, therefore we set $P(E) = \max(P(A), P(B))$. In other words, with respect to i, the probability of selecting j as one of i's neighbors is $\frac{k_j}{n-1}$. We cannot achieve a higher score unless $k_j > k_i$, thus the probability of the fact that two nodes are connected is decided by the node with the higher degree. Note that $P(E) \neq P(A) * P(B)$ since the two events A and B are dependent on each other.

8.4.2 Ordering Nodes to Visualize Networks

Now we can generate network visualizations by ordering nodes based on their rela-tion scores. Given the relationship function we defined above, for a node n_i, we create a list of nodes l_i ordered by their relation to n_i from high to low. (Note that we can limit candidate nodes to those which have $R > 0$, i.e., they are connected to or share at least one neighbor with n_i.) We define the kth value in this list to be l_{ik}. Here, our approach takes one input parameter s. However, as we will show in Section 8.5, s does not strongly affect the output. In practice, we usually generate several visualizations with s ranging from 2 to 8 and let the user make a choice based on their observations. For a node n_i, we define its community score C_s to be the sth value in its node list l_i, i.e., $C_s(n_i) = l_{is}$, and $C_s(n_i) = 0$ if there are less than s nodes in the list. Then we define the reachability of node j with respect to i as

$$\text{reach}_s(i,j) = \begin{cases} R(i,j) & \text{if } C_s(n_i) > R(i,j) \\ C_s(n_i) & \text{otherwise} \end{cases}$$

Intuitively, the parameter s represents the expected number of nodes that one node is similar with in order to be a member of any community. C_s is the lowest relation score between node i and its similar neighbors in one community. Then the reach-ability score from node i to j ($\text{reach}_s(i,j)$) is the relation score between nodes i and j if j is not among the top s nodes of l_i and is the community score of i otherwise. Thus, $\text{reach}_s(i,j)$ measures the community relationship between i and j. It is their direct distance score if i and j are far away from each other and equals the commu-nity radius of i if j is close enough. Therefore, a decreasing order of the reachability scores (RS) indicates a node list for i, starting from i's most related neighbors to the least ones.

We present our algorithm to generate node lists ordered by their reachability scores in Algorithm 1. More specifically, our algorithm creates an ordering of net-work nodes, additionally storing a reachability score RS(i) for each node i. It starts at a given node n_{start} and inserts n_{start} into a max-heap structure h, which is main-tained to store the reachability of candidate nodes. At each step, the node j, which has the highest reachability score in h, is chosen to be the next node in order and the popped score is stored as RS(j). All nodes that are in j's neighborhood are then inserted into h with their reachability according to j if they are not yet in h. The value in h is updated if the node is already in h and its new score is higher. Then h is updated to maintain its max-heap property. Therefore, the top node of heap h has the highest RS value to one of the nodes that has already been included in the list L, i.e., the RS score for each node in the list represents its highest reachability from any of the prior nodes in the sequence. The algorithm stops after all nodes in the network are visited.

Algorithm 1 The ONDOCS Algorithm: Network Visualization

Input: A social network G with n nodes and m edges, a start node n_{start} and possible s values $s_0, s_1, s_2 ....$
Output: A list of nodes L with their Reachability Scores RS for each s.
1. Sort a node list l_i for each node n_i, ordered by their relation score to n_i, from high to low.
2. For each s :
   Initialize a max-heap h, insert n_{start} in h with $RS = 0$.
   Select the sth largest element in l_i for each node n_i as its community score $C_s(n_i)$.
   While (there are still nodes in heap h) :
      Pop the node α in h with largest value ε.
      Store α in L_s with $RS_\alpha = \varepsilon$.
      For all nodes x in l_α :
         If $x \notin h$, insert x into h with $reach_s(\alpha, x)$.
         If $x \in h$, update its value if $reach_s(\alpha, x)$ is larger.
      Update max-heap h.
3. Return list L_s with RS values for each s value.

The computational complexity of ONDOCS is $O(n \log n)$ for dense graphs and $O(n)$ for sparse ones. The list generation and sort step takes $O(c \log cn)$ where constant c is the average number of similar nodes for each node. Note that based on our relationship function, one node can only be similar to another if they are connected or share one or more neighbors. In step 2, there are n insertions to the heap h and updating h for each insertion takes $O(\log n)$ time for dense graphs and $O(1)$ for sparse networks. Thus, the actual running time of our algorithm on experimental networks is $O(n)$ as shown in Section 8.5.

In summary, given a network with a list of s values, Algorithm 1 produces a sequence of nodes with their reachability scores for each s value, which can be visualized as a 2D graph by tools such as GNUPlot [11]. The visualizations show interesting community information such that nodes in the same communities are consecutive in the list with high RS scores, while the RS score apparently drops between two groups of community nodes (see Fig. 8.3). The goal of visual data mining is to help user acquire accurate parameters by observing this phenomenon, which is presented in the next section. (A detailed example of how to choose the parameters is given in Section 8.5.2 and Fig. 8.3 after explaining the experiments.)

8.4.3 Detecting Overlapping Community Structure: Communities, Hubs, and Outliers

We have generated lists of nodes given specific s values, where we found that the ordering of the corresponding RS values has interesting community properties. For example, if we start from one node i, we will first visit other nodes in i's community in sequence. This is because the reachability score from i to these nodes is higher than nodes outside i's community. Therefore, each community can be seen as a group of consecutive nodes with high RS scores. In a 2D visualization, these groups are represented as curves in a "mountain" shape or peak. A noticeable drop of subsequent RS scores after a "mountain" indicates that this community has ended, which is represented as a curve in a "valley" shape or trough. The "valley" between two "mountains" represents a set of hubs, which belong to several communities. For instance, if we start from nodes in community α, the fact that hubs have neighbors from different communities makes RS scores of hubs lower than that of those single-community nodes in α but still higher than nodes in communities other than α. Therefore, after all single-community nodes in α are visited, hubs are next to follow before nodes in other communities, which form the "valley" between "mountains."

As we have discussed in Section 8.1, there is no global community definition, thus communities in specific networks need to be defined by parameters given by the user. For this purpose, our visual data mining approach generates visualizations with different s values first. After the user selects the suitable one based on their observation, they need to further provide two parameters to define the communities in this network, *Community Threshold (CT)* and *Outlier Threshold (OT)*. While such parameters are usually hard to obtain for previous methods, parameter selection for our approach becomes easy since we provide a visualization of the network structure with "mountains" representing strongly related communities and "valleys" representing hub nodes that connect to both communities. Outliers are usually found at the end of the list, since their RS scores to any other nodes in the network are low. Examples of choosing parameters for real networks are presented in Section 8.5. Note that we do not require k, the number of communities to discover, as a parameter. The number of communities is a by-product of the mining process given the parameters OT and CT which are determined by the user after exploiting our visualization output. The visualization of the network helps the user understand the structure first and then decide about reasonable thresholds for communities and outliers, i.e., not the numbers per se but has a similar effect.

Given the two parameters CT and OT, our algorithm works as the following: from the first node in the sequence as the starting community, we scan all nodes along the list. One node n_i is merged into the current community if $RS(n_i) < CT$. If $CT \geq RS(n_i) > OT$, n_i is classified as a hub. If $OT \geq RS(n_i)$, it is an outlier. Since the first node of a community in the list has a low RS score, e.g., the starting node has $RS = 0$, we refine the outlier and hub nodes by moving any node n_i into corresponding communities if we have $RS(n_{i+1}) \leq CT$ (also see Algorithm 2). The complexity of Algorithm 2 is $\theta(n)$.

To represent that hubs can belong to k communities, for each hub node i, we use a vector of "belonging factors" $v = (f_{(i,1)}, f_{(i,2)}, \ldots, f_{(i,k)})$ where each coefficient $f_{(i,k)}$ measures the strength of the relationship between node i and community k. For every community C_k, we can quantify the overall relationship between i and C_k as

$$OR_{(i,k)} = \begin{cases} \sum_{x \in C_k} R(i,x) & \text{if } \sum_{x \in C_k} R(i,x) > 0 \\ 0 & \text{otherwise} \end{cases}$$

We then normalize the vector to get the coefficients so that we have $\sum_{x=1}^{k} f_{(i,x)} = 1$. Therefore, one node can belong to many communities at the same time,

Algorithm 2 The ONDOCS Algorithm: Overlapping Community Structure Detection

Input: A list L of nodes $n_0, n_1, \ldots$ and their RS scores, the Community Threshold CT and the Outlier Threshold OT.

Output: A list of communities $c_0, c_1, \ldots$, hubs $h_0, h_1, \ldots$ and outliers $o_0, o_1, \ldots$.

1. Create a community c, set $k = 0$.
2. **for** each $n_i \in L$ **do**
   If $RS(n_i) \geq CT$, classify n_i as a community node.
   else if $CT > RS(n_i) > OT$, classify n_i as a hub.
   else classify n_i as an outlier.
   end if
   If i is not classified as a community node but $RS(n_{i+1}) \geq CT$
   classify i as a community node.
   end if
   If n_i is a community node, insert n_i into c.
   else (n_i is a hub or an outlier)
     If $|c|! = 0$, save c as a community c_k for output
        reset c for the next community, increase index k by 1
    end if
   end if
  end for
3. Return communities $c_0, c_1, \ldots$, hubs $h_0, h_1, \ldots$ and outliers $o_0, o_1, \ldots$.

weighted by the relationship value in the range $[0,1]$ and the sum of belonging coefficients to communities is the same for all nodes in the network, except outliers.

In summary, the community mining process is aided by visual data mining in our approach. Instead of asking the user to arbitrarily provide vital parameters, we generate visualizations of the network in question so that the user is able to observe the structure and relations between communities before they give parameters. After appropriate parameters are determined, hubs and outliers are extracted together with communities. Note that another advantage of our approach is that while parameters are easy to be altered, the impact on the change of discovered communities can be clearly perceived by observing the visualization.

8.5 Experiment Results

Here we evaluate the ONDOCS approach using both synthetic and real-world data sets. The performance of ONDOCS is compared with CFinder [26] and CONGO [13], which are shown to be two of the most efficient algorithms for finding overlapping community structure [13]. The comparison is measured by the well-known F-measure score and adjusted rand index (ARI) [33]. All experiments were conducted on a PC with a 3.0 GHz Xeon processor and 4 GB of RAM.

8.5.1 ONDOCS Scalability

To evaluate the scalability of our algorithm, we generated ten random graphs of vertices ranging from 10,000 to 500,000 and the number of edges ranging from 20,000 to 1,000,000. The edges are randomly distributed in the network. Figure 8.2 shows the performance of our algorithm on those networks. It clearly shows that, although the running time of ONDOCS is $O(n \log n)$ in the worst case, our approach actually runs very close to linear time with respect to the number of vertices and edges.

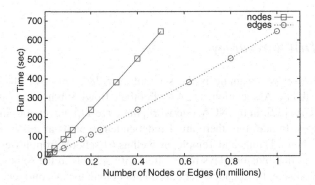

Fig. 8.2 ONDOCS algorithm running time

To further evaluate the efficiency of the algorithm, we apply three algorithms on several real-world networks. Table 8.2 shows the source of each network, its statistics, and the execution times for CONGO to compute the entire dendrogram, CFinder (v1.21) to generate solutions for $3 \le k \le 8$ and ONDOCS to create data set visualizations for $2 \le s \le 8$. From the table, we can see that ONDOCS works well overall, while CONGO's running time increases dramatically with respect to h and CF's clique detection becomes slow on some particular networks. (Note

Table 8.2 Comparing running time of CONGO, CF, and ONDOCS on real-world networks

Data sets	Vertices	Edges	CONGO [13] $h = 3$	$h = 2$	CF [26]	ONDOCS
Football [32]	180	787	8	2	1	<1
Protein_protein [26]	2640	6600	114	11	3	11
Blogs [13]	3982	6803	41	8	4	12
PGP [6]	10680	24316	772	104	>20000	62
Word_association [26]	7207	31784	15922	230	102	161
Blogs2 [13]	30557	82301	15148	380	319	269
Cond-mat [21]	27519	116181	>20000	1486	490	544

(Runtime / s)

that it may seem to be unfair to compare since ONDOCS merely generates visualizations but not communities yet. However, the intent of runtime comparison is to demonstrate that our approach is no more time consuming than previous methods but on the contrary in most cases faster. Additionally, the complexity of extracting communities after parameter setting, i.e., selecting CT and OT, is negligible compared to the visualization generation.) Unfortunately, we do not have ground truth to validate the accuracy of our results for these data sets, thus we turn to several real-world data sets with ground truth to evaluate the accuracy of our approach.

8.5.2 ONDOCS Accuracy

The first data set we examine is the schedule for 787 games of 2006 National Collegiate Athletic Association (NCAA) Football Bowl Subdivision (also known as Division 1-A) [32]. In the NCAA network, there are 115 universities divided into 11 conferences. In addition, there are 4 independent schools at this level, namely Navy, Army, Notre Dame, and Temple, as well as 61 schools from lower divisions. Each school in the division plays more often with schools in the same conference than schools outside. Independent schools do not belong to any conference and play with teams in different conferences, while lower division teams play only very few games. In our network vocabulary, this network contains 180 vertices (115 nodes as 11 communities, 4 hubs, and 61 outliers), connected by 787 edges.

First, the ONDOCS approach generates several visualizations with different s values for the user to choose. We show all visualizations for $2 \leq s \leq 8$ in Fig. 8.3. As we can see, most images are very similar to each other. The only one that shows a different structure is the visualization for $s = 8$. Recall that the parameter s represents the expected number of nodes that one node is similar with in order to be considered as a community member. When s is raised to a large value, some communities might disappear if their size is smaller than s. In this case, ONDOCS visualizations only show the structure of communities whose size is greater or equal to s. The larger the s value is, the smoother the curves are and the fewer "spikes" we have. Nevertheless, we have 7 visualizations that clearly represent the network structure, where there are 11 communities, a few hubs, and a set of outliers.

The parameter selection is solely based on users' visual interpretation of the visualized network. First we choose the visualization with $s = 2$, where the community structure is shown in most detail since pair relations are mostly measured as direct distance. In Fig. 8.4, we note that nodes in sequence from 120 to 180 are barely related to the rest and can be considered as outliers, therefore we set OT = 2. Note that OT can also be set as 2.5, or any other close number. Different OT values will not give completely different results and the impact can be perceived directly from the visualization. Furthermore, we see a community usually ends with a RS score between 3 and 5, thus we set CT = 4.5 so that all communities are separated. The range of possible thresholds is shown in the figure. Table 8.3 shows results of varying CT and OT in the range. As can be noticed, it is quite easy for one to select

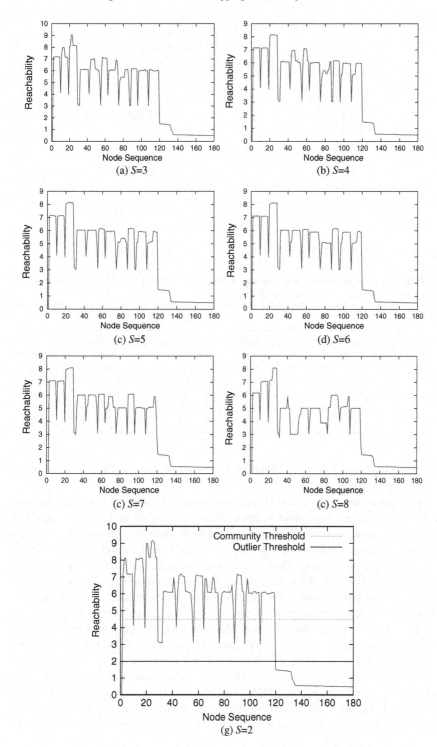

Fig. 8.3 Community visualizations of the football network with different S values

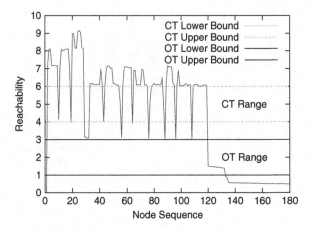

Fig. 8.4 Selecting CT and OT for ONDOCS

Table 8.3 Comparing ONDOCS accuracy with different CT and OT (H-FM means F-measure for Hubs and O-FM means F-measure for Outliers.x)

	OT = 2					CT = 4.5				
CT	Cluster	Hub	H-FM	Outlier	O-FM	OT	Cluster	Hub	H-FM	Outlier	O-FM
4.0	9	3	0.857	61	1.0	1.0	11	16	0.30	48	0.880
4.5	11	3	0.857	61	1.0	1.5	11	4	0.75	60	0.991
5.0	11	3	0.857	61	1.0	2.0	11	3	0.857	61	1.0
5.5	11	6	0.8	61	1.0	2.5	11	3	0.857	61	1.0
6.0	12	7	0.77	61	1.0	3.0	11	3	0.857	61	1.0

parameters given the network visualization, and the results are stable enough for a large range of parameters.

To evaluate how algorithms detect overlapping community structure, we provide the data to our algorithms in three different ways. At first, we give only 115 community nodes and connections between them, then we measure the accuracy of discovered communities by the ARI score based on the ground truth, which is the conference assignment. Then we add the four hubs and their connections into the network. Although these hubs clearly belong to multiple communities, we do not have exact ground truth for overlapping community structure, i.e., which communities these hubs should go. However, we do have ground truth for which nodes are hubs (outliers) and which are not. Therefore, we measure the accuracy of the output hubs and outliers by the F-measure score, which is defined as the harmonic mean of precision and recall. Finally we give the complete network with communities, hubs, and outliers. Table 8.4 shows the experimental results for the three algorithms. As we can see, the CONGO algorithm always detects overlaps, even for the first network where there are only community nodes. Additionally, it requires the cluster number as the input parameter, which is usually unavailable for real-world

Table 8.4 Comparing algorithm accuracy of CONGO, CF, and ONDOCS on the football data set

		Algorithms		
Data Setting		CONGO $(h = 2)$	CF $(k = 4)$	ONDOCS $(s = 2)$ $(CT = 4.5, OT = 2)$
115 nodes in	Cluster	11[a]	11	11
11 clusters	Hub	92	6	0
	ARI	0.047	0.945	1.00
Plus 4 hubs	Cluster	11[a]	12	11
	Hub	100	8	3
	Hub F-measure	0.038	0.167	0.857
Plus 4 hubs	Cluster	11[a]	12	11
and 61	Hub	96	8	3
outliers	Hub F-measure	0.04	0.167	0.857
	Outlier	0	61	61
	Outlier F-measure	0	1.00	1.00

[a]The right cluster number is provided as a parameter for the CONGO algorithm

networks, and it still fails to find any outliers. The CF algorithm gives its best result when $k = 4$, where it detects all outliers and finds 12 clusters, which is very close to the truth. However, CF also finds hubs when there is no overlap and the accuracy of its overlap detection is low with only a 0.167 F-measure score. Our ONDOCS algorithm works the best overall. It finds all outliers and only detects hubs when there is indeed some overlap between communities. The hub detection accuracy is not perfect; however, when we look into the data, we find out that the only missing hub team (Temple) plays half of its games (6 out of 12) with teams from the mid-American conference, which explains why it is classified into that community. Note that the result of our algorithm depends on two parameters (CT and OT); however, we believe that appropriate values are easy to find based on direct observation on network visualizations.

In ONDOCS, the node sequence might change if we choose different node n_{start} to start with. For previous experiments, we choose a community node to start the process. In Fig. 8.5, visualizations that start from hub nodes and outlier nodes are shown. However, as we can see, a community, represented by a "mountain" curve, is found first. It is because our algorithm intends to visit the closest nodes in the sequence, which have higher RS scores, before nodes that are far away. Thus, no matter where the start node is, the closest community is found first, followed by other communities ordered by their RS values. Hubs are found as "valley" between communities.

We also apply our algorithm on other real-world networks, including the Political Book network [17], the Mexican Politician network [25], the Dolphin network [24], and the Les Miserables network [16]. Although we do not have exact

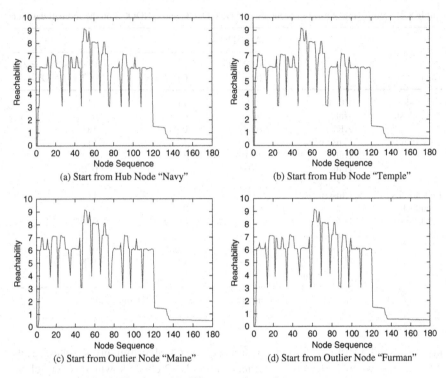

Fig. 8.5 ONDOCS visualizations with different starting nodes

overlapping truth for these networks, approximate community structure information is provided by previous research. In the Political Books data set, nodes represent political books sold by Amazon.com and edges represent frequent co-purchasing of books by the same buyers, as indicated by the "customers who bought this book also bought these items" feature on Amazon. Nodes are manually labeled as "Liberal," "Neutral," or "Conservative" by Mark Newman [20]. In the Mexican Politicians data set, edges indicate social relations between people and nodes represent politicians, who are classified based on their background as "Citizen" or "Military." The Dolphin Network gives the community structure of a group of bottlenose dolphins. The network can be approximately divided into four main groups [24]. Finally, the Les Miserables network represents the coappearance network of characters in the novel Les Miserables. Note that for these data sets, we only have indefinite community information instead of perfect ground truth, which is the common case for overlapping community detection and evaluation. We show visualizations for these data sets generated by ONDOCS in Fig. 8.6. One can see that the images correctly depict the approximate community information we have. Accurate CT and OT values should be easy to determine based on these figures. Also note that if the reachability plots are not clear for some data sets, the users may have problems

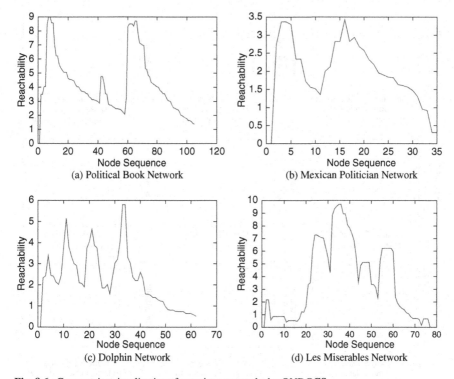

Fig. 8.6 Community visualizations for various networks by ONDOCS

selecting parameters. This could be the case when a large number of real communities exist, where the plot would present a jagged graph with many close peaks for a vague community structure. This is a limitation of the visualization and may be addressed by increasing the screen real-estate or a progressive hierarchical method, which selects parameters for each level of the community hierarchy. However, it is nevertheless reasonable to believe that other approaches with no visual data mining support, when faced with a large number of existing communities, would provide less information and do even worse in the mining process.

8.5.3 Comparing Metrics Within ONDOCS

We have reviewed previous community mining metrics (Q and S) and proposed our relational metric R. We then evaluated them from a theoretical perspective. Here we apply these three metrics to measure the similarity between two nodes in our ONDOCS system and compare the images generated for several real-world data sets, respectively, in order to further evaluate the effectiveness of the metrics.

The visualizations for four different data sets based on metrics Q, S, and R are shown in Fig. 8.7a–l, respectively (s is set to 2 for all metrics). We see that the plots

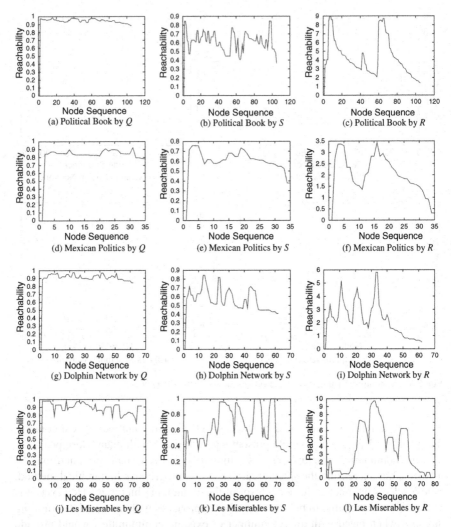

Fig. 8.7 Comparing metrics Q, S, and R with ONDOCS visualizations

using the R metric accurately depict the network structure since they match the vague community information that we have for those data sets. On the other hand, visualizations using the S metric are ambiguous and the community structure is hard to read. Also note that the R visualizations provide a much wider range for the user to observe accurate CT and OT values to detect the right number of communities than the S visualizations. Finally, visualizations based on the Q metric do not show any community structure. The reason is that Q does not consider local structure thus similarity scores of all node pairs are smaller than and close to 1 after node ordering, which makes the plots into a nearly horizontal line.

8.6 Conclusions

In this chapter, we first propose a general definition of communities in social networks and a list of requirements for a good similarity metric to detect those communities. We analyze existing metrics based on those criteria and then propose a new similarity metric R which satisfies all of those requirements. A visual data mining approach for overlapping community detection in networks is then proposed based on metric R. The method first generates lists of nodes, ordered by their reachability scores. Network visualizations are then provided to help the user determine important parameters. Finally, overlapping community structure, i.e., communities, hubs, and outliers, are extracted based on these parameters. Experiment results show that our approach not only scales well for large networks but also achieves a high accuracy for real-world networks. Unlike previous approaches, our method only detects overlap when it exists. Moreover, appropriate parameters are easy to obtain by means of visual data mining. The effectiveness of R over previous metrics is also confirmed by comparing ONDOCS visualizations.

Acknowledgments Our work is supported by the Canadian Natural Sciences and Engineering Research Council (NSERC), by the Alberta Ingenuity Centre for Machine Learning (AICML), and by the Alberta Informatics Circle of Research Excellence (iCORE).

References

1. Ankerst, M., Breunig, M.M., Kriegel, H.P., and Sander, J. Optics: Ordering points to identify the clustering structure. In *SIGMOD*, Philadelphia, PA, pp. 49–60, 1999.
2. Ankerst, M., Elsen, C., Ester, M., and Kriegel, H.P. Visual classification: An interactive approach to decision tree construction. In *KDD*, San Diego, CA, pp. 392–396, 1999.
3. Ankerst, M., Ester, M., and Kriegel, H.P. Towards an effective cooperation of the user and the computer for classification. In *KDD*, New York, NY, pp. 179–188, 2000.
4. Ankerst, M., and Keim, D.A. Visual data mining. San Francisco, CA, *Tutorial at SIAM Int. Conf on Data Mining*, 2003.
5. Baumes, J., Goldberg, M.K., and Magdon-Ismail, M. Efficient identification of overlapping communities. In *ISI*, New York, NY, pp. 27–36, 2005.
6. Boguñá, M., Pastor-Satorras, R., Díiaz-Guilera, A., and Arenas, A. Models of social networks based on social distance attachment. *Physical Review E*, 70(5):056,122, 2004.
7. Clauset, A., Newman, M.E.J., and Moore, C. Finding community structure in very large networks. *Physical Review E*, 70:066,111, 2004.
8. Danon, L., Duch, J., Diaz-Guilera, A., and Arenas, A. Comparing community structure identification. *Journal of Statistical Mechanics: Theory and Experiment*, 9:P09008–09008, 2005.
9. Ding, C.H.Q., He, X., Zha, H., Gu, M., and Simon, H.D. A min-max cut algorithm for graph partitioning and data clustering. In *ICDM*, San Jose, CA, pp. 107–114, 2001.
10. Duch, J., and Arenas, A. Community detection in complex networks using extremal optimization. *Physical Review E*, 72:027,104 2005.
11. Gnuplot: http://www.gnuplot.info/
12. Gregory, S. An algorithm to find overlapping community structure in networks. In *PKDD*, Warsaw, Poland, pp. 91–102, 2007.
13. Gregory, S. A fast algorithm to find overlapping communities in networks. In *PKDD*, Bristol, pp. 408–423, 2008.

14. Guimera, R., and Amaral, L.A.N. Functional cartography of complex metabolic networks. *Nature*, 433:895–900, 2005.
15. Han, J., and Cercone, N. Ruleviz: A model for visualizing knowledge discovery process. In *KDD*, Boston, MA, pp. 244–253, 2000.
16. Knuth, D.E. *The stanford graphbase: A platform for combinatorial computing*. Reading, MA, Addison-Wesley, 1993.
17. Krebs, V. http://www.orgnet.com/
18. Li, X., Liu, B., and Yu, P.S. Discovering overlapping communities of named entities. In *PKDD*, Heidelberg, pp. 593–600, 2006.
19. Nepusz, T., Petróczi, A., Negyessy, L., and Bazso, F. Fuzzy communities and the concept of bridgeness in complex networks. *Physical Review E*, 77:016107, 2008.
20. Newman, M. http://www-personal.umich.edu/~mejn/netdata/
21. Newman, M.E.J. The structure of scientific collaboration networks. In *Proceedings of the National Academy of Science USA*, 98:404–409, 2001.
22. Newman, M.E.J. Fast algorithm for detecting community structure in networks. *Physical Review E*, 69:066133, 2004.
23. Newman, M.E.J. Finding community structure in networks using the eigenvectors of matrices. *Physical Review E*, 74:036104, 2006.
24. Newman, M.E.J., and Girvan, M. Finding and evaluating community structure in networks. *Physical Review E*, 69:026113, 2004.
25. Pajek: http://vlado.fmf.uni-lj.si/pub/networks/pajek/
26. Palla, G., Derenyi, I., Farkas, I., and Vicsek, T. Uncovering the overlapping community structure of complex networks in nature and society. *Nature*, 435:814, 2005.
27. Ruan, J. and Zhang, W. An efficient spectral algorithm for network community discovery and its applications to biological and social networks. In *ICDM*, Omoha, NE, pp. 643–648, 2007.
28. Shi, J. and Malik, J. Normalized cuts and image segmentation. *IEEE. Trans. on Pattern Analysis and Machine Intelligence*, 22(8):888–905, 2000.
29. Teoh, S.T. and Ma, K.L. Painting class: Interactive construction, visualization and exploration of decision trees. In *Proceedings of the Ninth ACM SIGKDD International Conference on Knowledge Discovery and Data Mining*, pp. 667–672, 2003.
30. Wei, F., Wang, C., Ma, L., and Zhou, A. Detecting overlapping community structures in networks with global partition and local expansion. In *Detecting International Asia-Pacific Web Conference (APWeb)*, pp. 43–55, 2008.
31. White, S., and Smyth, P. A spectral clustering approach to finding communities in graphs. In *Proceedings of the 2005 SIAM International Conference on Data Mining*, pp. 274–286, 2005.
32. Xu, X., Yuruk, N., Feng, Z., and Schweiger, T.A.J. Scan: A structural clustering algorithm for networks. In *Proceedings of the 13th ACM SIGKDD International Conference on Knowledge Discovery and Data Mining*, pp. 824–833, 2007.
33. Yip, K.Y., and Ng, M.K. Harp: A practical projected clustering algorithm. *IEEE TKDE*, 16(11):1387–1397, 2004.
34. Zaïane, O.R., Foss, A., Lee, C.H., and Wang, W. On data clustering analysis: Scalability, constraints, and validation. In *Pacific-Asia Conference on Knowledge Discovery and Data Mining*, pp. 28–39, 2002.
35. Zhang, S., Wang, R., and Zhang, X. Identification of overlapping community structure in complex networks using fuzzy c-means clustering. *Physica A*, 374:483–490, 2007.

Chapter 9
Framework for Fast Identification of Community Structures in Large-Scale Social Networks

Yutaka I. Leon-Suematsu and Kikuo Yuta

Abstract One of the most important features of real networks is the presence of community structures or the subset of nodes that are densely connected to each other when compared to the rest of the networks, which encode the information about the organization and functionality of the nodes. Social networking sites (SNS), which allow the interaction of millions of users, have important scientific and practical implications; however, they require the development of fast algorithms. We focus on the algorithm developed by Clauset, Newman, and Moore (CNM) and its widely used modifications to analyze the behavior and effectiveness in terms of speed. This chapter describes the inefficiencies of CNM and shows that the determinant factor that impacts the speed is the number of interconnected communities (NIC) that represent the number of operations performed when merging two communities. We propose a new improvement of CNM that considers the NIC and a new implementation framework to accelerate CNM. Our improvements were compared with the former CNM and its variations when applied to large-scale networks from seven real data sets (Mixi, Facebook, Flickr, LiveJournal, Orkut, YouTube, and Delicious) and five synthetic networks with different structural properties. The experimental results demonstrate that the performance of all algorithms is impacted by the structural properties of the network and our proposed improvements outperform former algorithms in terms of speed and modularity in most network structures, thereby showing its applicability to real large-scale networks.

Y.I. Leon-Suematsu (✉)
National Institute of Information and Communications Technology (NiCT),
3-5 Hikaridai, Seika-cho, Soraku-gun, Kyoto 619-0289, Japan
e-mail: yutaka.leon@acm.org

Leon-Suematsu and Yuta are contributed equally to this work

N. Memon et al. (eds.), *Data Mining for Social Network Data*,
Annals of Information Systems 12, DOI 10.1007/978-1-4419-6287-4_9,
© Springer Science+Business Media, LLC 2010

9.1 Introduction

The last decade witnessed the advent of online societies where millions and even trillions of human communications took place. Social networking sites such as Facebook, MySpace, Orkut, and hi5, social bookmarking services such as Delicious and Digg, and sharing services such as Flickr and MySpace are online services that are becoming popular. These services have experienced an explosive growth; Facebook has 400 million active users, Delicious has 5 millions users and 180 million unique URLs, and MySpace has over 130 million users. Several social networks with connections represented by friendship relations or similar interest are available in these services that provide targets to social networks for scientific and practical purposes.

One of the most important features of real networks is the presence of community structures or the cohesive subset of nodes with a higher density of inner connections and a lower density of outer connections. These communities reveal the internal organization of the nodes, where nodes with similar properties are located in the same community. For instance, studies in the field of network science have shown that each community exhibits different structural properties [24], and studies in biological networks found a correspondence between communities of behavioral or functional units [13].

The identification of community structures in large-scale SNSs is a prominent approach to identify the communities of users with similar profiles or similar interest; another use is the identification of similar topics. The identification of communities can be employed to analyze the dynamics of the organization of users, to identify targets for marketing, or to even help improve user experience through recommendation services. Despite the size of these networks, fast algorithms are indispensable.

Recently, there have been a large number of algorithms for community extraction, which can be classified into two groups: local and global search techniques. Local search techniques require initial seeds in order to start the community extraction around these seeds; techniques such as max-flow/min-cut are commonly employed [15]. On the other hand, global search techniques use the entire network, which includes diverse methods based on clique analysis [9], betweenness centrality [12], modularity measure [6, 22, 25], and others.

We are interested in community extraction over the entire network containing millions of nodes; however, many algorithms are impractical for these scales due to their high computational cost. One of the faster and scalable algorithms is the one proposed by Clauset, Newman, and Moore (CNM) with $O(n \log^2 n)$ [6], which is an improvement of the original algorithm proposed by Newman that has $O(n^2)$ [22] applied to networks with n nodes and m edges in good conditions of sparse networks. Their algorithm is based on the concept of modularity proposed by Newman and Girvan [25] as a measure of evaluating how well the network is partitioned. Danon, Diaz, and Arenas (DDA) [7] proposed a modification to improve the modularity while retaining its speed. Furthermore, Wakita and Tsurumi(WT) proposed some modifications to accelerate CNM, but encountered a decrease in modularity [29] in their fastest algorithm.

We identify the limitations of CNM and propose a new algorithm that produces faster results with adequate modularity. The main contributions of this study are summarized as follows:

- We identify several factors that impact the speed of CNM. CNM becomes slow during the first part of the process due to a large number of operations it performs, which can be reduced, if not avoided. The number of operations is determined by the number of interconnected communities (NIC) of all tentative communities that are aggregated during the process. It was observed that large communities are created in an unbalanced manner where they absorb small ones such as a snowball involving more operations than when combining the same nodes in a different order.
- We present a new improvement of CNM that considers the NIC to prioritize the combination of communities that produce an increment in modularity while limiting the number of operations.
- Limitations in the available implementations of CNM were evaluated and a new framework was proposed that was seven times faster than CNM in its original implementation when applied to the same network.
- Our improvements were compared with CNM and its variations when used in seven large-scale networks from real SNSs (Mixi, Facebook, Flickr, LiveJournal, Orkut, YouTube, and Delicious) and five synthetic networks with different structural properties. Several benchmarks were proposed but none of them considered a full set of large-scale networks with different structural properties. The results showed that the structure of the network strongly impacts the performance of all algorithms, where our algorithm outperforms former algorithms in terms of speed and modularity in most network structures.

The remaining part of this chapter is organized as follows. Section 9.2 describes the concept of modularity and its research trends. The details of CNM and its two main modifications are presented in Section 9.3. In Section 9.4, we analyze the behavior of CNM and its implementation inefficiencies. In Section 9.5, we present our proposed improved algorithm followed by our implementation framework. In Section 9.6, we evaluate the effectiveness of our improvements while comparing to the former CNM and its variations when used in real and synthetic data sets. Finally, the conclusions are presented in Section 9.7.

9.2 Modularity

9.2.1 Definition

One of the most important issues in the extraction of communities is the evaluation of how well a particular network is partitioned into communities. Newman and Girvan [25] introduced the concept of modularity Q as an attempt to measure that quality for unweighted networks. Subsequently, Newman extended the concept to weighted networks [21]. It is to be noted that by assigning a weight of 1 to all edges, we can represent unweighted networks. In this chapter, we employ the weighted version.

Let A be the adjacent matrix of a network with N nodes and M edges whose elements are as follows:

$$A(u,v) = \begin{cases} w_{uv} & \text{if } u \text{ and } v \text{ are connected} \\ 0 & \text{otherwise} \end{cases} \quad (9.1)$$

where w_{uv} represents the weight of the edge that connects nodes u and v. The overall weight is $m = \sum_u \sum_v A_{uv}/2$; the sum of the weights of edges attached to u is $k_u = \sum_v A_{uv}$. For unweighted networks, the measures represent the total number of links and the degree of node u.

Assuming that the network is divided into communities, such as node v belongs to community c_v, it is possible to define e_{ij}, which represents the fraction of the overall weight of edges that connect nodes in community i to nodes in community j:

$$e_{ij} = \frac{1}{2m} \sum_u \sum_v A_{uv}\, \delta(c_u, i)\, \delta(c_v, j) \quad (9.2)$$

Here, $\delta(i,j)$ is 1, if $i = j$, and 0 otherwise. The fraction of the sum of weights of edges attached to i is calculated by

$$a_i = \sum_j e_{ij} \quad (9.3)$$

Similarly, the fraction of the overall weight of the edges within a community, the edges that connect nodes in the same community i, is calculated by

$$e_{ii} = \frac{1}{2m} \sum_u \sum_v A_{uv}\, \delta(c_u, i)\, \delta(c_v, i) \quad (9.4)$$

Intuitively, good partitions of a network should have higher values of $\sum_i e_{ii}$. However, this is not sufficient because in cases when all nodes are located in individual communities, the value becomes 0, whereas when all nodes are located in one unique community, the value becomes 1. To avoid this issue, and by assuming that random connections do not produce community structures, the modularity Q is defined as the fraction of the overall weight of edges that fall within communities contrasted to the expected fraction when the connections between nodes are random:

$$Q = \sum_i \left(e_{ii} - a_i^2\right) \quad (9.5)$$

9.2.2 Research Trends

Since its conception, several researches have been focused on measurement. There are three categories: (1) modularity optimization algorithms, (2) analysis of modularity and its extensions, and (3) fast algorithms.

9.2.2.1 Modularity Optimization Algorithms

The first category consists of the creation of algorithms to optimize the partition that produces higher modularity. For example, Massen and Doye presented an algorithm based on simulated annealing with $O((n + m) n)$ [19], Duch and Arenas proposed a technique that used external optimization with $O(n^2 \log n)$ [10], and Cappocci et al. and Newman et al. proposed techniques based on spectral analysis with $O(n^2)$ [5] and $O((n + m) n) \sim O(n^2)$ [23], respectively. However, Brandes et al. demonstrated that the community extraction is a NP-complete problem [4], and as a consequence, any efficient algorithm yields suboptimal partitions in many instances.

9.2.2.2 Analysis of Modularity

This category consists of extensions of the concept, such as extensions to weighted and directed networks [17, 21, 26], and the analysis of the properties and limitations of modularity. It has been realized that this modularity measurement has some limitations. For instance, Guimera et al. showed that the partitions of ordinary random networks may have high modularity [14], and Fortunato et al. demonstrated that modularity optimization has a resolution limit failing to identify modules smaller than a scale that depends on the total size of the network and on the degree of interconnectedness of communities [11]. As a consequence, the results of modularity optimization may produce communities that contain smaller communities connected even by only one edge.

9.2.2.3 Fast Algorithms

This category consists of the development of algorithms that provide fast results with relatively adequate modularity, which differs from the first category where higher modularity is the main concern. The first fast algorithm was proposed by Newman [22] with $O((m + n) n)$ or $O(n^2)$ in the case of sparse networks. This was improved by Clauset, Newman, and Moore(CNM) [6], thereby reducing the complexity of the algorithm to $O(n \log^2 n)$ and making it possible to apply it to larger networks (hundred thousand nodes). Danon, Diaz, and Arenas (DDA) [7] made a modification to CNM by improving its modularity while retaining its speed. Wakita and Tsurumi(WT) [29], on the other hand, proposed some heuristics to improve the speed of CNM, but with compromises in modularity in their fastest algorithm. Recently, Blondel et al. [3] proposed an algorithm (BGLL), which differs from CNM, that consisted of repeating two phases: the combination of communities and the development of networks with the resulting communities, until no further increment in modularity is possible. We will use this algorithm for comparison purposes.

Since our concern is with the identification of communities in large-scale networks from SNSs, such as 10 million friendship networks, then the possibility of using costly algorithms is out of scope. Thus, we focus on fast algorithms. As described in Section 9.2.2.2, for large-scale networks, there is a resolution limit described by Fortunato et al. where there is a tendency of producing larger communities that may contain small communities with high density but lower connectivity between them. These small communities are kept intact, and therefore, they can be extracted by recursively executing the algorithm to the resulting communities, thereby obtaining a hierarchical structure of communities. Therefore, this resolution limit does not affect our purpose of identifying communities in large-scale SNSs.

9.3 Details of CNM and its Variations

We describe the details of CNM and its variations that are required to analyze the limitations of these algorithms; we explain our contributions. For explanatory purpose, we use the word *in-process community* to refer a set of nodes combined during the extraction process, which will be part of a community in the final partition.

9.3.1 CNM Algorithm

Initially, Newman proposed a greedy algorithm for fast community extraction [22] with $O((n+m)\,n) \sim O(n^2)$. The algorithm first assigns each node of the network to its own in-process community. Then, the change in Q, ΔQ, which may occur if any pair of in-process communities i and j is combined, is calculated by

$$\Delta Q = 2(e_{ij} - a_i\,a_j) \tag{9.6}$$

The algorithm proceeds by selecting a pair of in-process communities i and j with the largest contribution to Q, max ΔQ_{ij}, and combines them. Then, all values of ΔQ are recalculated by Eq. (9.6). The process is repeated (counted as one iteration) until the maximum Q is reached, which happens when max $\Delta Q_{ij} < 0$.

This algorithm uses an additional matrix to record the values of e_{ij}, which are required to recalculate the values of ΔQ_{ij}.

Then, Clauset, Newman, and Moore (CNM) [6] demonstrated that the ΔQ values can be updated by using the values of ΔQ from the previous iteration, thereby avoiding recalculations and maintenance of e_{ij} required in the original algorithm.

There are three possible outcomes when combining two in-process communities i in j, as depicted in Fig. 9.1, where the values of ΔQ are updated by

Fig. 9.1 ΔQ update operations when combining two in-process communities i and j, triangle update when k is connected to both i and j, and chain update when k is connected to i or j

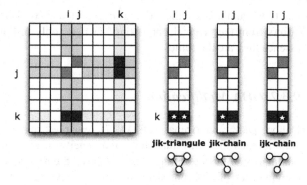

$$\Delta Q'_{jk} = \begin{cases} \Delta Q_{ik} + \Delta Q_{jk} & \text{if } k \text{ is connected to both } i \text{ and } j, \text{ jik-triangle} \\ \Delta Q_{ik} - 2a_j a_k & \text{if } k \text{ is connected to } i \text{ but not to } j, \text{ jik-chain} \\ \Delta Q_{jk} - 2a_i a_k & \text{if } k \text{ is connected to } j \text{ but not to } i, \text{ ijk-chain} \end{cases} \quad (9.7)$$

The resulting algorithm, which is used as a reference for explanations of CNM variations, is listed as follows:

step 1. Place each node in its own in-process community
step 2. Calculate initial ΔQ_{ij} for every edge (i, j) by Eq. (9.6)
step 3. Get a pair (i, j) that has $\max_{ij} \Delta Q_{ij}$
step 4. If $\Delta Q_{ij} < 0$, the max Q is reached and the algorithm terminates
step 5. Join community i and j
step 6. Update ΔQ of the resulting in-process community by Eq. (9.7)
step 7. Repeat step 3

Regarding the data structure, CNM uses three different data structures.

1. A matrix to store ΔQ, where each row i consists of a balanced binary tree to carry out insertion and search in $O(\log n)$; i represents the community id.
2. A max heap structure per row to locate and access the $\max_j \Delta Q_{ij}$ of row i in constant time, $O(1)$, while any update takes $O(\log n)$. It maintains another max heap H to store the $\max_j \Delta Q_{ij}$ element of every row i in order to access the overall maximum ΔQ in $O(1)$ and any update takes $O(\log n)$.
3. An ordinary vector array to store the values of a_i required chain-update operations of ΔQ.

The algorithm has an order of $O(md \log n) \sim O(n \log^2 n)$, where d is the depth of the dendrogram. Recently, Clauset[1] expressed that his implementation behaves

---

[1] http://cs.unm.edu/ aaron/blog/archives/2007/02/fastmodularity.htm

like $O(n^2)$ and not like the $O(n \log^2 n)$ reported in [6]. It should be noted that CNM differs from the original one, from Newman, only in how ΔQ is updated, but in essence they are the same.

9.3.2 DDA Modification

Danon, Diaz, and Arenas (DDA) [7] remarked that CNM combines in-process communities in a way that the heterogeneity in community sizes can affect the modularity of the algorithm. They proposed the normalization of ΔQ so as to treat communities of different sizes as equal by dividing ΔQ by k_i that represents the overall weight of all the edges of nodes in community i, or the degree for unweighted networks:

$$Q_{ij}^* = \frac{\Delta Q_{ij}}{k_i} \tag{9.8}$$

It should be noted that this measure is asymmetric, that is, $\Delta Q_{ij}^* \neq \Delta Q_{ji}^*$. DDA modifies step 3 of CNM by selecting a pair (i, j) with the $\max_{ij} \Delta Q_{ij}^*$; however, the update of ΔQ is kept the same as the former CNM. The new step 3 is as follows:

> step 3. Get a pair (i, j) that has $\max_{ij} \Delta Q_{ij}^*$

Danon et al. presented the experimental results showing that this modification produces an improvement in the modularity of 5.51% in average (S.D. = 5.35% in seven data sets.) It should be noted that the main purpose of this modification was to improve the modularity, not for the purpose of speed as they point out, "We propose a simple modification of the algorithm proposed by Newman which treats communities of different sizes on an equal footing, and show that it outperforms the original algorithm while retaining its speed" [7].

9.3.3 WT Modification

Wakita and Tsurumi (WT) [29] explained that CNM is slow because it combines in-process communities in an unbalanced way. They proposed some heuristics to speed up CNM by including a consolidation ratio based on the in-process community size. This ratio is defined as follows:

$$\text{ratio}(c_i, c_j) = \min \left(\frac{|c_i|}{|c_j|}, \frac{|c_j|}{|c_i|} \right) \tag{9.9}$$

where the size of the in-process community, $|c_i|$, can be represented by the composed number of nodes, or the degree of the in-process community. They modified step 3 of the CNM algorithm by selecting a pair (i,j) with the maximum value $\Delta Q_{ij} \times ratio(c_i, c_j)$ instead of the pair with the maximum ΔQ_{ij}. The new step 3 is as follows:

---

step 3. Get a pair (i,j) that has $\max_{ij} \Delta Q_{ij} \times ratio\,(c_i, c_j)$

WT becomes faster when compared to CNM by increasing the join priority between the communities of similar sizes. However, this modification compromises the modularity of the final result in their fastest algorithm.

Regarding the data structure, WT uses a matrix for ΔQ with rows consisting of double-linked list sorted by the node id.

9.4 CNM Speed Inefficiencies

As described previously, there are two main modifications of CNN–DDA that improves the modularity while retaining the speed, and WT that improves the speed but compromises the modularity. We analyze the behavior of CNM, WT, and DDA, discovering factors that make CNM inefficient in terms of speed.

9.4.1 Attractor of Large Communities

Wakita and Tsurumi [29] remarked that CNM combines unbalanced in-process communities by presenting a plot of the ratio between the degrees of combined in-process communities over the execution of the algorithm. Some intermittent fluctuations were found, showing that a combination of in-process communities is carried out in an unbalanced way by combining low-degree in-process communities with high-degree in-process communities. This inspired them to modify CNM by introducing a *consolidation ratio* explained in the previous section, giving more priority to the combination of in-process communities with similar sizes. Though their consolidation ratio provides good speed, there is no theoretical support to ensure its effectiveness. On the other hand, there is no explanation of what causes the fluctuations.

We assumed that the fluctuations might be caused by the creation of large in-process communities. We start analyzing the behavior of the CNM by observing how communities are combined during the process. The behavior of CNM during execution is depicted in Fig. 9.2a, when used in a friendship network of a SNS with 360,802 users and 1,904,641 friendship connections. The x-axis represents the iteration or the number of combination in the execution ofthe algorithm, while the

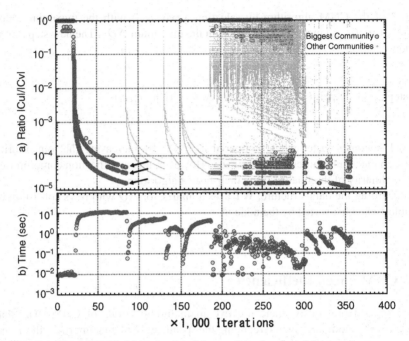

Fig. 9.2 Behavior of CNM. (a) The ratio of the number of nodes of the two in-process communities (c_u, c_v) that are selected for the combination in each iteration of the algorithm. (b) The accumulated elapsed time consumed in every 500 iterations

y-axis represents the ratio between the number of nodes of the combined pair of in-process communities. The small circles represent the ratio when combining in-process communities that will compose the resulting largest community, while the small dots represent the other cases.

It is observed that in the early phase of execution, nodes that compose the largest community are combined. The three curves marked with arrows reveal the creation of three large in-process communities that will be combined into one in further combinations. These curves clearly show that at a certain period of time large in-process communities attract smaller ones, such as a snowball, until they arrive to the point where further contributions to modularity are lower compared to other combinations. It should be noted that the first half of the graph displays the same phenomena for other large communities.

We analyze the attractor effect in terms of time consumption. Figure 9.2b presents the accumulated time required in every 500 iterations. By superposing Fig. 9.2(a, b), we observe that CNM becomes slow by the attractors of large communities. For instance, the attractor of the largest community is the one that produces the largest time consumption. The reason for this effect is explained in the next subsection.

9.4.2 Chain Effect

Wakita and Tsurumi improved the speed by including their ratio based on the community size or the community degree. Unfortunately, there is no proof that these variables directly influence the speed.

We assumed that the effect of attractors of large communities, in the execution time, is caused by the excessive number of update operations required when combining two in-process communities that have many connections with other in-process communities, regardless of their sizes and degrees. Figure 9.3a depicted the average number of update operations over every 500 iterations. As in Fig. 9.2a, the x-axis represents the iteration of the algorithm, while the small circles and small dots represent the number of chain updates and triangle updates generated when updating the values of ΔQ by Eq. (9.7).

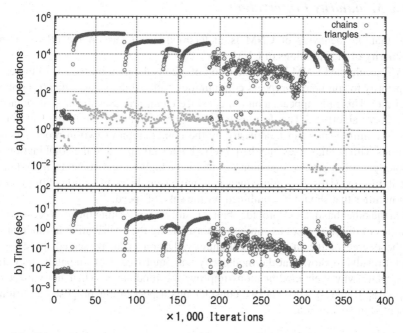

Fig. 9.3 Chain effect. (**a**) The average number of chain-update operations and triangle-update operations generated in every 500 iterations. (**b**) The accumulated elapsed time consumed in every 500 iterations

This figure clearly reveals that the number of chain updates is excessively higher in the first part of the execution that corresponds to the operations required by the attractors of large communities. When the attractor of the larger in-process communities absorbs smaller communities, it may increase the number of connections with other in-process communities; thus, the number of operations in further combinations of this in-process community may increase. For visual analysis, Fig. 9.2b was repeated as in Fig. 9.3b that presents the accumulated time required in every 500 iterations.

By superposing Fig. 9.3(a, b), we observe that the average number of generated chain updates and the execution time required for every 500 iterations have the same tendency; therefore, it proofs the direct influence the chain-update operation has over the execution time of the algorithm.

As a consequence, the determinant of speed is the number of chain operations required in every combination of in-process communities, which can be approximated by the number of interconnected communities (NIC) of in-process communities. The higher the NIC of an in-process community, the slower is the algorithm. We conclude that in order to accelerate CNM, it is necessary to manipulate the NIC of in-process communities.

9.4.3 Modularity Preservation

Now that the behavior of CNM is understood, we focus on the effect in the modularity of the variations of CNM.

WT accelerated CNM by the inclusion of a consolidation ratio so as to increase the priority to combine in-process communities with similar sizes, which is applied to all ΔQ. This ratio appears a bit radical since it compromises the final modularity in its faster algorithm. The decrement in modularity may be due to the fact that a very low improvement in modularity by the combination of two in-process communities with similar sizes may be preferred when compared to the combination of another pair of in-process communities that have higher improvements in modularity but different sizes. As a consequence, it may avoid the combination of in-process communities that should be combined for the sake of speed.

On the other hand, DDA provides better results when treating the in-process communities of different sizes as similar by normalizing the contribution in modularity by the degree of the in-process community. Danon et al. presented the experimental results to show that the modularity was improved. Unfortunately, they did not explain why their modifications improve the modularity. Their normalization process appeared to work and we consider this aspect in our proposed algorithm presented in Section 9.5.

9.4.4 Implementation Inefficiencies

Another important aspect for considering the analysis of inefficiencies of the algorithm is the implementation phase. There are two implementation frameworks – one for CNM and another for WT. We observed that they perform unnecessary calculations that can be reduced, if not avoided, which are considered in our proposed implementation framework presented in Section 9.5.

For undirected networks, the adjacency matrix is symmetric, and therefore, the information can be stored in a triangular sparse matrix. However, CNM and WT basically maintains the full adjacency matrix, storing both symmetric values ΔQ_{ij} and ΔQ_{ji}, which produces unnecessary operations because they must be permanently kept consistent. Therefore, when inserting any value ΔQ_{ij}, the insertion of its symmetric ΔQ_{ji} is also required, where each operation takes $O(\log n)$ for inserting column j in row i, with an additional cost of $O(\log n)$ for updating the max heap of the row in the case of CNM. A similar situation occurs when deleting an element.

During, or after, the combination of two in-process communities i and j, the updates in every pair (j, k) take $O(1)$ but updates in its symmetric pair (k, j) take $O(\log n)$ because it requires searching column j in row k. Additionally, these updates may search $\max_l \Delta Q_{kl}$. In the case of CNM, the max heap of every row is updated in every modification of ΔQ that takes $O(\log n)$, while WT takes $O(1)$ or $O(n)$ because it maintains a reference to the max value of the row.

9.5 Proposed Improvements

9.5.1 Acceleration of CNM

In Section 9.4.2, we concluded that the NIC of in-process communities is the determinant in the speed of the algorithm. Our analysis showed that CNM exhibits the attractor effect in large communities, which may increase the NIC after absorbing small ones, and therefore, slow down CNM.

We propose other improvement to CNM that reduces the number of operations while trying to maintain the modularity levels by using the following factor:

$$\text{factor}(i, j) = \frac{1}{\max(\text{nic}_i, \text{nic}_j)} \quad (9.10)$$

where nic_i is the number of interconnected communities of the in-process community i, which is simply the number of elements in row i. The dividend uses the maximum of both NICs because it approximates the number of operations required in the combination. The bigger the nic, the lower is the faction. Instead of nic_i, it is preferable to use the number of update operations that will be generated when combining i and j; however, recalculations of these values will be required for every possible combination of in-process communities, which is impractical for our purpose.

This factor is not applied to all the values of ΔQ because it may prioritize the combinations of in-process communities with reduced *nic* and low contributions of Q instead of combinations of in-process communities with high contribution and relative high nic.

In order to avoid the reduction of modularity Q, we first identify $\max_k \Delta Q_{ik}$ for an in-process community i and then apply the described factor only to the $\max_k \Delta Q_{ik}$, in contrast to WT in which the ratio is applied to all elements in the row (we applied to all elements and observed that modularity decreases as we expected). The resulting value is the one inserted to the max heap H in order to give priority to in-process communities with lower NIC, thereby reducing the number of chain operations. It must be noted that the factor is applied only for the updates of the max heap H, but the recalculation of ΔQ is the same as the former algorithms. The resulting algorithm is as follows:

step 1. Place each node in its own in-process community
step 2. Calculate initial ΔQ_{ij} for every edge (i,j) by Eq. (9.6)
step 3. Get a pair (i,j) that has

$$\max_i \left[(\max_j \Delta Q_{ij}) \times factor(c_i, c_{k_i}) \right] ; k_i = \arg\max_j \Delta Q_{ij}$$

step 4. If $\Delta Q_{ij} < 0$, the max Q is reached and the algorithm terminates
step 5. Join community i and j
step 6. Update ΔQ of the resulting in-process community by Eq. (9.7)
step 7. Repeat step 3

In this Chapter, this algorithm will be referred as LY.

The reduction of update operations obtained when used in the same data set employed to explain the inefficiencies of CNM is presented in Fig. 9.4. Similar to

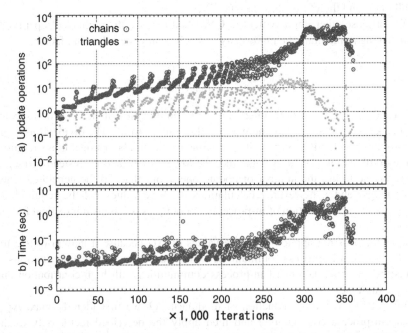

Fig. 9.4 Our LY algorithm behavior. (a) The average number of chain-updates and triangle-updates operations generated in every 500 iterations. (b) The accumulated elapsed time consumed in every 500 combinations

Figs. 9.3, 9.4(a, b) represent the average number of operations required in every 500 iterations and the time consumed for every 500 iterations, respectively. As expected, we observe a strong reduction in the number of chain-update operations compared to the results of CNM shown in Fig. 9.3 (Section 9.4.2). The algorithm starts combining in-process communities with lower NIC, and at the final part, it combines the remaining in-process communities with higher NIC, thereby obtaining a strong reduction in the overall execution time.

9.5.2 Implementation Improvements

9.5.2.1 Data Structure

Regarding implementation improvements, we employ two triangular matrices so as to avoid the previously described issues presented in Section 9.4.4. A lower triangular matrix stores ΔQ values in the form (i,j) where $i > j$; if $i < j$, the ΔQ values are stored in (j, i). A second triangular matrix (upper triangular matrix) stores the references of the symmetric values in the lower triangular matrix in order to access the data over the columns of the lower triangular matrix at a constant time $O(1)$, as depicted in Fig. 9.5a.

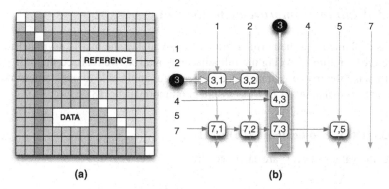

(a)   **(b)**

Fig. 9.5 A new framework. (**a**) Two triangular matrices–a lower triangular matrix (data) for values of ΔQ and an upper triangular matrix for references of their symmetric values located in the data matrix. (**b**) Data structure and how to iterate the elements of community 3

We use a balanced binary tree for rows in both triangular matrices – data and reference. The advantage of this structure is that deletions and updates of ΔQ are done in $O(1)$.

In order to iterate all the neighbors of community i, or the row in the symmetric matrix, it is necessary to iterate the elements in the lower triangular matrix and then switch to elements of the upper triangular reference matrix, thereby obtaining the position and access of the symmetric cell in the lower triangular matrix. The iteration is shown by the filled area in Fig. 9.5b, where the horizontal arrows represent the sequence over the lower triangular matrix and the vertical arrow represents the iteration of references stored in the upper triangular matrix to access its symmetric cell in the lower triangular matrix. This process can be carried out easily by the creation of a special *iterator* to switch the matrix when required.

We track the $\max_j \Delta Q_{ij}$ of row i for only the lower triangular matrix, thereby reducing the search space for the recalculation of the maximum ΔQ in the row when required.

9.5.2.2 Reduction of Unnecessary Operations

When all the values of ΔQ_{ij} in the lower triangular matrix are negative, for a certain in-process community i, its maximum value is assigned to a constant negative value in order to avoid unnecessary updates in the max heap H.

Similarly, when combining two in-process communities i and j, we keep track of the $\max_k \Delta Q_{jk}$ for the community j. In the case that this value is negative, this in-process community will produce no positive value under any circumstances (Eq. (9.7)); therefore, this row can be eliminated. In our framework, we eliminate these rows, thereby reducing unnecessary operations.

9.5.3 Additional Improvements to DDA

It was explained that the normalization of DDA makes the matrix asymmetric, and therefore, it requires storing the full adjacency matrix. We realized that it is possible to make the matrix symmetric, and therefore, applicable to our framework. We present two variations of DDA to assure good modularity [18].

9.5.3.1 DDA Modification 1 (DDA-M1)

Here, the values of ΔQ^* are calculated by

$$\Delta Q_{ij}^* = \frac{\Delta Q_{ij}}{\min(k_i, k_j)} \qquad (9.11)$$

This modification does not compromise the result since under any circumstances, for any pair i and j, the maximum value between ΔQ_{ij}^* and ΔQ_{ji}^* is produced by the minimum value of k_i and k_j. Therefore, only the maximum of both values is necessary to store in the triangular matrix. The new step 3 is as follows:

step 3. Get a pair (i,j) that has $\max_{ij} \Delta Q_{ij}^*$

9.5.3.2 DDA Modification 2 (DDA-M2)

Since DDA applies the normalization to all values of ΔQ, we assume that the modified ΔQ^* must be applied only to the maximum of ΔQ_{ij} per row rather than to all the elements of the matrix. The new step 3 is as follows:

step 3. Get a pair (i,j) that has

$$\max_i \left[\frac{\max_j \Delta Q_{ij}}{\min(k_i, k_{l_i})} \right] \; ; \; l_i = \arg\max_j \Delta Q_{ij}$$

9.6 Large-Scale Network

Here, we evaluate the effectiveness of our framework when compared to the original implementation of CNM. Then, we compare the performance of our algorithm with CNM, its variations, and a recently proposed method. These comparisons have been performed in large-scale networks from seven SNSs and five theoretical models. All programs were implemented in standard C++ and executed in a PC with the following configuration: CPU Xeon 2.8 GHz, 64 GB Ram, and Red Hat Linux. We should note that all the programs are single processes. For WT, we implemented the faster version and the one with better modularity, i.e., WT1 and WT2, respectively.

9.6.1 Data Set

9.6.1.1 Real-World Networks

1. *Mixi:* We use a data set of Mixi, the largest Japanese SNS, when it was at its earlier phase of uniform growth. The network consists of 360,802 users and 1,904,641 friendship connections. Ahn et al. expressed that SNSs presented multi-scaling behaviors [1]; however, our data set presented a uniform degree distribution that made it a special case.
2. *Delicious:* We crawled the user relationship from delicious during the period March 9-11, 2007. Our data set consists of 165,344 users and 417,179 friendship connections.
3. *Flickr:* We use a data set from Flickr, the largest photo-sharing site based on social networks, crawled by the Max-Planck Institute [20]. The undirected network consists of 1,715,255 users and 22,613,981 friendship connections.
4. *YouTube:* We use a data set from YouTube, the largest video-sharing site with social networks, crawled by the Max-Planck Institute [20]. The undirected network consists of 1,138,499 users and 4,945,382 friendship connections.

5. *LiveJournal:* We use a data set from LiveJournal, a popular blogging site whose users form a social network, crawled by the Max-Planck Institute [20]. The undirected network consists of 5,204,176 users and 77,402,652 friendship connections.
6. *Orkut:* We use a data set from Orkut, a popular SNS run by Google, crawled by the Max-Planck Institute [20]. The undirected network consists of 3,072,441 users and 223,534,301 friendship connections.
7. *Facebook:* We use a data set from Facebook, the largest worldwide SNS, crawled by the Max-Planck Institute [28] that focused on the New Orleans regional network. The undirected network consists of 63,731 users and 1,545,686 friendship connections.

9.6.1.2 Theoretical Models

For an appropriate analysis of the influence of the structural properties of networks, we use the following theoretical models that exhibit different structural properties.

1. *Beta model:* The beta model [30] proposed by Watts-Strogatz (WS) had the rewiring probability of 25%.
2. *Preferential attachment model:* The preferential attachment model [30] proposed by Barabási-Albert (BA) had each new vertex with degree $m = 5,6$.
3. *Connecting nearest neighbor model:* The connecting nearest neighbor (CNN) model proposed by Vázquez [27] had the single parameter $\mu = 0.81$.
4. *Connecting nearest neighbor with random linkage:* The connecting nearest neighbor with random linkage (CNNR) model proposed by Yuta, Fujiwara, and Ono [31] had random rewiring of 16%. This model extends CNN by introducing random linkage between nodes. Its authors expressed that the CNNR model produces SNS-like networks.
5. *Fully randomized CNN model:* Fully randomized CNN (CNN-FR), which consists of creating a network with the CNN model with the single parameter $\mu = 0.81$ and randomizing the entire network but maintaining the same degree distribution, thereby keeping it as a single connected component without parallel edge and self-loops.

9.6.2 Framework Effectiveness

First, we evaluate the effectiveness of our framework by comparing the original CNM, implemented and distributed by Clauset[2], with the CNM implemented under our framework. The effectiveness is evaluated using the same networks. Due to the

---

[2]http://www.cs.unm.edu/ aaron/research/fastmodularity.htm

scalability limitations of the original CNM for applying it to networks with over million nodes, we evaluate them in networks from 10 nodes to 3 million nodes ($k = 5$) generated by the CNNR model ($r_{ccnr} = 4\%$) that produces SNS-like networks rather than the real large data sets.

Comparative results are displayed in Fig. 9.6. Figure 9.6a presents the execution time of each implementation in different network sizes. We fit the execution time vs. the network size per implementation; the curves are displayed for reference. These results indicate that the CNM under our framework is seven times faster than the original implementation of CNM. Further, it is observed that the order of CNM for this experiment is $O(n^2)$. The original CNM was executed for up to 1 million nodes, which took around 45 h. In the case of a network with 10 million nodes, the original CNM will require about 183 days, while the CNM under our framework will take about 25 days. This confirms that CNM is impractical to apply to large-scale networks.

Figure 9.6b presents a snapshot when applied to a network with 1 million nodes and 5 million edges. Both implementations produce similar results in modularity and number of communities; thus, our implementation is correct. The number of communities is slightly different due to the fact that for large networks, CNM produces slightly different results when a different order of combinations of pairs of in-process communities with the same high ΔQ is taken. This is reproduced by simply shuffling the node id labels in the network. This variation in the selection order also brings a difference in the number of nodes in the largest community in the experiment. It may be caused by composed small communities that are weakly connected to others (explained by the resolution limit) that may be grouped with other weakly connected communities since the selection order was changed. In our implementation, since we employ a triangular matrix for the data, the real maximum ΔQ

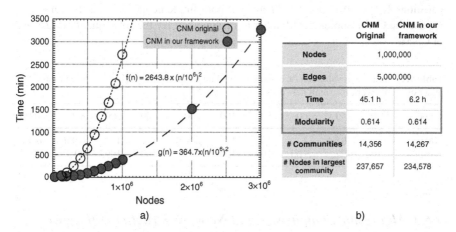

Fig. 9.6 Comparison of the effectiveness of the original CNM implemented by its proposer and the CNM implemented under our framework; two reference curves that fit the execution time in both implementations are included

of a row, in the symmetric matrix, may be located in its symmetric position; therefore, the position in the max heap H can be different among equal ΔQ, and so is the selection order of the pairs.

We evaluate how similar the resulting partitions of the network are by the normalized mutual information (NMI) measurement used in the information theory and arranged for community structures in [8], which uses a confusion matrix M where rows correspond to the communities of the baseline partition and columns correspond to the target partition. M_{ij} corresponds to the number of nodes in the baseline community i that appears in the target community j. The NMI is calculated by

$$\text{NMI}(A, B) = \frac{-2 \sum_{i=1}^{c_A} \sum_{j=1}^{c_B} M_{ij} \log \left(\frac{M_{ij} N}{M_{i.} M_{.j}} \right)}{\sum_{i=1}^{c_A} \log \left(\frac{M_{i.}}{N} \right) + \sum_{j=1}^{c_B} \log \left(\frac{M_{.j}}{N} \right)} \tag{9.12}$$

where c_A and c_B are the number of communities in partitions A and B, respectively, N is the number of nodes in the network, $M_{i.}$ is denoted as the sum over row i of Matrix M_{ij}, and $M_{.j}$ is denoted as the sum over column j. This NMI measure is 0, if a partition consists of a unique community, and the NMI measure is 1, in a perfect match of the partitions.

We obtain NMI $= 0.91$ for the network with 1 million nodes, which indicates that both partitions obtained from the two implementations are quite similar. Similar result was obtained when comparing the results of the original CNM in a node id shuffled version of the network. Further analysis about the details of the communities were performed in small networks from 20 nodes to 1000 nodes to see if both implementations produce the same communities, which are presented in Table 9.1. We compare all communities and evaluate a recall measure that represents the percentage of correct nodes assigned to the community by using the results of the original CNM as baseline. It is observed that both algorithms produce near-equal partitions for small networks. Therefore, both implementations are the same and we use the CNM implemented under our framework for the subsequent evaluations of CNM.

Table 9.1 Similarity evaluation of communities obtained from the original CNM and the CNM under our framework for small networks

# nodes	20	40	60	80	100	200	400	600	800	1000
NMI	1	0.94	1	1	1	0.675	1	1	0.996	0.944
recall(%)	100	97	100	100	100	73	100	100	99	80

9.6.3 Algorithm Comparison and Network Structure Influence

We compare our algorithm with CNM and its variations in seven real data sets from SNSs and five theoretical models that exhibit different structural properties. There are benchmarks such as [8, 16] to compare the algorithms when used in small networks or a synthetic model with a predefined structural property. However, none of them considers a set of networks with different structural properties, which impact the algorithm performance, as shown in the results. For an appropriate analysis of the influence of the network structure, we use the previously mentioned models (Section 9.6.1.2) to create networks with the same size as the real data from *Mixi* (360,802 nodes and 1,904,641 edges). The structural characteristics of all data sets are presented in Table 9.2.

Table 9.2 Comparison of degree correlation r_{cor}, average local clustering coefficient C, and the characteristics of SF (scale-free), HT (high-transitivity), Gap (in the distribution of community-sizes), and Rnd (randomness) for the real data sets and synthetic networks

	Nodes	Edges	r_{cor}	C	SF	HT	Gap	Rnd
Mixi	360,802	1,904,641	0.121	0.330	+	+	+	+
Delicious	165,344	417,179	−0.022	0.165	+	+	+	+
Flickr	1,715,255	22,613,981	0.024	0.184	+	+	+	+
YouTube	1,138,499	4,945,382	−0.034	0.081	+	+	+	+
LiveJournal	5,204,176	77,402,652	0.094	0.275	+	+	+	+
Orkut	3,072,441	223,534,301	0.017	0.167	+	+	+	+
Facebook	63,731	1,545,686	0.172	0.221	+	+	+	+
WS	360,802	1,904,641	0.222	0.373	−	+	−	++
BA	360,802	1,904,641	−0.009	0.000	+	−	−	+++
CNN	360,802	1,904,641	0.100	0.398	+	+	−	−
CNNR	360,802	1,904,641	0.124	0.346	+	+	+	+
CNN-FR	360,802	1,904,641	−0.010	0.007	+	+	−	+++

The experimental results are presented in Tables 9.3, 9.4, and 9.5, which shows the number of updates conducted, execution time, and the modularity of all algorithms in each data set, respectively.

In Table 9.3, we observe that the CNM produced the largest number of update operations due to its attractor of large communities, while our algorithm produced the lowest number of update operations except in YouTube and the CNN model where DDA-M2 and DDA-M1 had the largest reduction, respectively. This table demonstrates that the reduction of chain updates of our LY is larger than WT in its fast version (WT1) for all data sets.

For instance, our algorithm reduced the number of operations by factors of 81, 21, 12, and 24 times when compared to the number of operations required by CNM in Mixi, Delicious, YouTube, and Facebook, respectively, while WT1 reduced the number of operations by a factor of 17, 3, 4, and 21 times when compared to the number of operations required by CNM in Mixi, Delicious, YouTube, and Facebook, respectively. The same is observed in the synthetic networks where our algorithm reduces the number of operations by a factor of 576, 506, and 69 times for BA, CNN, and CNNR, respectively. In the case of YouTube, DDA-M2 produces the largest reduction, which requires further analysis.

Table 9.3 Number of update operations produced by CNM and all the variations in the seven real data sets and five theoretical models with different network structures

Data set	Update	Algorithm					
		CNM	DDA-M1	DDA-M2	WT1	WT2	LY
Mixi	Triangles	1,539,730	1,537,774	1,537,075	1,543,092	1,542,605	1,541,642
	Chains	10,355,932,452	524,745,069	450,932,381	602,975,558	706,072,445	126,398,966
Delicious	Triangles	167,713	164,607	163,961	168,696	168,478	165,723
	Chains	531,182,126	57,438,076	29,676,206	142,691,992	110,488,616	25,107,624
Flickr	Triangles	13,837,181	13,842,658	13,843,752	13,848,662	13,855,105	13,857,208
	Chains	115,784,586,398	44,612,770,494	4,541,224,894	20,080,179,146	30,737,647,015	4,316,797,276
YouTube	Triangles	1,839,708	1,842,773	1,844,149	1,848,272	1,851,074	1,848,426
	Chains	39,423,523,516	5,617,517,423	914,019,813	9,323,840,026	7,844,836,918	3,086,624,755
LiveJournal	Triangles	43,466,371	43,499,728	43,499,282	43,503,515	43,507,121	43,504,719
	Chains	2,341,181,918,814	272,076,454,511	189,370,191,429	61,643,924,566	110,741,652,579	21,918,377,509
Orkut	Triangles	–	114,112,099	114,111,896	114,110,439	114,112,234	114,112,041
	Chains	–	879,433,211,692	296,013,615,033	40,593,499,779	310,377,076,975	14,634,450,605
Facebook	Triangles	752,335	752,655	752,348	752,770	753,249	753,124
	Chains	434,976,055	118,779,119	115,825,317	20,401,187	56,289,334	17,530,448
WS	Triangles	1,540,851	1,535,067	1,532,832	1,533,400	1,513,868	1,490,270
	Chains	11,734,690,496	853,999,724	800,322,554	20,607,028	29,124,232	20,226,236
BA	Triangles	1,543,582	1,543,409	1,543,216	1,540,680	1,543,375	1,540,672
	Chains	14,284,541,959	1,808,565,920	1,925,453,076	132,501,522	260,722,906	23,512,618
CNN	Triangles	1,543,799	1,542,926	1,543,102	1,543,002	1,543,623	1,543,352
	Chains	2,139,819,544	72,412,382	79,833,945	357,734,445	617,766,679	101,548,731
CNNR	Triangles	1,539,431	1,540,388	1,540,157	1,543,064	1,543,109	1,542,360
	Chains	6,902,115,985	107,439,892	139,014,872	296,570,881	457,633,271	100,654,466
CNN-FR	Triangles	1,539,240	1,543,291	1,543,186	1,542,664	1,543,401	1,540,984
	Chains	17,048,231,791	1,714,038,340	672,156,817	454,989,933	407,806,207	32,099,818

The gray cells represent the algorithm producing the best results per network structure.

Table 9.4 Execution time in seconds required for each algorithm in different network structures, including the level of randomness of the network structure as reference

Data set	CNM	DDA-M1	DDA-M2	WT1	WT2	LY	Rnd
Mixi	4,747	417	509	639	884	288	+
Delicious	139	24	17	26	54	17	+
Flickr	36,191	17,090	12,236	11,422	31,688	7,986	+
YouTube	11,892	2,091	959	3,852	8,062	2,631	+
LiveJournal	810,302	114,898	339,544	56,767	195,982	43,059	+
Orkut	–	275,154	561,527	41,961	562,761	26,960	+
Facebook	72	15	58	11	41	11	+
WS	2,788	459	154	75	60	59	++
BA	3,312	607	2,178	122	359	94	+++
CNN	573	91	324	383	1,075	186	–
CNNR	4,039	163	274	494	630	265	+
CNN-FR	6,301	1,044	1,043	383	601	160	++

Table 9.5 Modularity obtained from each algorithm in different network structures, including the degree correlation of the network as reference

Data set	CNM	DDA-M1	DDA-M2	WT1	WT2	LY	r_{cor}
Mixi	0.601	0.666	0.662	0.466	0.602	0.615	0.121
Delicious	0.771	0.796	0.790	0.714	0.760	0.775	−0.022
Flickr	0.626	0.623	0.603	0.463	0.529	0.542	0.024
YouTube	0.705	0.703	0.694	0.552	0.644	0.646	−0.034
LiveJournal	0.686	0.737	0.731	0.433	0.631	0.648	0.094
Orkut	–	0.663	0.648	0.380	0.606	0.540	0.017
Facebook	0.606	0.592	0.596	0.385	0.510	0.500	0.172
WS	0.654	0.763	0.763	0.642	0.701	0.757	0.222
BA	0.257	0.233	0.234	0.200	0.220	0.205	−0.009
CNN	0.685	0.685	0.699	0.512	0.650	0.678	0.100
CNNR	0.596	0.632	0.626	0.400	0.598	0.600	0.124
CNN-FR	0242	0.225	0.219	0.194	0.217	0.204	−0.010

The strong difference in the reduction can be observed in the execution time presented in Table 9.4, where our algorithm performs faster in almost all cases with the exception of YouTube, where DDA-M2 is faster, and CNN and CNNR, where DDA-M1 performs better. For instance, our algorithm took only 1 min to extract communities in the WS network while DDA-M1 required 7 min, the same happens in the real data, where the community extraction of Mixi was done in less than 5 min in LY, 1.5 times faster than DDA-M1 that took 7 min. Similarly for the largest data set from Orkut, LY required 7 h while WT1 and DDA-M1 required 11.6 h and 3 days, respectively. It is to be noted that all modifications of CNM outperform the former CNM.

From the results, for synthetic networks that have the same sizes but different structural properties, it is observed that the speed of LY and DDA-M1 are influenced in opposite ways by the level of the randomness of the network structure. The larger the level of randomness, the slower is DDA-M1, because DDA-M1 prioritizes the pair of communities that have one in-process community with lower degree regardless of the degree of the pair, which may be larger in randomized networks and therefore impact the speed of DDA-M1. It should be noted that our LY algorithm, while slower in CNN compared to DDA-M1, is still faster and applicable to large-scale networks generated by CNN and CNNR.

Table 9.5 shows that lower modularity is obtained when the network has lower degree of correlation. DDA-M1 and DDA-M2 provide even better modularity, but its speed is strongly influenced by the network structure. We should remember that DDA was proposed to improve the modularity and not speed [7]. These results demonstrate that WT1 produces the lowest modularity and its time improvement was outperformed by our LY algorithm.

Our algorithm, developed for speed, produces modularities comparable to the former CNM. These results demonstrate that our LY algorithm in combination with our framework produced large reductions in the number of operations in almost any network structure, thereby making it practical for community extraction in large-scale networks. If modularity is the main concern, DDA-M1 and DD1-M2 can be employed; however, the execution time is increased and not practical for mega-sized networks. Another possibility is merging LY and DDA-M2 by means of combining both factors, experimental results showed improvements in modularity, close to DDA-M2, with slight impact in speed, compared to LY.

The code is freely available at http://sites.google.com/site/communityextraction/

9.6.4 Competing Algorithm

Finally, we compare our improvements with the recently proposed BGLL [3] that differs from CNM. For BGLL, we employed the program distributed by its authors,[3] which is divided in to two main modules–a conversion that pre-processes the adjacency network to perform some preliminary calculations required for the algorithm and the main module that performs the community extraction. It differs with the current implementation of our algorithms, where all calculations are performed in the same process (no pre-processing) and we record several logs for the performance analysis while BGLL does not record any log at all. Some results are presented in Table 9.6. It is observed that BGLL produces modularity comparable to DDA-M1 and DDA-M2, and the algorithm is fast, except in the case of BA where took it longer.

The aim of this chapter is to understand the behavior of the widely used CNM and its variations and to propose a solution to overcome the inefficiencies of CNM.

---

[3]http://findcommunities.googlepages.com/

Table 9.6 Some results of BGLL

Data set	Delicious	WS	BA	CNN	CNNR	CNN-FR
Pre-processing time (s)	0.72	3.11	3.73	3.43	3.98	4.05
Extraction time (s)	2.71	2.81	331.26	5.50	9.74	36.84

BGLL appears to be a promising approach and further research on the analysis of the behavior of this algorithm is recommendable, including a fair comparison, by using a similar framework for similar conditions and with the same level of optimization. Future studies for BGLL should consider and explain the key issues such as its speed and modularity, similar to what we analyze in this chapter for CNM.

9.7 Conclusions

We have analyzed the behavior of CNM and found that the number of interconnected communities (NIC) of an in-process community is the determinant factor that affects the speed in CNM. We found the existence of attractors of large communities in the early part of the process, where CNM tends to absorb small communities, such as snowballs, which may produce a surge in its NIC. A new improvement to CNM was proposed based on the manipulations of the NIC, which prioritizes the combinations of in-process communities with less NIC, thereby reducing the number of update operations. We presented a new implementation framework that is seven times faster than the original CNM implemented by Clauset. All variations of CNM under our framework were evaluated with real data sets from seven SNSs and five theoretical models with different structural properties. Experimental results show the strengths and weaknesses of the algorithms against different network structures. Our proposed LY algorithm was the fastest among the several network structures, and the most comprehensive in terms of modularity and speed, which is practical for application to large-scale networks.

Acknowledgments The authors are grateful to Yoshi Fujiwara from ATR for his ever-inspiring discussions and helpful comments on preliminary versions. We would like to thank the anonymous reviewers for their invaluable comments and for letting us know about the competing algorithm. We also thank Alan Mislove from the Max-Planck Institute for providing his data sets. Finally, we would like to thank Mixi, Inc., for providing the data set, in which users were all encrypted. The data set is handled under a Non-Disclosure Agreement. Our work does not evaluate the personality of participants or services in any SNSs. We declare no competing interests.

References

1. Ahn, Y., Han, S., Kwak, H., Moon, S., and Jeong, H. Analysis of topological characteristics of huge online social networking services. In *Proceedings of the 16th International Conference on World Wide Web*, Banff, Alberta, Canada, pp. 835–844, 2007.
2. Albert, R. and Barabási, A.-L. Statistical mechanics of complex networks. *Review of Modern Physics*, 74(1):47–97, Jan 2002.

3. Blondel, V.D., Guillaume, J.-L., Lambiotte, R. and Lefebvre, E. Fast unfolding of communities in large networks, *Journal of Statistical Mechanics: Theory and Experiment*, 10:P10008,
   2008.
4. Brandes, U., Delling, D., Gaertler, M. Goerke, R., Hoefer, M., Nikoloski, Z., and Wagner, D.
   Maximizing modularity is hard. arXiv: physics/0608255, 2006.
5. Capocci, A., Servedio, V.D.P., Caldarelli, G., and Colaiori, F. Detecting communities in large
   networks. arXiv:cond-mat/0402499v2, 2004.
6. Clauset, A., Newman, M.E.J., and Moore, C. Finding community structure in very large
   networks. *Physical Review E*, 70:066111, 2004.
7. Danon, L., Diaz-Guilera, A., and Arenas, A. Effect of size heterogeneity on community
   identification in complex networks. arXiv:physics/0601144, 2006.
8. Danon, L., Duch, J., Diaz-Guilera, A., and Arenas, A. Comparing community structure
   identification. *Journal of Statistical Mechanics: Theory and Experiment*, 09:P09008, 2005.
9. Derenyi, I., Palla, G., and Vicsek, T. Clique percolation in random networks. *Physical Review
   Letters*, 94:160202, 2005.
10. Duch, J. and Arenas, A. Community detection in complex networks using extremal optimiza-
    tion. *Physical Review E*, 72:027104, 2005.
11. Fortunato, S. and Barthelemy, M. Resolution limit in community detection. *Proceedings of
    the National Academy of Sciences of the United States of America*, 104:36, 2007.
12. Girvan, M. and Newman, M.E.J. Community structure in social and biological networks.
    Proceedings of the National Academy of Sciences of the United States of America, 99:7821,
    2002.
13. Guimera, R. and Nunes Amaral, L.A. Functional cartography of complex metabolic networks.
    Nature, 433(895), 2005.
14. Guimerà, R., Sales-Pardo, M., and Amaral, L.A.N. Modularity from fluctuations in random
    graphs and complex networks. *Physical Review E*, 70(2):025101, 2004.
15. Kumar, R., Raghavan, P., Rajagopalan, S., and Tomkins, A. Trawling the web for emerging
    cyber-communities. *Computer Networks*, 31(11–16):1481–1493, 1999.
16. Lancichinetti, A., Fortunato, S., and Radicchi, F. Benchmark graphs for testing community
    detection algorithms. *Physical Review E*, 78:046110, 2008.
17. Leicht, E.A. and Newman, M.E.J. Community structure in directed networks.
    arXiv:0709.4500v1, 2007.
18. Leon-Suematsu, Y.I. and Yuta, K. A framework for fast community extraction of large-scale
    networks. In *Proceeding of the 17th International Conference on World Wide Web*, Beijing,
    China, pp. 1215–1216, 2008.
19. Massen, C.P. and Doye, J.P.K. Identifying "communities" within energy landscapes. *Physical
    Review E*, 71:046101, 2005.
20. Mislove, A., Marcon, M., Gummadi, K. P., Druschel, P., and Bhattacharjee, B. Measurement
    and analysis of online social networks. In *Proceedings of the 7th ACM SIGCOMM Conference
    on Internet Measurement*, San Diego, California, USA, pp. 29–42, 2007.
21. Newman, M.E.J. Analysis of weighted networks. *Physical Review E*, 70:056131, 2004.
22. Newman, M.E.J. Fast algorithm for detecting community structure in networks. *Physical
    Review E*, 69(6):066133, 2004.
23. Newman, M.E.J. Finding community structure in networks using the eigenvectors of matrices.
    Physical Review E, 74:036104, 2006.
24. Newman, M.E.J. Modularity and community structure in networks. *Proceedings of the
    National Academy of Sciences of the United States of America*, 103(23):8577–8582, 2006.
25. Newman, M.E.J. and Girvan, M. Finding and evaluating community structure in networks.
    Physical Review E, 69(2):026113, 2004.
26. Palla, G., Farkas, I.J., Pollner, P., Derenyi, I., and Vicsek, T. Directed network modules. *New
    Journal of Physics*, 9:186, 2007.
27. Vázquez, A. Growing networks with local rules: Preferential attachment, clustering hierarchy
    and degree correlations. *Physical Review E*, 67:056104, 2003.

28. Viswanath, B., Mislove, A., Cha, M., and Gummadi, K. P. On the evolution of user interaction in Facebook. In *Proceedings of the 2nd ACM Workshop on online Social Networks*, Barcelona, Spain, pp. 37–42, 2009.
29. Wakita, K. and Tsurumi, T. Finding community structure in mega-scale social networks. arXiv:cs/0702048, 2007.
30. Watts, D.J. and Strogatz, S.H. Collective dynamics of 'small-world' networks. *Nature*, 393(6684):440–442, June 1998.
31. Yuta, K., Ono, N., and Fujiwara, Y. A gap in the community-size distribution of a large-scale social networking site. arXiv:physics/0701168v2, 2007.

Chapter 10
Geographically Organized Small Communities and the Hardness of Clustering Social Networks

Miklós Kurucz and András A. Benczúr

Abstract Spectral clustering, while perhaps the most efficient heuristics for graph partitioning, has recently gathered bad reputation for failure over large-scale power law graphs. In this chapter we identify the abundance of small-size communities connected by long tentacles as the major obstacle for spectral clustering. These subgraphs hide the higher level structure and result in a highly degenerate adjacency matrix with several hundreds of eigenvalues very close to 1. Our results on clustering social networks, telephone call graphs, and Web graphs are twofold. (1) We show that graphs generated by existing social network models are not as difficult to cluster as they are in the real world. For this end we give a new combined model that yields degenerate adjacency matrices and hard-to-partition graphs. (2) We give heuristics for spectral clustering for large-scale real-world social networks that handle tentacles and small dense communities. Our algorithm outperforms all previous methods for power law graph partitioning both in speed and in cluster quality. In a combination of heuristics for the contraction of tentacles as well as the removal of community cores that involve the recent SCAN (Structural Clustering Algorithm for Networks) algorithm, we are able to efficiently find balanced partitioning of over 10 million edge power law graphs. In particular, our heuristics promise similar or better performance than semidefinite relaxation with orders of magnitude lower running time.

10.1 Introduction

Clustering covers a wide class of methods to partition a set of data in order to locate relevant information by grouping and organizing similar elements in an intelligible way. The purpose of clustering members of a social network may include user

M. Kurucz (✉)
Data Mining and Web search Research Group, Informatics Laboratory, Computer and Automation Research Institute, Hungarian Academy of Sciences, Budapest, Hungary
e-mail: mkurucz@ilab.sztaki.hu

N. Memon et al. (eds.), *Data Mining for Social Network Data*,
Annals of Information Systems 12, DOI 10.1007/978-1-4419-6287-4_10,

segmentation, selection of communities with desired or undesired properties as, e.g., high ADSL penetration, viral marketing planning [36], or high recent churn rate. In a survey, Newman [31] observes that in social network research "particular recent focus has been the analysis of communities."

Spectral graph partitioning, a method based on the singular value decomposition (SVD) of the adjacency matrix, is a widely used heuristics for finding good balanced cuts in real-world graphs [1]. It is natural to apply the spectral method for large social networks as well. In addition to partitioning, the singular vectors themselves serve the purpose of understanding the organizing principles of the contacts between the members of the network [30].

Spectral graph partitioning has recently gathered bad reputation for failure over large-scale social networks. Lang [28] observes that for

> many power law graphs, the spectral method produces cuts that are highly unbalanced,
> thus decreasing the usefulness of the method for visualization or as a basis for divide-and-
> conquer algorithms.

He recommends semidefinite programming (SDP) to yield stricter balance constraints and a flow-based rounding cleanup step to find the best cuts.

In our experiments the existing models are insufficient to explain the failure of spectral partitioning. While Lang [28] in part suggests this may be due to the expansion and the power law degree distribution in these networks, in our experiments graphs generated by known models for social-like networks, the preferential attachment model of Barabási et al. [4], the evolving copy model of Kumar et al. [23], and the small-world model of Kleinberg [22] are all easily partitioned in a balanced way by the spectral method.

We identify *dense communities* interconnected by long *tentacles* as the main reason for the hardness of clustering. We call a subgraph a *tentacle* if it can be built by recursively adding low-degree nodes. A tree is an obvious example of a tentacle; we may, however, have cycles or even somewhat wider objects built by degree 3 or higher nodes in a tentacle. Notice that our notion of a tentacle is reminiscent to the octopus structure described by Lang [28], although key is that the tentacles connect a large number of dense regions.

Another blocker of the partitioning method is the abundance of relative small, local dense communities that attract most of the first principal vectors. These dense regions are seemingly similar to the dense bipartite communities described by the evolving copy model [23]; surprisingly, however, this model does not generate sufficiently dense communities needed for the observed bad behavior of spectral partitioning.

Our key result is a new combined model of social networks. Graphs generated by our model are hard to partition with the spectral method and in addition the size distribution of dense communities and tentacles fits those of the hardest real-life graphs. As the first step we generate a large number of small dense regions modeling densely settled geographic regions. We generate a graph over the 2D grid by Kleinberg's geographic small-world model [22] and replace some of its randomly selected nodes by small cliques. In the second step we achieve power law degree distribution over this graph by generating a degree sequence. The required number of edges is generated as in Kleinberg's model independent with probability proportional to the Euclidean distance in the underlying grid.

The clustering hardness measurements rely on our recent results [24] that extend the applicability of spectral clustering to very large social networks. In this chapter we summarize heuristics that prevent low-level communities from overtaking the first principal vectors. Our method is based on the combination of the removal of Tightly Knit Communities (TKC) [29] and the contraction of long tentacles. We build on the dense community finder algorithm of Xu et al. [40] who identify bridges across TKCs as the main reason for the failure of graph partitioning methods. Even though in our observations community finder algorithms are insufficient in themselves for partitioning very large networks, these methods, however, can be used prior to spectral partitioning to remove a large number of cores that act as TKCs by attracting a large number of principal vectors.

Our experiments are performed on the LiveJournal Friends network of more than three million users as in [24] and extended by two additional data sets: the call graph of more than two million Hungarian Telecom users with close 50 million directed edges [27] and the host graph of the UK2007-WEBSPAM graph of Boldi et al. [6] that contains more than 100,000 hosts and near two million directed weighted edges. Our networks form the largest power law graph attacked by graph partitioning. In earlier experimentation on social networks [17, 32, and many more], networks are smaller by orders of magnitude so that hierarchical community structures or even the graphs themselves could easily be visualized. The largest graph partitioning benchmark has only 448 K nodes and 3.3 M edges and Kevin Lang [28] considered the Yahoo IM graph with less than 10 M edges.

The rest of this chapter is organized as follows. After discussing related results, in Section 10.2 we describe the components of our spectral partitioning algorithm. Then in Section 10.3 we describe the real networks used in our experiments. A central result of the chapter in Section 10.4 describes existing and new social network models and their properties related to dense communities and tentacles. Finally, the key running time and cluster quality measurements are in Section 10.5.

10.1.1 Related Results

The applicability of spectral methods to graph partitioning is observed in the early 1970s [14]. The methods are then rediscovered for netlist partitioning, an area related to circuit design, in the early 1990s [1, 2, 10] and a large number of results appeared in the "Spectral Clustering Golden Age" [42, etc] 2001.

Prior to our work, spectral clustering was known to fail for large power law graphs with several partly successful attempts [26, 28]. When clustering large social networks, spectral methods tend to chop off tentacles attached loosely to a densely connected larger subset, resulting in a disconnected part and keeping the dense component in one [28]. While even the optimum cluster ratio cut might have this structure, the disconnected cluster consists of small graph pieces that each belong strongly to certain different areas within the dense component. Since the only practically meaningful interpretation of a disconnected cluster is to treat each connected component separately, we obtain an undesired very uneven distribution of cluster sizes.

The first ingredient of our algorithm relies on our recent result [26] where we obtain good quality clusters by heuristics for rejecting uneven splits and small clusters. The algorithm is based on k-way hierarchical clustering as described among others by Alpert et al. [2].

One solution proposed to solve the problem of accidental unbalanced low-quality splits with possibly disconnected parts is the Divide-and-Merge algorithm [11] that simply produces more clusters than requested and merges them in a second phase. The applicability of this algorithm for some of the easier-to-partition social networks with certain modifications is demonstrated in [26].

While spectral methods are key in top-down clustering, as a different possibility agglomerating strategies are used for bottom-up clustering [1]. However, these latter methods are known to be unstable [33], in particular for the blogger network where small communities are in abundance while the interpretation of a next layer of super-communities over communities is missing. We show that the top-down approach is probably the right choice to analyze very large-scale social networks.

As a related area, the HITS [21] ranking algorithm is a direct application of the SVD since the hub and authority ranks correspond to the first left and right singular vectors. It has been known for long that HITS is unstable [33] and it should be applied for subgraphs only. We believe that the reason is the same as for the failure of spectral partitioning. In particular, by using our preprocessing method, we avoid the Tightly Knit Community (TKC) phenomenon caused by communities that are small on a global level but still grab the first (or, as we show, even the first many) principal vectors. Lempel et al. [29] are probably the first who identify the TKC problem in the HITS algorithm, their algorithmic solution (SALSA), however, turns out to merely compute in- and out-degrees [7]. In contrast we keep SVD as the underlying matrix method and filter the relevant high-level structural information by removing TKCs and concentrating the network by contracting long tentacles.

10.2 Components of the Algorithm

First we describe the graph bisection relaxation methods, the singular value decomposition (SVD) and semidefinite programming (SDP) following the discussion of Lang [28], and then our combination of heuristics to filter out the globally relevant network structure prior to spectral clustering. The pre-filtering heuristics (Sections 10.2.1 and 10.2.2) are applicable in general to obtain globally meaningful principal vectors.

Spectral clustering refers to a set of a heuristic algorithms, all based on the overall idea of computing the first few singular vectors and then clustering in a low (in certain cases simply one [14]) dimensional subspace. As input, partitioning takes L, the graph Laplacian defined as

$$L = D - A$$

where A is the graph adjacency matrix and D is a diagonal matrix such that D_{ii} is the sum of the edge weights at node i. The Laplacian L is positive semidefinite and its first eigenvector is the all-one vector with eigenvalue 0.

The standard Quadratic Integer Program for graph bisection is

$$1/4 x^T L x$$

where x is the ± 1 cut indicator vector. In order to avoid the trivial cut with all nodes on one side, we have $x^T e = 1$ where e is a vector of all ones. When relaxing x to arbitrary real values between -1 and $+1$, the optimum is known to be the second eigenvector (the Fiedler vector) of L [14]. We may also relax indicator values to be arbitrary norm 1 n-dimensional vectors. In this case, the resulting optimization problem can be solved by semidefinite programming [28].

In our experiments, we use hierarchical spectral clustering algorithms that project the graph into a d-dimensional vector space [10] and divide it into more than two parts by the k-means clustering algorithm in one step, as suggested first by [42]. In order to obtain the projection, we test both the SDP relaxation in d dimensions and the first d singular vectors. As suggested by [12, 38], instead of the Laplacian $L = A - D$ we use the *weighted Laplacian* $L = D^{-1/2} A D^{-1/2}$. By using the weighted Laplacian, we may produce better quality partitioning [26].

The two main ingredients of our algorithm consist of the removal of small dense regions and the contraction of long interconnecting tentacles. In Fig. 10.1 we see typical subgraphs of the entire network of several small community cores, two of which is seen, with low degree nodes loosely connected to some of them or interconnecting pairs of them. Since SVD is unable to select from the abundance of small cores, it falls into the trap of the Tightly Knit Community effect [29] by selecting the most dominant such structure that is still very small on the scale of the entire network. We will demonstrate that after the proposed preprocessing these traps are avoided and meaningful principal vectors are found.

10.2.1 Tentacles and Small Component Heuristics

We use two heuristics for handling tentacles, one for pre- and another for postprocessing. The postprocessing is identical to the one discussed in [26]: we test the resulting partition for small clusters and try to redistribute nodes to make each component connected. Preprocessing consists of eliminating tentacles so that related communities are moved in the proximity of each other.

In a recursive definition we say that a node belongs to a *tentacle* if its degree is not more than a prescribed value d_{max}; we use $d_{max} = 3$. As long as there are

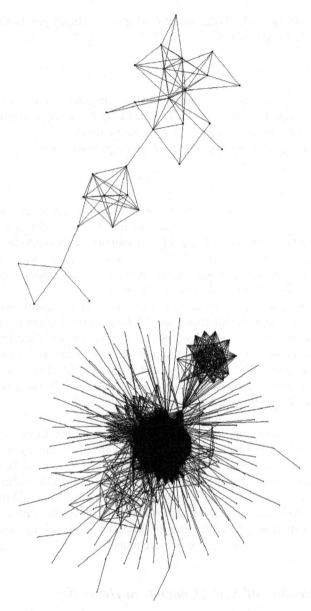

Fig. 10.1 *Top*: A 82-node subgraph of the LiveJournal Friends network, with two cores and several short tentacles. *Bottom*: A similar 317-node subgraph of the UK2007-WEBSPAM host graph

tentacle nodes in the graph, we contract them into (one of) their neighbors with smallest degree. In this way, we may create new small degree nodes and the procedure may recursively continue. By recording the contractions we may also reconstruct all nodes that get contracted into a final node. Such a set of nodes is called a tentacle. The procedure is described in Algorithm 1. We note that the definition of a tentacle depends on the order of contractions and we use this notion only for the preprocessing heuristic and not for characterizing a particular node.

Algorithm 1 Tentacle contraction.
input: d_{max}: maximum degree of a tentacle node.
output: graph G' with all tentacles contracted.

---

    while node v of degree $\leq d_{max}$ exists in G' **do**
        Contract v to its neighbor u with lowest degree in G'
        Record $v \rightarrow u$ for tentacle set reconstruction

---

In addition to preprocessing by tentacle removal, in Algorithm 2 we also give a postprocessing subroutine to reject very uneven splits identical to that of [26]. Given a split of a cluster (that may be the entire graph) into at least two clusters $C_1 \cup \ldots \cup C_k$, we first form the connected components of each C_i and select the largest C_i'. We consider vertices in $C_i - C_i'$ as outliers. In addition, we impose a relative threshold limit and consider the entire C_i outlier if C_i' is below limit.

Algorithm 2 redistribute$(C_1, \ldots, C_k)$: Small cluster redistribution

---

    for all C_i **do**
        $C_i' \leftarrow$ largest connected component of C_i
        if $|C_i'| <$ limit $\cdot |C_1 \cup \ldots \cup C_k|$ **then**
            $C_i' \leftarrow \emptyset$
    Outlier $= (C_1 - C_1') \cup \ldots \cup (C_k - C_k')$
    for all $v \in$ Outlier **do**
        $p(v) \leftarrow j$ with largest total edge weight $d(v, C_j')$
    for all $v \in$ Outlier **do**
        Move v to new cluster $C_{p(v)}$
    return all nonempty C_i

Next we redistribute outliers and check if the resulting clustering is balanced. In one step we schedule a single vertex v to component C_j with $d(v, C_j)$ maximum where $d(A, B)$ denotes the number of edges with one end in A and another in B. Scheduled vertices are moved into their clusters at the end so that the output independent of the order vertices v is processed. By this procedure, we may be left with less than k components; we will have to reject clustering if we are left with the entire input as a single cluster. In this case, we either try splitting it again with modified SVD parameters or completely give up forming subclusters.

10.2.2 Tightly Knit Communities and the SCAN Algorithm

The second main ingredient of our algorithm consists of the removal of community cores seen in Fig. 10.1 or, in another terminology, Tightly Knit Communities (TKC) before singular value decomposition. Several authors observe difficulties caused by the TKCs: Lempel and Moran [29] investigate hyperlink-based ranking on the Web and recently [40] identifies hubs that bridge between several TKCs as the main difficulty in network partitioning.

Several algorithms are proposed to identify community cores. Flake et al. use network flows [15] or min-cut trees [16] and Xu et al. [40] uses an agglomerating method that prefers core nodes and avoids bridges that connect more than one TKC. All these methods suffer from the abundance of very small communities with no superimposed larger scale structure that network flow-based heuristics could exploit. Some experiments on the failure of community core-based approaches are found in [27].

Our heuristic solution is based on the Structural Clustering Algorithm for Networks (SCAN) algorithm [40]; however, instead of using moderate parameters to build large clusters directly as community cores, we use SCAN with restrictive values and remove 1–5% of the nodes that belong to TKC prior to SVD.

The assumption of Xu et al. [40] is that hub vertices bridge many clusters. Therefore they define the SCAN algorithm that selects pairs of vertices with a concentration of common neighbors as candidate intra-cluster nodes limited by parameter ε. Hubs, as opposed to intra-cluster nodes, are then characterized by the distraction of neighbors. Finally, cores are formed by nodes that have at least μ neighbors within the core.

The key step in the SCAN algorithm is the selection of edges between pairs of nodes whose neighborhood similarity is above a threshold ε. In the original algorithm of Xu et al. [40], with $\Gamma(u)$ denoting the neighbors of u, the similarity is measured as

$$\sigma(u,v) = |\Gamma(u) \cap \Gamma(v)|/\sqrt{|\Gamma(u)||\Gamma(v)|}.$$

For power law graphs, in particular for the Web graph in our experiments, however, the running time for computing $\sigma(u,v)$ is very large due to the huge neighborhood sets $\Gamma(u)$ involved. Hence we use the Jaccard similarity

$$\mathrm{Jac}(u,v) = |\Gamma(u) \cap \Gamma(v)|/|\Gamma(u) \cup \Gamma(v)|$$

that we approximate by 100 min-hash fingerprints [8].

The modified SCAN Algorithm 3 proceeds as follows. First it discards edges that connect pairs of dissimilar nodes below threshold ε: these edges may bridge different dense regions [40]. Then nodes with more than μ remaining edges are considered as community cores. We use $\mu = 4$ in our experiments. Finally, connected components of cores along remaining edges augmented by neighboring non-core nodes. The resulting components $\mathcal{C}$ may overlap at these augmented vertices that are considered hubs in [40].

Algorithm 3 Modified SCAN.

input: ε: similarity threshold of neighbors within same core, μ: size threshold of neighborhood within core

output: list of communities

---

for all edges uv **do**

    compute approximate $\mathrm{Jac}(u,v)$ by min-hash fingerprints

$E' \leftarrow \{(uv) : \sigma(u,v) \geq \varepsilon\}$

$V' \leftarrow \{u : \deg_{E'}(u) \geq \mu\}$

compute the connected components $\mathscr{C}$ of V' with edges E'

for all components C of $\mathscr{C}$ **do**

    Add all vertices to C that are connected to C by edges of E'

return $\mathscr{C}$

Our main algorithm (Algorithm 4) combines the previous three heuristics. First, community cores $Q_1, \ldots, Q_s$ are identified by the SCAN algorithm and discarded from the graph. Then tentacles are contracted prior to the actual SVD procedure. SVD is performed on the normalized Laplacian. The singular vectors are normalized before the actual partitioning by k-means. The SVD and normalization steps can also be replaced by solving the semidefinite relaxation. Finally, as the last heuristic, we feed all k-means clusters and SCAN cores to the small component redistribution procedure that merges the SCAN cores into the final components.

For SVD we use the Lanczos code of `svdpack` [5] and for SDP we use Burer and Monteiro's solver [9].

Algorithm 4 Spectral Clustering.

input: k: desired branching factor of the cluster hierarchy.

output: hierarchical clustering

---

while desired number or cluster size is not reached **do**

    Select largest cluster C_0 and induced subgraph G

    $Q_1, \ldots, Q_s \leftarrow$ cores given by $\mathrm{SCAN}(G, \varepsilon, \mu)$

    $G' \leftarrow G - \bigcup Q_i$

    $G'' \leftarrow$ Contract all tentacles in G'

    $A \leftarrow$ adjacency matrix of G''

    Project $D^{-1/2}AD^{-1/2}$ into first d eigenvectors

    For each node i form vector $v'_i \in R^d$ of the projection

    $v_i \leftarrow v'_i / ||v'_i||$

    $(C_1, \ldots, C_k) \leftarrow$ output of k-means$(v_1, \ldots, v_{|C_0|})$

    Call `redistribute`$(C_1, \ldots, C_k, Q_1, \ldots, Q_s)$

    Discard C_0 if C_0 remains a single cluster

return all discarded and remaining clusters

10.3 Data Sets

10.3.1 LiveJournal Friends Network

Our first data set consists of the LiveJournal friends network downloaded in a 2-week period of November 2007.[1] The total number of users is 3,583,332 with 44,913,072 directed edges, out of which 14,286,827 M is reciprocal. In contrast, the data set of Backstrom et al. [3] has 4.2 M users with no major reason for difference between the two collections. By manual analysis we observed certain users missing due to timeouts, some users renamed, also some friends changed. The union of the two collections has 4,720,668 users, less than 28% of the 14 million listed by LiveJournal as of November 2007.

In our analysis below we rely solely on our crawl since no user data is collected in [3]. We keep only bidirectional edges; this procedure leaves us with a giant component with 2,379,267 nodes and 14,286,827 reciprocal edges. Since graph partitioning requires a connected graph, we discard all other nodes.

In this chapter we only summarize the most important results related to the hardness of clustering. More detailed analysis of LiveJournal clusters is described in [24].

The available metadata provided via a LiveJournal XML interface and the percentage of users who provide the information is summarized in Table 10.1 with a list of characteristic country locations in Table 10.2.

Table 10.1 Availability of metadata over the LiveJournal friends network

Country	Age	Interest	School
76.03	39.79	62.82	47.31

Table 10.2 Top list of country location

Country	Number	% known	% all
US	1 463 654	76.9	40.9
CA	87 609	4.6	2.4
RU	82 801	4.3	2.3
UK	73 789	3.8	2.1
AU	32 508	1.7	0.9
SG	14 986	0.7	0.4
DE	11 329	0.6	0.3
PH	10 380	0.5	0.3
UA	10 260	0.5	0.3
JP	7 778	0.4	0.2
FI	7 104	0.4	0.2
NL	5 970	0.3	0.2
NZ	4 958	0.3	0.1
FR	3 747	0.2	0.1

---

[1] Available for research purposes upon request from the second author, benczur@sztaki.hu

To illustrate our data set, we have performed six-way partitioning on the LiveJournal graph and illustrated the clusters by the country, age, and religious interest (Jesus, atheist, pagan) in the clusters in Fig. 10.2. We find the characteristic Russian cluster [18, 41] as well as two international clusters, one with European connection, the other with mostly English-speaking countries. The English-speaking cluster consists of the UK, CA, and AU; in addition they are clustered together with SG and PH. The US-only clusters predominantly consisted of high school or college-aged people. We find three US clusters, two with predominant interest in Jesus, while the third with Jesus in minority compared to Paganism and Atheism (this last cluster is also more international). We also noticed an apparent correlation with younger age and interest in Jesus. We note that certain clusters such as the Russian one are underrepresented for this type of interest.

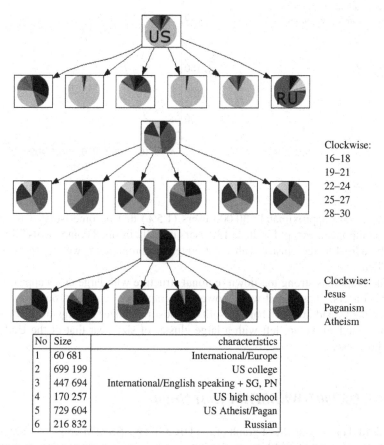

Clockwise:
16–18
19–21
22–24
25–27
28–30

Clockwise:
Jesus
Paganism
Atheism

No	Size	characteristics
1	60 681	International/Europe
2	699 199	US college
3	447 694	International/English speaking + SG, PN
4	170 257	US high school
5	729 604	US Atheist/Pagan
6	216 832	Russian

Fig. 10.2 Partition of LiveJournal users into six, with the distribution of location (*top*), age (*middle*), and religious interest (*bottom*). Characteristics of the parts 1–6 (*left to right*) are shown in the table

10.3.2 Telephone Call Graph

Our second data set consists of the telephone call graph of the Hungarian Telecom used in [26]. For a time range of 8 months, after aggregating calls between the same pairs of callers we obtained a graph with $n = 2,100,000$ nodes and $m = 48,400,000$ directed edges that include 10,800,000 bidirectional pairs.

Settlement sizes (Fig. 10.3) follow a distribution very close to log normal with the exception of a very heavy tail of Hungary's capital Budapest of near 600,000 users. In a rare number of cases the data consists of subpart names of settlements resulting in a relatively large number of settlements with one or two telephone numbers; since the total number of such nodes is negligible in the graph, we omit cleaning the data in this respect.

Fig. 10.3 Distribution of the number of telephone lines by settlements in the telephone data

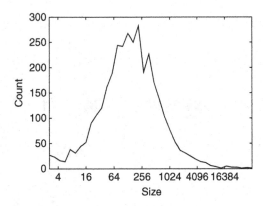

We discard approximately 30,000 users (1.5%) that become isolated from the giant component; except for those 130 users initially in small components all nodes can be added to the cluster with most edges in common but we ignore them for simplicity.

The graph has strong top-down regional structure with large cities appearing as single clusters. These small-world power law graphs are centered around very large degree nodes and are very hard to split. In most parameter settings of the original spectral method we are left with a large cluster of size near that of the Budapest telephone users.

10.3.3 UK2007-WEBSPAM Host Graph

The third data set is the host graph of the UK2007-WEBSPAM crawl of Boldi et al. [6] that contains 111,149 hosts and 1,836,441 directed weighted edges. The hosts are labeled with the top-level Open Directory [34] categories as in [19]. The list of the largest categories is seen in Fig. 10.4, right.

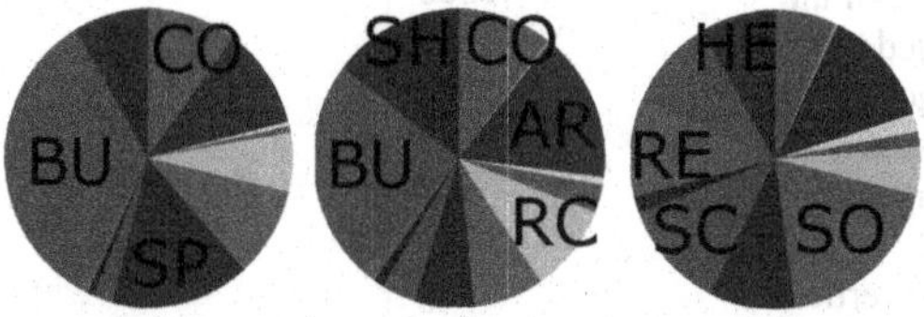

AR	arts
BU	business
CO	computers
HE	health
RC	recreation
RE	reference
SC	science
SH	shopping
SO	society
SP	sports

hosts	labeled
23595	2622
13111	8754
38279	14964
111149	35814

Fig. 10.4 The size of the three largest remaining clusters and the number of labeled hosts within the cluster and in the entire crawl (*bottom*) as well as the distribution of categories within these clusters in the same order, left to right, with the list of abbreviations (*left*)

Over this host graph plain spectral clustering into 100 clusters leaves three giant clusters unsplit as seen in Fig. 10.4. The distribution of the 14 categories is shown in the pie charts. The first cluster has a very low fraction of known labels, most of which belongs to business (BU), computers (CO), and sports (SP), likely a highly spammed cluster. The second cluster has high ODP reference rate in business (BU), shopping (SH), computers (CO), arts (AR), and recreation (RC). Finally, the largest cluster has an opposite topical orientation with high fraction of health (HE), reference (RE), science (SC), and society (SO). Among the less frequent four more categories, this latter cluster has a high fraction of kids and home while the second cluster contains games; news is negligible in the three clusters.

10.4 Social Network Models

Network models such as the preferential attachment [4], evolving copy [23], or Kleinberg's small world [22] describe certain properties of social networks and Web graphs such as the degree distribution, low diameter, geographic concentration of the contacts, and even certain dense communities.

We show that the above models do not explain the hardness of clustering. In what follows, we describe our procedures to generate graphs according to these models and also give our new model based on Kleinberg's small world [22] combined with power law degree and community distributions. Throughout the discussion, we will refer to the following measurements. In Fig. 10.5 we show the distribution of the sizes of community cores and tentacles in the models as well as the real graphs in Section 10.3. In addition, in Table 10.3 we show the 15th largest singular value under different heuristics as an indicator of the hardness for partitioning. We also mark instances where no balanced bipartitioning is possible by a heuristics-free spectral method.

Barabási et al. [4] define the preferential attachment model that generates graphs with power law degree distribution. In their model, new vertices arrive and they

Fig. 10.5 *Top*: the distribution of the size of the tentacles identified by Algorithm 1. *Bottom*: the distribution of the size of the communities identified by the modified SCAN Algorithm 3. Both charts are on the log–log scale and the horizontal axis shows the size of the component while the vertical the number of components with that size

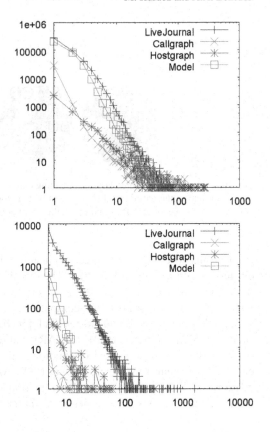

Table 10.3 The 15th largest singular value for different inputs and the choice of the heuristics for tentacle contraction (tent) and core removal (SCAN)

σ_{15}	Plain	Tentacle removal	Core removal	Both
Kumar	**0.956**	0.783	**0.956**	0.783
Kleinberg	**0.980**	0.811	**0.980**	0.811
New Model	**0.997**	**0.994**	0.988	0.810
LiveJournal	**0.999**	0.989	0.993	0.987
Telephone	0.897	0.886	0.897	0.881
UK2007-WEBSPAM	**0.894**	0.856	0.867	0.698

Figures in boldface denote cases when no balanced partitioning is possible at the first split by Algorithm 2

choose edges among old vertices proportional to their degree. This model generates power law degree distribution with the exponent -3; if random noise is added to the edge selection procedure, we may obtain different exponents as well [35]. By generating graphs according to these models, we obtain neither cores nor tentacles and all such graphs can be partitioned by the basic spectral method.

In the evolving copy model of Kumar et al. [23], whenever new vertices arrive, they select an old vertex uniform at random and copy their edges with noise. In addition to achieving power law degree distribution, the graphs in this model have a large number of dense bipartite cliques. Dense bipartite cliques are characteristic to Web graphs and as our particular interest they may yield dense regions with imbalanced spectral clusters. This model already generates hard instances for spectral partitioning; to however, they can be resolved by tentacle removal itself (Table 10.3). We observe no cores; tentacle size distributions are similar to the hard instances (Fig. 10.5).

The small-world graph model of Kleinberg [22] captures a different property of social networks, the fact that short paths not just exist but can efficiently be found by using only local information. In his model there is an underlying 2D grid, and nodes select a constant number of neighbors inversely proportional to their squared Euclidean distance in the grid. The model has a density parameter; if an intermediately large number of edges are generated from each node, then, similar to the evolving copy model, tentacles appear and partitioning is possible only after contracting them (Table 10.3). This model generates no cores.

Our new model is a power-law-degree-and-clique small world, defined as follows. The starting point is the small-world graph model of Kleinberg [22] with nodes placed over a 2D grid.[2] Next we generate geographically dense regions over the grid by assigning density to each node according to a power law distribution with exponent -3. Finally, as in Kleinberg's model, we connect nodes with probability inversely proportional to their squared Euclidean distance. However, in Kleinberg's model the degree is constant; in our model for each vertex we generate a number t by a power law distribution with exponent -3 and add t edges independent with probability as in Kleinberg's model.

Graphs generated in this new model are hard to partition, as seen in Table 10.3. In order for spectral partitioning to produce balanced enough partitions to pass the small component redistribution heuristics (Algorithm 2), both dense community removal and tentacle contraction are required for preprocessing. The distribution of community and tentacle sizes follows close power law very similar to those of the real graphs and in particular to LiveJournal, the hardest instance.

We remark that a simpler version itself suffices as a hard example for spectral partitioning. Instead of a power law density generation, we may simply select roughly 1% of the grid points and add 10 element clusters to these points. The tentacle size distribution remains the same and spectral partitioning remains hard. We also remark that power law and log-normal distributions are similar in their heavy tail; a power law community size distribution may hence follow from the log-normal settlement size distribution as seen in Fig. 10.3.

---

[2]To simplify generation we in fact used a 2D torus.

10.5 Experiments on Cluster Quality and Running Time

In this section we compare the solution of an SVD and an SDP-based relaxation of the graph partitioning problem with and without the heuristics for removing tentacles (Section 10.2.1) and dense communities (Section 10.2.2).

As an initial observation, we show how different projection methods on the Russian cluster of the LiveJournal friends network may or may not distinguish between Russians and other nations within the Russian cluster (Ukraine, Belarus, Estonia etc.). In [26] it is observed that direct spectral partitioning of this cluster is impossible, since in the singular value sequence even the 100th largest one is above 0.99. In accordance, the weighted Laplacian of the unmodified graph has non-characteristic principal vectors as seen in Fig. 10.6. However, the distinction between Russian and non-Russian nationalities becomes strongly visible by using our preprocessing algorithm prior to SVD (Fig. 10.6, middle). Finally, in the bottom of Fig. 10.6 we also see why the semidefinite relaxation outperforms SVD: since it projects nodes on a unit ball, most of the time a balanced partitioning may be constructed, although it does not necessarily corresponds to a good quality one. In our example, locations other than Russia tend to shift to the upper left part of the projection, although they strongly mix near the central dense diagonal hyperplane.

In our main experiments we measure clustering quality in a hierarchical partitioning of the three real-world graphs into 500 clusters. The branching factor in k-means is set to $k = 8$; note that the actual number of sub-clusters may be smaller. The initial number of dimensions is set to $d = 15$. The SVD-based algorithms include the option to give up clustering if the number of dimensions becomes so high that they run out of memory. As seen in Table 10.3, this happens for the heuristics-free SVD at a second-level split both for LiveJournal and for the Web graph. As another distinction, SDP always produces balanced partitioning while SVD stays, with the above exceptions, within the limit parameter of Algorithm 2. The size distribution hence varies for the algorithms used that introduce certain noise in the output.

We use four commonly used cluster quality measures, some based on the ground truth and others purely on graph-based properties. Although all four measures include correction factors for cluster sizes, we stress again that due to the varying cluster size distribution, small differences in the quality measures are inconclusive.

First we define entropy and purity, both measuring goodness with respect to the available ground truth information. For LiveJournal, ground truth is the country, for the telephone call graph, it is the settlement, and for the Web graph, it is the DMOZ top-level category. To define, let $N_{i,\ell}$ denote the cluster confusion matrix, the number of elements in cluster $\ell \leq m$ with ground truth attribute i and let $p_{i,\ell} = N_{i,\ell}/N_\ell$ denote the ratio within the cluster. Then the *entropy E* and *purity P* are defined as

$$E = (-1/\log m) \sum_\ell (N_\ell/N) \sum_i p_{i,\ell} \log p_{i,\ell} \quad \text{and}$$
$$P = \frac{1}{N} \sum_\ell \max_i N_{i,\ell},$$

where the former is the average entropy of the distribution of the property (e.g., country or DMOZ category) within the cluster while the latter measures the ratio of the "best fit" within each cluster.

Fig. 10.6 Principal
directions 4 and 5 within the
Russian cluster before (*left*)
and after (*middle*) the removal
of cores and tentacles as well
as two dimensions of the SDP
relaxation solution (*right*)

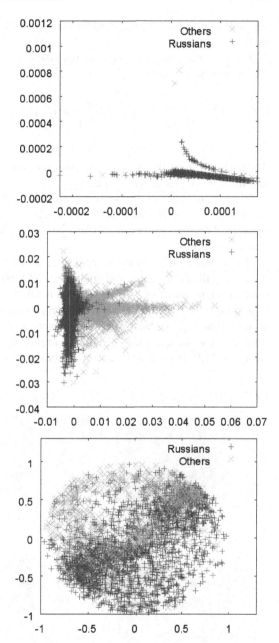

We use two more quality measures that rely solely on the graph, both based on
the number of edges inside and across clusters. First we considered *modularity*, a
measure known to suit social networks well [40] defined as follows:

$$Q = \sum_{\text{clusters } s} \left[\frac{|E(C_s, C_s)|}{|E|} - \left(\frac{|E(C_s, \overline{C_s})|}{2|E|} \right)^2 \right], \qquad (10.1)$$

where E is the set of all edges and $E(X, Y)$ is the set of edges with tail in X and head in Y.

Unfortunately, this measure does not take different cluster sizes into account, so we use *normalized network modularity* [39]:

$$Q_{\text{norm}} = \sum_{\text{clusters } s} \frac{N_s}{N} \left[\left(\frac{|E(C_s, C_s)|}{|E|} - \frac{|E(C_s, \overline{C_s})|}{2|E|} \right)^2 \right]. \qquad (10.2)$$

The larger the normalized modularity, the more edges remain within the same cluster and the less connect different clusters.

We also measure the *cluster ratio* defined as follows. Let there be N nodes with N_ℓ of them in cluster l for $\ell = 1, \ldots, m$. The *cluster ratio* is the number of edges between different clusters divided by $\sum_{i \neq j} N_i \cdot N_j$. Smaller values correspond to better clustering.

As for the reliability of the measures, we tested the behavior of our four measures by varying the dimension d and branching k of hierarchical SVD-based partitioning over the telephone call graph. As in the general settings of this section, we produced 500 clusters. We used SVD with small component redistribution only, an experiment similar to [27] where 3000 clusters were used. As seen in Fig. 10.7, purity and entropy show the expected behavior of improving quality with increasing dimensionality d [2]. In contrast, cluster ratio is very noisy and, to less extent, the same

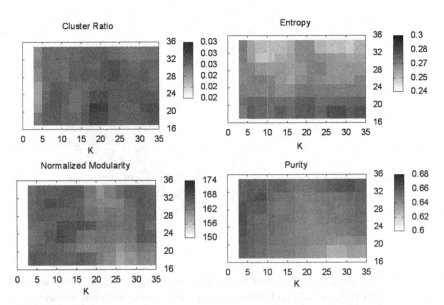

Fig. 10.7 Relation between dimensions d (*vertical*), branching k (*horizontal*) and quality (*darkness*) for purity (*top left*), entropy (*top right*), cluster ratio (*bottom left*, multiplied by 10^3), and normalized modularity (*bottom right*) of the telephone call graph. The darker the region, the better the clustering quality except for purity where larger values denote better output quality

holds for normalized modularity. Cluster ratio in our experiment seems inappropriate to measure clustering quality. Also notice that purity is expected to vary by roughly 10%, entropy by 50%, and normalized modularity by 10% with the internal parameters of the algorithms. This amount of variance hence needs to be taken into account when comparing the quality of various clustering procedures.

The running times and cluster quality measures are summarized in Table 10.4. The most important observation is the huge running time difference between SDP and SVD with only minor differences in cluster quality. The only large SVD running time appears for LiveJournal with no heuristics; here partitioning is possible only in very large dimensions.

Table 10.4 The running time, entropy, purity, normalized modularity, and cluster ratio over the three real data sets. We test four algorithms: SVD with small component redistribution heuristic only, with all heuristics, semidefinite relaxation (SDP), and SDP with core and tentacle removal, all with parameters $k = 8$ and $d = 15$. Best and near-best results are shown with boldface

LiveJournal	Runtime	Entropy	Purity	n.mod.	Cluster ratio
SVD small component redistribution only	1980m	0.105	0.812	**2339**	$2 \cdot 10^{-6}$
SVD small comp + tentacle + core	**150m**	**0.073**	**0.853**	2561	$8 \cdot 10^{-6}$
SDP no heuristics	1755m	0.111	**0.857**	272	$6 \cdot 10^{-6}$
SDP tentacle + core	675m	**0.072**	**0.854**	2537	$4 \cdot 10^{-6}$

Telephone	Runtime	Entropy	Purity	n.mod.	Cluster ratio
SVD small component redistribution only	**80m**	0.263	**0.653**	257	$1.5 \cdot 10^{-5}$
SVD small comp + tentacle + core	**87m**	**0.239**	**0.648**	206	$1.2 \cdot 10^{-5}$
SDP no heuristics	2520m	**0.237**	0.634	237	$1.4 \cdot 10^{-5}$
SDP tentacle + core	2865m	0.252	0.628	**251**	$1.3 \cdot 10^{-5}$

UK2007-WEBSPAM	Runtime	Entropy	Purity	n.mod.	Cluster ratio
SVD small component redistribution only	**3m**	0.362	0.199	35.69	$1.16 \cdot 10^{-4}$
SVD small comp + tentacle + core	**5m**	**0.277**	**0.416**	**101.14**	$2.38 \cdot 10^{-4}$
SDP no heuristics	45m	**0.266**	0.426	51.77	$8.64 \cdot 10^{-4}$
SDP tentacle + core	47m	**0.277**	**0.410**	82.38	$2.08 \cdot 10^{-4}$

When comparing the quality of the partitions given by different algorithms in Table 10.4, we observe that the three meaningful measures entropy, purity, and normalized modularity, although noisy in certain cases, do not show major differences in judgment.

First we compare SVD to SDP. SVD with the heuristics works always nearly as good as SDP. For LiveJournal, the hardest instance, it outperforms SDP in entropy and normalized modularity and for the other two data sets it is better in terms of purity and normalized modularity.

Next we compare tentacle and core removal to the heuristics-free versions. The telephone call graph is the only "easy" instance where small component redistribution itself achieves a solution that is beaten only in terms of entropy. For the other two graphs, as noted in Table 10.3, SVD fails for certain large components without tentacle and core removal. For LiveJournal, the hardest instance, even SDP appears to require heuristics. The very low normalized modularity of SDP here may indicate an unfortunate split. Note that the purity values are very close to 0.8, the fraction of US location that corresponds to a random split. Here our heuristics greatly improve SDP as well but for the other data sets SDP performs in general better without them.

In summary, SVD with heuristics achieves cluster qualities comparable or better than SDP at an order of magnitude lower running time. LiveJournal definitely requires the tentacle and core removal heuristics while our telephone call graph is an easy instance best solved perhaps by small component redistribution SVD. For the Web graph SDP and full-heuristics SVD both perform good quality clusters, the former at a price of a very high running time. The exact quality differences are inconclusive in favor of one method or another in part because of their strong dependence on the internal parameters of the algorithms and in part because of the noise introduced by varying cluster sizes in all quality measures.

10.6 Conclusion

We demonstrated that spectral graph partitioning can be performed on very large power law networks after appropriate preprocessing heuristics. Our preprocessing steps include the removal of densely connected communities that are of small size on the global scale as well as the contraction of long "tentacles," loosely connected users that form large chains out of the center of the network.

Our central findings are related to the comparison of the SVD vs. semidefinite programming relaxation of the graph partitioning problem [28]. We show the SVD-based partitioning quality can be improved to at least as good as the semidefinite one with large gains in speed. In particular. the Lanczos algorithm-based SVD can be parallelized since it consists of the multiplication of a vector with the input Laplacian [25]. In addition, SVD has good approximate solutions [13, 37]. In future work we plan to test distributed approximate SVD for very large graphs such as the UK2007-WEBSPAM page level graph with over three billion edges.

Of independent interest is our top-level analysis of the LiveJournal blogger Friends network, a data set of over three million users, in near 80% from US, 6% from Western Europe, and 5% from Russia and East Europe. Here the components reveal global aspects of the network such as location, age, or religious belief. In future work, more types of interest can be analyzed and the techniques presented here can be applied to blog posts or other large social networks.

Acknowledgments We would like to thank Jon Kleinberg and Lars Backstrom for providing us with the LiveJournal friends and communities data used in [3]. Thanks to Zoltán Gyöngyi for providing us with the host graph with labels from the Open Directory top hierarchy for the UK2007-WEBSPAM crawl of the UbiCrawler [6]. This work was supported by grants OTKA NK 72845 and NKFP-07-A2 *TEXTREND*.

References

1. Alpert, C.J. and Kahng, A.B. Recent directions in netlist partitioning: A survey. *Integration the VLSI Journal*, 19(1–2):1–81, 1995.

2. Alpert, C.J. and Yao, S.-Z. Spectral partitioning: the more eigenvectors, the better. In *DAC '95: Proceedings of the 32nd ACM/IEEE Conference on Design Automation*, New York, NY: ACM Press, pp. 195–200, 1995.

3. Backstrom, L., Huttenlocher, D., Kleinberg, J., and Lan, X. Group formation in large social networks: Membership, growth, and evolution. In *KDD '06: Proceedings of the 12th ACM SIGKDD International Conference on Knowledge Discovery and Data Mining*, New York, NY: ACM Press, pp. 44–54, 2006.

4. Barabási, A.-L., Albert, R., and Jeong, H. Scale-free characteristics of random networks: The topology of the word-wide web. *Physica A*, 281:69–77, 2000.

5. Berry, M.W., SVDPACK: A Fortran-77 software library for the sparse singular value decomposition. Technical report, University of Tennessee, Knoxville, TN, 1992.

6. Boldi, P., Codenotti, B., Santini, M., and Vigna, S. Ubicrawler: A scalable fully distributed web crawler. *Software: Practice & Experience*, 34(8):721–726, 2004.

7. Borodin, A., Roberts, G.O., Rosenthal, J.S., and Tsaparas, P. Finding authorities and hubs from link structures on the world wide web. In *Proceedings of the 10th World Wide Web Conference (WWW)*, pp. 415–429, 2001.

8. Broder, A.Z. On the resemblance and containment of documents. In *Proceedings of the Compression and Complexity of Sequences (SEQUENCES'97)*, pp. 21–29, 1997.

9. Burer, S. and Monteiro, R.D.C. A nonlinear programming algorithm for solving semidefinite programs via low-rank factorization. *Mathematical Programming*, 95(2):329–357, 2003.

10. Chan, P.K., Schlag, M.D.F., and Zien, J.Y. Spectral k-way ratio-cut partitioning and clustering. In *DAC '93: Proceedings of the 30th International Conference on Design Automation*, pp. 749–754, New York, NY, ACM Press, 1993.

11. Cheng, D., Vempala, S., Kannan, R., and Wang, G. A divide-and-merge methodology for clustering. In *PODS '05: Proceedings of the 24th ACM SIGMOD-SIGACTSIGART Symposium on Principles of Database Systems*, pp. 196–205, New York, NY: ACM Press, 2005.

12. Ding, C.H.Q., He, X., Zha, H., Gu, M., and Simon, H.D. A minmax cut algorithm for graph partitioning and data clustering. In *ICDM '01: Proceedings of the 2001 IEEE International Conference on Data Mining*, pp. 107–114, Washington, DC: IEEE Computer Society, 2001.

13. Drineas, P., Mahoney, M.W., and Kannan, R. Fast Monte Carlo algorithms for matrices II: Computing a low rank approximation to a matrix. *SIAM Journal on Computing*, 36:158–183, 2006.

14. Fiedler, M. Algebraic connectivity of graphs. *Czechoslovak Mathematical Journal*, 23(98), 1973.

15. Flake, G., Lawrence, S., and Giles, C.L. Efficient identification of web communities. In *Sixth ACM SIGKDD International Conference on Knowledge Discovery and Data Mining*, pp. 150–160, Boston, MA, August 20–23 2000.

16. Flake, G.W., Tarjan, R.E., and Tsioutsiouliklis, K. Graph clustering and minimum cut trees. *Internet Mathematics*, 1(4):385–408, 2003.

17. Girvan, M. and Newman, M.E. Community structure in social and biological networks. *Proceedings of the National Academy of Sciences of the USA*, 99(12):7821–7826, June 2002.

18. Gorny, E. Russian LiveJournal. The Impact of Cultural Identity on the Development of a Virtual Community. In H. Schmidt, K. Teubener, and N. Konradova, (eds), *Control and Shift: Public and Private Usages of the Russian Internet*, pp. 73–90, 2006.

19. Gyöngyi, Z., Garcia-Molina, H., and Pedersen, J. Web content categorization using link information. Technical report, Stanford University, 2006–2007.

20. Hopcroft, J., Khan, O., Kulis, B., and Selman, B. Natural communities in large linked networks. In *KDD '03: Proceedings of the 9th ACM SIGKDD International Conference on Knowledge Discovery and Data Mining*, pp. 541–546, New York, NY: ACM Press, 2003.

21. Kleinberg, J. Authoritative sources in a hyperlinked environment. *Journal of the ACM*, 46(5):604–632, 1999.

22. Kleinberg, J. The small-world phenomenon: An algorithmic perspective. In *Proceedings of the 32nd ACM Symposium on Theory of Computing*, 2000.

23. Kumar, R., Raghavan, P., Rajagopalan, S., Sivakumar, D., Tomkins, A., and Upfal, E. Stochastic models for the web graph. In *Proceedings of the 41st IEEE Symposium on Foundations of Computer Science (FOCS)*, pp. 1–10, 2000.

24. Kurucz, M., Benczúr, A.A., and Pereszlényi, A. Large-scale principal component analysis on live journal friends network. In *Workshop on Social Network Mining and Analysis Held in Conjunction with the 13th ACM SIGKDD International Conference on Knowledge Discovery and Data Mining (KDD 2008)*, 2008.

25. Kurucz, M., Benczúr, A.A., and Csalogány, K. Methods for large scale SVD with missing values. In *KDD Cup and Workshop in Conjunction with KDD 2007*, 2007.

26. Kurucz, M., Benczúr, A.A., Csalogány, K., and Lukács, L. Spectral clustering in telephone call graphs. In *WebKDD/SNAKDD Workshop 2007 in Conjunction with KDD 2007*, 2007.

27. Kurucz, M., Siklósi, D., Lukács, L., Benczúr, A.A., Csalogány, K., and Lukács, A. Telephone call network data mining: A survey with experiments. In *Handbook of Large-Scale Random Networks to be published by Springer Verlag in conjunction with the Bolyai Mathematical Society of Budapest*, 2008.

28. Lang, K. Fixing two weaknesses of the spectral method. In *NIPS '05: Advances in Neural Information Processing Systems*, volume 18, Vancouver, BC, 2005.

29. Lempel, R. and Moran, S. The stochastic approach for link-structure analysis (SALSA) and the TKC effect. *Computer Networks*, 33(1–6):387–401, 2000.

30. McGlohon, M., Leskovec, J., Faloutsos, C., Hurst, M., and Glance, N. Finding patterns in blog shapes and blog evolution. In *Proceedings International Conference on Weblogs and Social Media (ICWSM-2007)*, 2007.

31. Newman, M. Detecting community structure in networks. *The European Physical Journal B – Condensed Matter,* 38(2):321–330, March 2004.

32. Newman, M.E.J. and Girvan, M. Finding and evaluating community structure in networks. *Physical Review E,* 69(2):26113, 2004.

33. Ng, A.Y., Zheng, A.X., and Jordan, M.I. Link analysis, eigenvectors and stability. In *Proceedings International Joint Conference on Artificial Intelligence*, Seattle, WA, August 2001.

34. Open Directory Project (ODP). http://www.dmoz.org.

35. Pennock, D.M., Giles, C.L., Flake, G.W., Lawrence, S., and Glover, E. Winners don't take all: A model of web link accumulation. *Proceedings of the National Academy of Sciences,* 99:5207–5211, April 2000.

36. Richardson, M. and Domingos, P. Mining knowledge-sharing sites for viral marketing. In *KDD '02: Proceedings of the 8th ACM SIGKDD International Conference on Knowledge Discovery and Data Mining*, pp. 61–70, New York, NY: ACM Press, 2002.

37. Sarlós, T. Improved approximation algorithms for large matrices via random projections. In *Proceedings of the 47th IEEE Symposium on Foundations of Computer Science (FOCS)*, 2006.

38. Shi, J. and Malik, J. Normalized cuts and image segmentation. *IEEE Transactions on Pattern Analysis and Machine Intelligence (PAMI)*, 2000.

39. Shiga, M., Takigawa, I., and Mamitsuka, H. A spectral clustering approach to optimally com-
    bining numerical vectors with a modular network. In *KDD '07: Proceedings of the 13th ACM
    SIGKDD international conference on Knowledge discovery and data mining*, pp. 647–656,
    New York, NY: ACM press, 2007.
40. Xu, X., Yuruk, N., Feng, Z., and Schweiger, T.A.J. Scan: A structural clustering algorithm for
    networks. In *KDD '07: Proceedings of the 13th ACM SIGKDD International Conference on
    Knowledge Discovery and Data Mining*, pp. 824–833, New York, NY: ACM Press, 2007.
41. Zakharov, P. Structure of LiveJournal social network. In *Proceedings of SPIE Volume 6601,
    Noise and Stochastics in Complex Systems and Finance*, 2007.
42. Zha, H., He, X., Ding, C.H.Q., Gu, M., and Simon, H.D. Spectral relaxation for k-means
    clustering. In T.G. Dietterich, S. Becker, and Z. Ghahramani (eds), *NIPS*, pp. 1057–1064.
    Cambridge, MA: MIT Press, 2001.

Chapter 11
Integrating Genetic Algorithms and Fuzzy Logic for Web Structure Optimization

Iltae Lee, Negar Koochakzadeh, Keivan Kianmehr, Reda Alhajj, and Jon Rokne

Abstract This chapter addresses the restructuring of Websites by an approach that integrates fuzziness weighted page rank (WPR) index and log rank index for pages of the considered Website. Fuzzy logic gives a degree of a membership to a problem and, hence, more adequately describes reasoning to a problem than a numeric deviation value does (the difference between the WPR index and log rank index), which does not give accurate human reasoning. Using fuzzy logic, the computational program translates a deviation value to a fuzzy representation by producing statements like "page *A* has a low restructuring factor by degree 0.8." However, without well-defined membership functions, a fuzzy value can be as meaningless as or even worse than a deviation value. Accordingly, we have shown how genetic algorithms (GA) can be applied to optimize the fuzzy membership functions. This chapter demonstrates how fuzzy logic can be applied to a deviation value to better represent the degree of restructuring.

11.1 Introduction

Usability is one of the keys to the success of a Website. If the link structure is not well organized for Websites that have many pages linked together internally, it may be difficult for users to find the information they want. As the complexity of the link structure grows, it becomes more important to optimize the internal link structure so that users can navigate the site easily.

Search engines such as Google have used Web mining to retrieve relevant information from the Web. Among several Web-mining techniques, our work described in [14] uses Web log mining and Web structure mining technique to get the insight on how a site's internal link structure can be improved.

R. Alhajj (✉)
Department of Computer Science, University of Calgary, Calgary, AB, Canada; Department of Computer Science, Global University, Beirut, Lebanon
e-mail: alhajj@ucalgary.ca

N. Memon et al. (eds.), *Data Mining for Social Network Data*,
Annals of Information Systems 12, DOI 10.1007/978-1-4419-6287-4_11,
© Springer Science+Business Media, LLC 2010

In [14], we used the weighted page rank (*WPR*) algorithm [25] for Web structure mining to analyze the hyperlink structure of a Website. The WPR algorithm considers the fact that the page rank of popular page should have a higher weight than the one of an unpopular page. In addition, we demonstrated how to use Web log mining to obtain data on the site users' specific navigational behavior. We then presented a scheme describing how to interpret and compare these intermediate results to measure the Website's efficiency in terms of usability. Eventually, based on the results, we outlined how to make recommendations to Website owners' in order to assist them in improving their sites' usability. In order to achieve our goal of recommending changes to the link structure of a Website, we identified two main subproblems which we had to solve before moving forward with the overarching problem: first to determine which pages were important, as implied by the structure of the Website and, second to conclude which pages the users of the Website consider to be important, based on the information amassed from the Web log. Once we solved these two subproblems, we had methods in place to rank the same Web pages. The ranking method introduced in [14] can be summarized as follows. Assume that v_i is the number of visitors for a page i and t_i is the total time spent by all visitors on this page; the log rank value d_i is defined as

$$d_i = 0.4v_i + 0.6t_i;$$

d_i represents the importance of a page relative to the others. Pages that are frequently visited and accessed for long periods of time will have a larger log rank than pages with an insignificant number of visits and think time. Rather than giving time and visits equal importance as discussed above, the difference is quantified through a constant, in this case being a 60/40 split, respectively. The numeric deviation value d_i is calculated for each page and is presented to the site owner. Website owners can then use these deviations in order to find out problematic Website structures. Three sample result data from [14] are shown in Table 11.1.

Table 11.1 Sample result data from [14]

Url	Log rank index	Page rank index	d_i
/manufacturers/index.html	2	0	2
/dr-660/index.html	21	476	−455
/images/index.html	1515	7	1508

Although the results obtained from our previous study are promising, analyzing numerical values of d_i may make the process of the conceptual decisions very unattractive and sometimes even confusing when non-technical users are concerned. The value of d_i from Table 11.1 does not represent human reasoning accurately. What does it mean to the end user whether d_i is −455 or 1508? This research paper addresses this problem and represents d_i as the restructuring factor using fuzzy logic so that site owners can have better understanding of d_i, when presented in fuzzy linguistic terms, which will consequently result in a better conceptual decision making.

Fuzzy logic gives a degree of membership to a problem and, hence, more adequately describes reasoning to a problem than a numeric value does. We will apply fuzzy logic to d_i to give better human reasoning to it. However, a fuzzy value can be meaningless without well-defined membership functions. GA is a process used to optimize membership functions. We will apply GA to our fuzzy logic to better represent the restructuring factor. Using optimized membership functions, we can obtain the fuzzified restructuring factor shown in Table 11.2 The degree of membership ranges from 0 to 1. A high restructuring factor indicates that it is likely that the page should be restructured. It is harder to indicate whether the restructure will make the page harder or easier to reach.

Table 11.2 Fuzzified restructuring factor

Url	Log rank index	Page rank index	Harder	Fuzzy value
/manufacturers/index.html	2	0	True	Low by degree 0.03
/dr-660/index.html	21	476	False	High by degree 0.7
/images/index.html	1515	7	True	High by degree 0.9

Here the term "harder to reach" for a page means that it is not necessary that there exists a hyperlink to this particular page from the homepage, or this page should not be placed in a location where it plays the role of a bridge that allows user to only pass trough this page to reach some other pages. Actual test result will be further discussed in Section 11.3.1.

The rest of this chapter is structured as follows. Section 11.2 contains the previous work related to the Web structure optimization. The proposed solution is described in Section 11.3. The result derived from using our proposed solution is demonstrated in Section 11.3.1. Finally, we conclude this chapter with a summary of the proposed method in Section 11.3.2.

11.2 Previous Work

As described in the literature, numerous approaches have been taken to analyze a Website's structure and correlate these results with usability, e.g., [3, 4, 6, 7, 8, 9, 15, 19, 22, 23]. For instance, the work described in [18] devised a spatial frequent itemset data mining algorithm to efficiently extract navigational structure from the hyperlink structure of a Website. The navigational structure [5] was defined as a set of links commonly shared by most of the pages in a Website. The approach was based on a general purpose frequent itemset data mining algorithm, namely ECLAT [2]. ECLAT was used to mine only the hyperlinks inside a window with adaptive size that slides along the diagonal of the Website's adjacency matrix. The authors compared the results of their algorithm with results from a user-based usability evaluation. The evaluation method gave certain tasks to a user (like finding a specific piece of information on a Website) and recorded the time needed to accomplish a task and failure ratios. The researchers found a correlation between the size of the navigational structure set and the overall usability of a Website, specifically the more navigational structure a Website has, the more usable it is.

In [21], the authors proposed to analyze the Web log using data mining techniques to extract rules and predict which pages users will be going to visit based on their prior behavior, and then showed how to use this information to improve the Website structure. By its use of data mining techniques, this approach is related to our approach, although the details of the method vary greatly, due to their use of frequent itemset data mining algorithms. The main difference between our approach and the method described in [21] is that the authors did not consider the time spent on a page by a visitor in order to measure the importance of that particular page. Their approach applies frequent itemset mining that discovers navigation preferences of the visitors based on the most frequently visited pages and the frequent navigational visiting patterns. However, we believe that in a particular frequent navigational pattern there might exist some pages which form an intermediate step on the way to the desirable page that a user is actually interested in. Therefore, the time spent on a page by a visitor is considered an important measure to quantify the significance of a page in a Website structure.

The work described in [12] proposed two hyperlink analysis-based algorithms to find relevant pages for a given Web page. The work is different in nature from our work; however, it applies Web mining techniques. The first algorithm extends the citation analysis to Web page hyperlink analysis. The citation analysis was first developed to classify core sets of articles, authors, or journals to different fields of study. In the context of the Web mining, the hyperlinks are considered citations among the pages. The second algorithm makes use of linear algebra theories to extract more precise relationships among the Web pages in order to discover relevant pages. By using linear algebra, they integrate the topologic relationships among the pages into the process to identify deeper relations among pages for finding the relevant pages. The work in [10] describes an expanded neighborhood of pages with the target to include more potentially relevant pages.

In the approach described in [18], the standard page rank algorithm was modified by distributing rank among related pages with respect to their weighted importance, rather than treating all pages equally. This change results in a more accurate representation of the importance of all pages within a Website. We used the weighted page rank formula outlined in [18] to complement the Web structure mining portion of our approach, with the hope of returning more accurate results than the standard page rank algorithm. The result obtained from the weighted page rank is validated by applying HITS [17] to check the consistency of the results.

In [26], the authors outline a method of preparing Web logs for mining specific data on a per session basis. This way, an individual's browsing behavior can be recorded using the time and page data gathered. Preparations to the log file such as stripping entries left by robots are also discussed.

There are Websites that have complex internal link structure. As the complexity of a site's link structure grows, it becomes more important to structure the site in such a way that users can navigate the site easily. The following list shows three reasons that Website structure optimization is important [20]:

1. Increase Website spidering index range
2. Increase page rank of internal pages
3. Increase user experience and overall Website navigation and usability

Web-mining is the application of data mining techniques to discover patterns from the Web. Web-mining techniques are categorized as Web usage mining, Web content mining, and Web structure mining. Major search engines such as Google, Yahoo, and MSN have successfully used Web-mining techniques. To optimize the site structure, [14] uses two types of Web-mining technique, Web structure mining and Web usage mining (i.e., Web log mining.)

In order to perform Web structure mining in [14], at first, hyperlinks contained within a set or root page are extracted using regular expressions. Then the crawler recursively continues crawling the pages. Once the entire site or the user defined part of the site is completely crawled, the WPR is calculated for each page and each page is assigned a page rank value, p_i.

The weighted page rank algorithm is an extension to the standard page rank algorithm implemented by the two founders of Google. The page rank algorithm uses the dampening factor, the page rank of the sets of the pages that point to the page and the number of outgoing links from each set of pages that point to the page in order to calculate the rank of a page. However, the standard page rank algorithm evenly divides the rank among its outgoing links [25]. To improve the standard page rank algorithm, the larger rank value is given to more important pages instead of dividing the rank value of a page evenly among its outlinked pages [25]. In addition, the weighted page rank computes the weight of inbound links using the same algorithm used to calculate the outbound link weight. The weight of inbound links and the weight of outbound links are weighted equally when calculating the WPR [25].

Frequency (number of visits) and time (total time spent by users) are the two parameters that we have already used in [14] for Web log mining. Each page is given a log rank value (l_i), and d_i is calculated by subtracting the index of the log rank value, index (l_i) from the index of the WPR value, index (p_i). If the deviation value of a particular page is low, our work described in [14] suggests that the page needs to be harder to reach. On the other hand, if the deviation value for a page is high, our work described in [14] recommends the site owner to restructure the page so it is more easily reachable. However, d_i is likely to be meaningless to most site owners. Fuzzy logic can give a degree of a membership to the nominal output, hence, aid a site owner to identify which pages need how much degree of restructuring.

Optimizing fuzzy logic membership functions is important because non-optimized membership functions may return inaccurate degree of a membership. GA is a process to find the optimal solution to a given problem by processes such as parent selection, genetic operations, and evolvement. The work described in [1] illustrates the process of optimizing fuzzy logic membership functions by using GA. The authors of [1] discuss various GA operations in developing a single input and output fuzzy system. We will develop a GA application for a two inputs and a single output fuzzy system.

11.3 The Proposed Solution

To apply fuzzy logic to d_i, we need to determine the membership functions for two inputs (index (p_i) (WPR index), index (l_i) (Log rank index)), and a single output (restructuring factor.) The two inputs are provided from [14]. Let us call the membership function for the WPR value, $\mu(x)$, and the membership function for the log rank value, $\mu(y)$.

Our work in [14] defines d_i as follows:

$$d_i = \text{index}(l_i) - \text{index}(p_i) \tag{11.1}$$

An output of a fuzzy membership function is usually positive. However, d_i can be negative. In order for us to produce only positive d_i, the absolute d_i value is calculated as follows. We would like to call the absolute d_i value as the restructuring factor, rf_i. Greater rf_i indicates that it is likely that the page needs to be restructured by using the following (but not limited to) methods described in [14]:

– Removing links to that page, especially on those pages with high page rank.
– Linking to the page from places with low page rank value instead.

However, by changing d_i to rf_i, information as to whether the page needs to be restructured so the page is harder or easier to reach is lost. As our previous work described in [14] mentions, if d_i for a page is low (if the page rank index is higher than the log rank index), the page needs to be restructured so it is easier to reach. On the other hand, if d_i for a page is high (if page rank index is lower than the log rank index), the page needs to be restructured so it is harder to reach. Therefore, when taking the absolute value of d_i, it is necessary to preserve the information as a bit. If the log rank index is higher than the WPR index, the bit is false or else, it is true. Let us name the bit, *harder*. This boolean bit will be output to the result file.

11.3.1 Define Input and Output

Each input and output membership function can have any number of memberships greater than one. However, as the number of membership grows, GA performance decreases because the number of base increases. We will define four memberships, namely low, medium left, medium right, and high for both the input functions ($\mu(x)$,

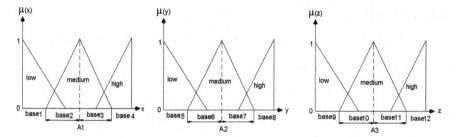

Fig. 11.1   Initial membership functions

$\mu(y)$) and the output function ($\mu(z)$). Figure 11.1 demonstrates the initial, non-optimized membership functions. There are two rules to use when determining the output value.

Rule 1:   When x or y intersects two points, the output is determined as follows [13].
Fig. 11.2 shows how output x can be determined using this rule.

Fig. 11.2   Rule #1

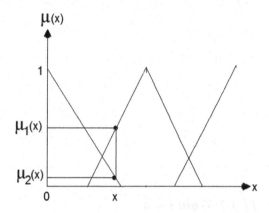

$$\mu(x) = \min(\mu_1(x), \mu_2(x)), \mu(y) = \min(\mu_1(y), \mu_2(y)) \qquad (11.2)$$

Rule 2: $\mu(x)$ and $\mu(y)$ will possibly intersect four points when applied to $\mu(z)$ as shown in Fig. 11.3. In such a case, the originating membership of $\mu(x \text{ or } y)$ determines which intersection point is to be chosen. For example, if $\mu(x)$ was originated from membership low, point 1 from Fig. 11.3 is selected.

Rule 3:   Output z is determined using the following rule. Figure 11.4 demonstrates this rule.

$$\text{Output} z = \min(z_1, z_2) \qquad (11.3)$$

Fig. 11.3 Rule #2

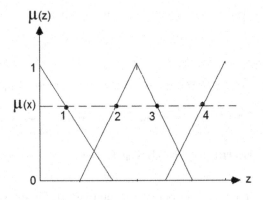

Fig. 11.4 Rule #3

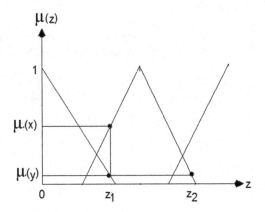

11.3.2 Train Data

For experiments, we used a medium size Website ($\approx$ 631 pages) obtained from [24], which provides reference for HiFi devices. Its structure is wider than deep, as for example when it lists the manufacturers of documented devices. Since this Website has been provided for experiments with data mining techniques, it already came with a log file that had been parsed into sessions. Let us define training data as the sample data used to optimize membership functions. The optimum solution gets better as the number of training data increases [1]. The following five data show the training data we will use for this chapter to demonstrate how they are used.

$$\text{Input}_1 : x_i = \{11, 132, 182, 369, 476\}$$
$$\text{Input}_2 : y_i = \{11, 56, 375, 7, 2003\}$$
$$\text{Output} : z_i = \{0, 76, 193, 362, 1527\} i = 1, 2, 3, 4, 5$$

11.3.3 Encoding

Chromosome is the representation of the input and output membership functions and consists of unassigned integers (uint). Each membership function needs five points to represent them; one point for the center of medium membership and four points for four bases. Therefore, in total, 15 uints are required to form a single chromosome. Each chromosome's points are generated such that $\mu(x)$, $\mu(y)$, or $\mu(z)$ does not yield zero for any input x, y, or z [1]. This is a requirement of a chromosome.

11.3.4 Population

It is necessary to choose the population size (number of chromosomes) for a generation. Increasing population size results in longer computation time. However, a small population size decreases the accuracy of the solution because of reduced variation of chromosomes. Therefore, there should be a balance [1]. An experiment can be conducted with different population sizes to find the optimal size. Finding the optimal size of chromosome is out of the scope of this research page and we will use population size ten. Table 11.3 shows a sample chromosome that has membership function information.

Table 11.3 Sample chromosome

$\mu(x)$					$\mu(y)$					$\mu(z)$				
base1	base2	A1	base3	base4	base5	base6	A2	base7	base8	base9	base10	A3	base11	base12
142	87	320	354	235	34	1082	1208	803	923	12	23	69	70	15

11.3.5 Error Score Calculation

The error score for each chromosome can be calculated using the following formula [1]. The chromosome that has the least error score becomes the best chromosome:

$$\sum_{j=1}^{n}(rf_i - z_j)^2, i = ith \text{ chromosome}, n = \text{total number of data} \qquad (11.4)$$

11.3.6 Parent Selection

Different parent selection methods are discussed below [11]. We chose to use sorted roulette method, but it is possible that other methods can optimize the output better. Investigating other opportunities and finding the best parent selection method is a future work.

1. Fitness Roulette: The probability of an individual being selected in the population is equal to the fitness value normalized with respect to the total fitness of the
   population.
2. Sorted Roulette: Sort the population by fitness, and then select for reproduction
   with some bias toward the front of the list.
3. Fitness Generational: Individuals should be mated with individuals that are *close*
   to them
4. Sorted Generational: This selection method is the same as fitness generational,
   but it uses a sorted roulette method to select the first individual.
5. Elitist Random Search: It moves the best individual to the next population and
   generates random values for the remainder.

11.3.7 Crossover

Crossover is an information exchange from two parents. Crossover rate can range
from zero (no crossover) to one.

   After two parents (=chromosomes) are selected, the program randomly decides
whether crossover should occur. When crossover occurs, a random position (pos_1)
is chosen and every unit after the position will be switched between the two parents.
The children are checked to see if they fulfill the requirement of a chromosome
mentioned earlier. A new random uint is generated if any position in any of the
children does not fulfill the requirement.

11.3.8 Mutation

A random change without a reason is mutation. If the information from parents is
exchanged only without any mutation, children can only inherit genes from their
parents. A mutation gives a variation to a chromosome in order for children to find
information that their parents do not have. A mutation rate can be set from zero (no
mutation) to one (all values on each position are re-generated).

   Every position of the children chromosomes is tested to see whether mutation
should occur. If a value is selected for mutation, a random value is generated
and replaces the value. If the new value violates the requirement of chromosome
mentioned in Section 11.3.3, it is re-generated until it meets the requirement of
chromosome.

11.3.9 Evolvement

The previous four steps (from Section 11.3.5 to Section 11.3.8) combine to create a
complete reproduction process. The application continues the reproduction process
until the pre-defined numbers of generations are reached.

The generation that has the chromosome with the least error score among ten chromosomes is stored and becomes the best chromosome when the application terminates.

11.3.10 Optimal Fuzzy Membership Functions

If the best chromosome of the best generation meets the requirement of a chromosome, the chromosome becomes the optimal solution and the optimal fuzzy membership functions. However, if it does not meet the requirement, the second best chromosome is checked to see if it meets the requirement, and so on until the one that meets the requirement is found. If none of the chromosomes in the best generation meets the requirement, the application exits without outputting the result.

11.3.11 Calculating Error Ratio

Total possible error score (TPE) is calculated as follows [1]:

$$\sum_{j=1}^{n}(\max_z - z_j)^2, i = i^{th}\text{chromosome}, n = \text{total number of data} \qquad (11.5)$$

By using the equation described in Section 11.3.5, total error score (TE) can be computed. The error ratio is computed using the following equation:

$$(\frac{TE}{TPE}) \times 100 \qquad (11.6)$$

Experiments can be conducted to obtain a better solution (a chromosome that has smaller error score) by choosing different population size, generation size, parent selection method, crossover rate, and mutation rate.

11.3.12 General Rules

After the optimal chromosome is found, the fuzzy rule for each data can be determined. If there are n number of data(=pages) available, we will have n number of rules. Table 11.4 shows several sample rules.

To determine the general fuzzy rules, we need to calculate the strength score for each data using the following equation:

$$\sum_{i=1}^{n}(\text{output}\mu(x) \times \text{output}\mu(y)), n = \text{total number of data.} \qquad (11.7)$$

Table 11.4 Example of fuzzy rules for two input-single output fuzzy System

Page#	Rule	Strength score
1st Page	If x is low and y is high, then the restructuring factor z is low.	300
2nd Page	If x is medium and y is low, then the restructuring factor z is high.	540
3rd Page	If x is high and y is low, then the restructuring factor z is high.	150
4th Page	If x is medium and y is high, then the restructuring factor z is medium left.	720
5th Page	If x is medium and y is high, then the restructuring factor z is medium right.	320
6th Page	If x is low and y is high, then the restructuring factor z is low.	1150

We can only define maximum of four general fuzzy rules (low, medium left, medium right, and high) from these rules because our fuzzy system has four memberships namely low, medium left, medium right, and high. The following rules from [16] determine the general fuzzy rules among n rules.

– Rule #1: If the output membership of the fuzzy rule does not match any of the output membership of any of the existing general fuzzy rules, the rule becomes a general fuzzy rule.
– Rule #2: If the output membership of the fuzzy rule matches an output membership of any of the existing general fuzzy rules, the rule with the greater strength score becomes the general fuzzy rule.

Suppose we apply the above conditions to Table 11.4. The first page is a general rule because there is no general fuzzy rule with a low restructuring factor is defined by rule #1. The second page is also a general rule by rule #1. For the third page, rule #2 is applied because the second page's restructuring factor was high as well. The second page's strength score is higher so second page remains to be a general fuzzy rule. The fourth page and the fifth page become general rules by rule #1. The sixth page page's strength score is greater than the first page's strength score. Therefore, the sixth page overrides the first page and becomes a new general fuzzy rule.

11.4 Evaluation

The proposed solution described in this chapter is implemented using C#. Six hundred thirty-one page data with their WPR index and log rank index were input to the application, which used population size of ten, 15 maximum generations, an 85 crossover rate, a 0.09 mutation rate, and a sorted roulette method. Figure 11.5 was obtained from the above data and configuration. The best chromosome for this result had 2.73% error ratio. The general fuzzy rules for this result were found to be the followings:

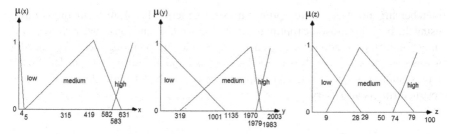

Fig. 11.5 Best chromosome

1. If x is LOW and y is LOW, then the restructuring factor is LOW;
2. If x is LOW and y is MED LEFT, then the restructuring factor is HIGH;
3. If x is MED LEFT and y is LOW, then the restructuring factor is MED LEFT;
4. If x is HIGH and y is LOW, then the restructuring factor is MED RIGHT.

The effectiveness of incorporating fuzzification into the process reveals where the information obtained during the analysis of the Website in terms of link structure and logs is summarized in the form of simple if–then fuzzy rules. It can be easily seen that the above if–then rules are easily understandable by non-technical users since the antecedents of the rules are simply conjunctions of the two ranking factors shown by their values in form of fuzzy linguistic terms that are precisely chosen during the fuzzification process of the proposed method and the consequents are the deviation (restructuring) factors. Table 11.5 shows fuzzy representation of four random data obtained from the above result. As an example, the restructuring factor of the page */images/index.html* is *High* with the degree of membership computed as 0.95 reveals that this particular page is essentially problematic in terms of its link structuring in the Website and suggests to the Website owner to reconsider the link structure of this particular page within the Website.

Table 11.5 Sample fuzzy representation

Page URL	Harder	Membership	Degree
/manufacturers/linn/index.html	false	MED LEFT	0.36
/manufacturers/yamaha/cs-30/index.html	false	MED RIGHT	0.95
/manufacturers/arp/explorer/index.html	false	LOW	0.82
/images/index.html	false	HIGH	0.95

11.5 Conclusions

In this chapter, we demonstrated that fuzzy logic can be applied to the deviation value using genetic algorithms. First, we converted deviation value to the restructuring factor value. Second, we defined the initial random fuzzy memberships using the WPR index, the log rank index, and the restructuring factor value. Third, the membership functions were optimized using genetic algorithm techniques. Last, using the best chromosome (optimal fuzzy membership functions), we derived fuzzy rules for each page and selected general fuzzy rules from among them. As a result, it was possible to assign the fuzzified restructuring factor for each page. The fuzzy representation of each page can help site owners to better understand how much restructuring is necessary.

References

1. Arslan, A., and Kaya, M. Determination of fuzzy logic membership functions using genetic algorithms. In *Fuzzy Sets and Systems 118*, pp. 297–306. Department of Computer Engineering, Faculty of Engineering, Firat University, 23279, 1998.
2. Borgelt, C. Efficient implementations of apriori and eclat. In *Proceedings of the Workshop of Frequent Item Set Mining Implementations,* Melbourne, FL, Nov. 2003.
3. Borodin, A., Roberts, G.O., Rosenthal, J.S., and Tsaparas, P. Link analysis ranking: algorithms, theory, and experiments. *ACM Transactions on Internet Technology*, 5(1):231–297, 2005.
4. Bradley, J.T., de Jager, D.V., Knottenbelt, W.J., and Trifunovic, A. Hypergraph partitioning for faster parallel pagerank computation. In *Proceedings of Formal Techniques for Computer Systems and Business Processes, European Performance Engineering Workshop*, Versailles, France, pp. 155–171, 2005.
5. Browne, G., and Jermey, J. *Website indexing: Enhancing Access to Information Within Websites,* 2nd ed. Adelaide, SA: Auslib Press, 2004.
6. Chakrabarti, S., Dom, B., Gibson, D., Kleinberg, J., Raghavan, P., and Rajagopalan, S. Automatic resource compilation by analyzing hyperlink structure and associated text. In *Proceedings of the International Conference on World Wide Web*, Brisbane, Australia, 1998.
7. Chen, Y.-Y., Gan, Q., and Suel, T. I/o-efficient techniques for computing pagerank. In *Proceedings of ACM International Conference on Information and Knowledge Management*, Mclean, VA, pp. 549–557, 2002.
8. Cho, J., Roy, S., and Adams, R.E. Page quality: In search of an unbiased Web ranking. In *Proceedings of ACM SIGMOD*, Baltimore, Maryland, pp. 551–562, 2005.
9. Chirita, P.-A., Diederich, J., and Nejdl, W. Mailrank: Using ranking for spam detection. In *Proceedings of ACM International Conference on Information and Knowledge Management*, Bremen, Germany, pp. 373–380, 2005.
10. Dean, J., and Henzinger, M. Finding related pages in the World Wide Web. In *Proceedings of the International Conference on World Wide Web*, Toronto, Canada, 1999.
11. Genetic algorithm experiment. http://www.oursland.net/projects/PopulationExperiment/.
12. Hou, J., and Zhang, Y. Effectively finding relevant Web pages from linkage information. *IEEE Transactions on Knowledge and Data Engineering*, 15(4):940–951, 2003.
13. Jantzen, J. Tutorial on fuzzy logic. page 10. Technical University of Denmark, Oersted-DTU, Automation, Bldg 326, 2800, 2006.
14. Jeffrey, J., Karski, P., Lohrmann, B., Kianmehr, K., and Alhajj, R. Optimizing Web structures using Web mining techniques. In *Proceedings of the International Conference on Intelligent Data Engineering and Automated Learning*, Birmingham, UK, 2007.
15. Jiang, X.-M., Xue, G.-R., Song, W.-G., Zeng, H.-J., Chen, Z., and Ma, W.-Y. Exploiting pagerank at different block level. In *Proceedings of the International Conference on Web Information Systems Engineering*, pp. 241–252, 2004.
16. Klir, G.J., Clair, U.S., and Yuan, B. *Fuzzy Set Theory: Foundations and Applications*. Upper Saddle River, NJ: Prentice Hall, 1997.

17. Kleinberg, J.M. Authoritative sources in a hyperlinked environment. In *Proceedings of the Ninth Annual ACM-SIAM Symposium on Discrete Algorithms*, San Francisco, CA, pp. 668–677, 1998.
18. Li, C.H., and Chui, C.K. Web structure mining for usability analysis. In *Proceedings of IEEE/WIC/ACM International Conference on Web Intelligence*, Compiègne, France, pp. 309–312, 2005.
19. Massa, P., and Hayes, C. Page-rerank: Using trusted links to re-rank authority. In *Proceedings of IEEE/WIC/ACM International Conference on Web Intelligence*, Compiègne, France, pp. 614–617, 2005.
20. P. S. Production. Internal linking and Website structures for seo. http://www.pixelsquare.com.au/seo-articles/internal-linking-Website-str%uctures-for-seo.html/.
21. Renáta Iváncsy, I.V. Frequent pattern mining in web log data. *Journal of Applied Sciences at Budapest Tech*, 3(1):77–90, 2006.
22. Soucy, P., and Mineau, G.W. Beyond TFIDF weighting for text categorization in the vector space model. In *Proceedings of the International Joint Conference on Artificial Intelligence*, Edinburgh, Scotland, UK, pp. 1130–1135, 2005.
23. Steinberger, R., Pouliquen, B., and Hagman, J. Cross-lingual document similarity calculation using the multilingual thesaurus EUROVOC. In *Proceedings of the International Conference on Computational Linguistics and Intelligent Text Processing*, Mexico City, Mexico, pp. 415–424, 2002.
24. U. of Washington Artificial Intelligence Research. Music machines Website. http://www.cs.washington.edu/ai/adaptive-data/.
25. Xing, W., and Ghorbani, A.A. Weighted page rank algorithm. In *CNSR*, pp. 305–314. IEEE Computer Society, 2004.
26. Yu, J.X., Ou, Y., Zhang, C., and Zhang, S. Identifying interesting customers through Web log classification. *IEEE Intelligent Systems*, 20(3):55–59, 2005.